Encyclopedia of MATLAB: Science and Engineering

Volume V

Encyclopedia of MATLAB: Science and Engineering Volume V

Edited by **Louis Young**

LANRYE
INTERNATIONAL

New Jersey

Published by Clanrye International,
55 Van Reypen Street,
Jersey City, NJ 07306, USA
www.clanryeinternational.com

Encyclopedia of MATLAB: Science and Engineering
Volume V
Edited by Louis Young

International Standard Book Number: 978-1-63240-193-9 (Hardback)

This book contains information obtained from authentic and highly regarded sources. Copyright for all individual chapters remain with the respective authors as indicated. A wide variety of references are listed. Permission and sources are indicated; for detailed attributions, please refer to the permissions page. Reasonable efforts have been made to publish reliable data and information, but the authors, editors and publisher cannot assume any responsibility for the validity of all materials or the consequences of their use.

The publisher's policy is to use permanent paper from mills that operate a sustainable forestry policy. Furthermore, the publisher ensures that the text paper and cover boards used have met acceptable environmental accreditation standards.

Trademark Notice: Registered trademark of products or corporate names are used only for explanation and identification without intent to infringe.

Printed in the United States of America.

Contents

Preface

This book has been a concerted effort by a group of academicians, researchers and scientists, who have contributed their research works for the realization of the book. This book has materialized in the wake of emerging advancements and innovations in this field. Therefore, the need of the hour was to compile all the required researches and disseminate the knowledge to a broad spectrum of people comprising of students, researchers and specialists of the field.

This book discusses MATLAB based applications in nearly every branch of science. The collection of insightful chapters will provide beneficial results to the readers in their spheres of work. It deals with MATLAB general applications and the use of MATLAB for educational purposes. This compilation of valued chapters covers a wide range of professional fields and can be used for applications in science as well as for various educational purposes.

At the end of the preface, I would like to thank the authors for their brilliant chapters and the publisher for guiding us all-through the making of the book till its final stage. Also, I would like to thank my family for providing the support and encouragement throughout my academic career and research projects.

Editor

MATLAB General Applications

Micro-Robot Management

Wael A. Al-Tabey

Additional information is available at the end of the chapter

1. Introduction

Micro-Robots have been and continue to be essential components of medical field. Micro-Robots are used in medical field to surgical applications. Knowledge of the kinematics, dynamics and trajectory planning of these Micro-Robots is most important for their design and control. MATLAB is a modern tool that has transformed the mathematical calculations methods because MATLAB not only provides numerical calculations but also facilitates analytical calculations using the computer. The present textbook uses MATLAB as a tool to solve problems from micro-robots. The intent is to show the convenience of MATLAB for micro-robots analysis. Using example problems the MATLAB syntax will be demonstrated. MATLAB is very useful in the process of deriving solutions for any problem in micro-robots. The chapter includes a most problem of micro-robots for surgical applications that are being solved using MATLAB. The programs are available at the end of this chapter.

Robots are widely used in medical field for getting minimally invasive surgery efficiently and accurately. Minimally invasive surgery is an innovative approach that allows reducing patient trauma, postoperative pain and recovery time [1]. The kinematic and dynamic analysis of the robot, for any applications whether in medical field or another, are very important. The direct aim is to properly select the workspace and the actuator size. Frumento [1] designed a minimally invasive robot for heart surgery. They concentrated mainly on the kinematic analysis and the workspace of the robot. Tsai and Hsu [3] investigated a parallel surgical robot having six degrees of freedom. They studied the kinematics only, to obtain the workspace of surgical robot and control it using Fuzzy Logic control. Miller and Christensen [4] analyzed the dynamics of the Multi-rigid-body robot using Newton's second law of motion and used the results to design the controller. Featherstone and Orin [5] investigated the robot dynamics and used Newton-Euler technique to obtain the equation and algorithms of robot motion. Wang, et al [6] designed the dimensional synthesis of 6-DOF Micro-surgery manipulator (Micro Hand) .They studied the kinematics and the workspace of the manipulator they considered by an Optimal design method. Alici and Shirinzadeh [7] obtained the singularity loci of parallel manipulators exemplified by a 3-DOF spherical parallel manipulator. They utilized the inverse kinematics, and Jacobian matrices to obtain the velocity equation of the actuator and the end effector. The determinants of the manipulator Jacobian matrices were evaluated for a specified set of geometric parameters. Finally, the singularity loci of the manipulator in Cartesian space were generated. Ben-Horin, et al [8] analyzed the kinematics and dynamics of parallel robot consisting of three plenary actuated links [6-DOF parallel manipulator]. They investigated by direct kinematic analysis and obtained the dynamics equations and algorithms using Newton's second law and presented the system performance. Bonnifait and Garcia [9] studied the 6-DOF dynamic localization of an outdoor mobile robot. They obtained the robot dynamics equations and algorithms using the numerical method (Taylor method) and used the azimuth and elevation angles of known landmarks, collected by a rotating linear camera to obtain the simulation results of the robot. They finally presented and analyzed the results of real experiments, performed with an outdoor mobile robot. Abdellatif and Heimann [10] investigated the inverse dynamics equations of 6-DOF fully parallel manipulators using the Lagrangian formalism. With respect to a proposed set of generalized coordinates and velocities they obtained the final form with respect to the robot's active coordinates. Attention was paid to the transformation of the sub chains dynamics. Finally, a systematic study of the resulting computational effort was presented and discussed with respect to results of other methods and approaches of other researches. Zhu, et al [11] investigated the kinematic and dynamic modeling for a newly developed parallel robot with the proposed Tau configuration and used the inverse kinematics method to obtain the kinematic equations of end effector of 3-DOF parallel robot. The dynamic modeling of 3-DOF parallel robot was derived by analytical solutions, which were verified by both numerical simulation and actual experiments. This analytical approach enabled the real-time control of this parallel robot with high positioning accuracy. Gouliaev and Zavrazhina [12] investigated the dynamic and kinematic control of the spatial movements of a flexible multi-link manipulator. They focused on the dynamics of a flexible multi-link manipulator by Euler-Bernoulli method, so that each element was in a compound motion. A technique for the numerical construction of solutions for an essentially non-linear hybrid-type system of constituent equations was proposed. They used the linear control method. Eliodoro and Serna [13] investigated the inverse dynamics of flexible robots. They focused on the new and general technique for solving the inverse dynamics of flexible robots. The proposed method finds the joint torques that must be applied by the actuators to obtain a specified end-effector trajectory. The inverse dynamics of flexible robots are derived by using the Euler-Bernoulli beam theory and Lagrange's equations. The finite element method was utilized to discretize space variables. They finally established the global dynamic equations of the robot. Kinematic constraints were introduced in the dynamic equations by means of a penalty formulation. The system performance was drawn for different tip trajectories.

Martins et al [14] examined an adaptive controller to guide a unicycle-like mobile robot during trajectory tracking. They concentrated, mainly on the kinematic analysis to design the adaptive controller using Lyapunov theory. The kinematic equations of mobile robot were found by inverse kinematics method to obtain the desired values of the linear and angular velocities, which represented the input to adaptive controller. Valero et al [15] investigated a trajectory planner for 3-DOF industrial robots that have to operate in workspaces with obstacles. They found the workspace modeling analytically using the differential equations of all joints angle and solved them in Cartesian coordinates system. The trajectory planner for 3-DOF industrial robots they found by workspace model using the finite element method for joints and end effector. Integrating all elements, the function of the trajectory planner for 3-DOF industrial robots was obtained. Finally they minimized the objective function of the trajectory planner to attain the minimum time. Geng [16] investigated the dynamics and trajectory planning of a planar flipping robot with two feet and one-leg robot. Geng made a dynamic analysis to obtain the trajectory planning using Lagrange's formulation. Geng presented the simulation results for joints kinetic variables with time. Alessandro and Vanni [17] investigated a technique for optimal trajectory planning of robot manipulators to minimize the jerk. They concentrated on the trajectory planning of robot manipulators. In order to get the optimal trajectory, an objective function composed of two terms was minimized. The first term was proportional to the total execution time, and the second was proportional to the integral of the squared jerk. Finally, they minimized the time of trajectory planning to minimize energy (or actuator effort) and jerk of manipulator joints. They represented the Simulation results for joints kinetic variables and jerk against the minimized time. Pires et al [18] tested a manipulator trajectory planning with multiple objectives and obstacle avoidance (MOEA).It is a non-trivial optimization problem. They concentrated on the trajectory planning of 2-DOF robot manipulators using MOEA method and simulated for several ranges of joint angle. Finally they gave the simulation results for joints kinetic variables with minimized time. Chettibi et al [19] studied the problem of minimum cost trajectory planning for 2-DOF industrial manipulators. They studied the optimal control via direct parameter optimization of joint positions then they concentrated on the trajectory planning of 2-DOF industrial manipulators for six ranges of joint angle. Finally, they represented the simulation results for joints kinetic variables, jerk and torque with minimized time, to obtain the optimum parameters of joint positions and minimum cost trajectory planning. Alessandro and Vanni [20] investigated a method for smooth trajectory planning of robot manipulators. In order to ensure that the resulting trajectory is smooth enough they used the same method used by them in reference. They also presented in their work a new method to obtain the smooth jerk by composing the overall trajectory with respect to other trajectory optimization techniques.

1.1. Introductory remarks on robots for medical field applications

Robots in medicine are recent entry, beginning as generic instrumental aides and aiming at specialized duties once technology sophistication enables effective settings. Several classifications are used, mainly, dressing taxonomy by means of the expected accomplishments [1]:

1. Patients and disabled aid: bed automation, walking assistants, delivery servants, etc.
2. Laboratory support: clinical testers, radiation therapies assistants, etc.
3. Soundness care: pace-makers, health-monitors, drugs dosing up suppliers, etc.
4. Surgery help: surgeon's servants, remote effectors, autonomous actors, etc.

Moreover, roughly speaking, the example taxonomy distinguishes extra corporeal fixtures, mainly derived out of conventional technologies, from in-body active devices, generally requiring invasive actions, thus, critically dependent on micro-mechanics and nanotechnologies. With focus on surgery robots, four kinds of tasks are, generally, considered:

1. Organ inspection: cerebral probing, laparoscopic monitoring, etc.
2. Organ nursing or repair: internal anastomosis, obstruction relief, etc.
3. Organ removal: cysts excision, lymph node dissection, etc.
4. (Artificial) organ implant: prosthesis insertion, etc.

Surgical robotic systems are commonly classified according to the degree of direct control the surgeon has over the machine [2].Under this classification there are three principal types of robots Table 1:

1. Autonomous: performs a preoperative plan without any immediate control from the surgeon.
2. Surgical Assist Device: surgeon and robot share control.
3. Teleoperator: function of the robot completely controlled by the surgeon.

Type of system	Examples	Function(s)	Clinical Discipline(s)
Autonomous	Robodoc	Percutaneous renal needle placement	Orthopedic surgery
	PAKY-RCM	Prostatectomy	Urology
	ProBot	Hip surgery	Urology
Surgical Assist	Caspar	Voice controlled telescope	Orthopedic surgery
	AESOP	Stereotactic	Multiple
	NeuroMate	Neurosurgery	Neurosurgery
Teleoperator	Acrobat	Knee arthroplasty	Orthopedic surgery
	PUMA (Programmable Universal Machine for Assembly)	Multiple	Multiple
	Da Vinci	Multiple	Multiple
	Zeus	Multiple	Multiple
	Neurobot	Multiple	Neurosurgery

Table 1. Classification of robotic surgical systems

The systems in study at this present work are Zeus and Da Vinci robotic arms which are usually attached to a patient-side tower structure and consists of two to three arms that control the operative instruments and a separate arm that controls the video endoscope as shown in the Figure 1.

Figure 1. Zeus and Da Vinci robotic arms

Both the Zeus and Da Vinci systems enhance dexterity in several ways. Internal software filters out the natural tremor of a surgeon's hand, which becomes particularly evident under high magnification and problematic when attempting fine maneuvers in very small fields. In addition, the system can scale movements such that large movements of the control grips can be transformed into smaller movements inside the patient. Finally the system group has 7-DOF. The Surgery arm has 6-DOF plus 1-DOF for the tool actuation. Arrangement, the DOF "a" and "b" are respectively the last DOF at the carrier and the 6-DOF robot joints has Roll-Yaw-Pitch motions as shown in the Figures .2, 3 and 4.

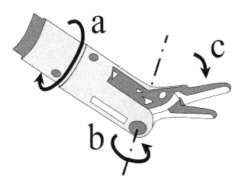

Figure 2. The ZEUS® surgery tools

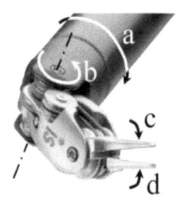

Figure 3. Da Vinci® surgery tools

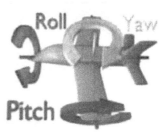

Figure 4. Roll-Yaw-Pitch motions

2. The kinematic model

2.1. The forward kinematics

The forward kinematics problem is concerned with the relationship between the individual joints of the robot manipulator and the position and orientation of the tool or end effector. Stated more formally, the forward kinematics problem is to determine the position and orientation of the end effector, given the values for the joint variables of the robot. The joint variables are the angles between the links in the case of revolute or rotational joints, and the link extension in the case of prismatic or sliding joints.

The solution is always unique: one given joint position vector always corresponds to only one single end effector pose. The FK problem is not difficult to solve, even for a completely arbitrary kinematic structure.

There are different methods for a forward kinematic analysis: like using straightforward geometry and using transformation matrices.

2.1.1. The Denavit-Hartenberg convention

The D-H modeling rules:

1. Find and identify all joint axes: Z_0 to Z_{n-1}.
2. Establish the base frame. Set base origin anywhere on the Z_0 axis. Choose X_0 and Y_0 conveniently and to form a right hand frame.
3. Locate the origin O_i where the common normal to Z_{i-1} and Z_i intersects Z_i.
   If Z_i intersects Z_{i-1} locate O_i at this intersection.
   If Z_{i-1} and Z_i are parallel, locate O_i at Joint (i+1).
4. Establish X_i along the common normal between Z_{i-1} and Z_i through O_i, or in the direction normal to the plane Z_{i-1} - Z_i if these axes intersect. See Figure 5.
5. Establish Y_i to form a right hand system
6. Repeat Steps 3 to 5 for i= 1 : n-1.
7. Establish the end effector (n) frame: $O_nX_nY_nZ_n$. Assuming the nth joint is revolute.
   Set K_n = a along the direction Z_{n-1} and establish the origin O_n conveniently along Z_n, at center of tool tip. Set $j_n=o$ in the direction of tool closure (opening) and set $i_n= n$, such that n=oxa.
   If the tool is not a simple gripper, set X_n and Y_n conveniently to form a right hand frame.
8. Create a table of "Link" parameters: See Figure 5.
   Joint Angle θ_i : angle between X_{i-1} and X_i about Z_i.
   Link Offset d_i : distance from X_{i-1} and X_i along Z_i.
   Link Twist α_i : angle between Z_i and Z_{i+1} about X_i.
   Link length a_i : distance between Z_i and Z_{i+1} along X_i.
9. Form HTM matrices $A_1, A_2 \ldots A_n$ from the information contained in each row of the LP table by substituting θ, d, α and a into the general model.
10. Build forward kinematic solution: $T_1^n = A_1{}^* A_2{}^* \ldots {}^* A_n$.

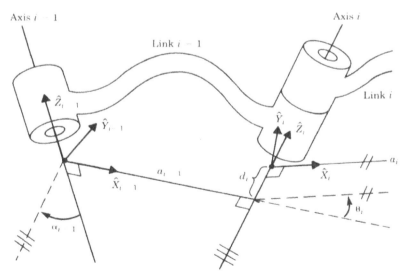

Figure 5. Construction of the link frame

2.2. The kinematics of Zeus and Da Vinci robotic arms

The geometrical model of the surgical robot in this study has 6 degrees of freedom (DOF) and an extra one for tool action. The end-effector has 3 rotations (Roll, Pitch and Yaw) as shown in Figure 6 and the frame assignment of 6-DOF surgical manipulator is represented in Figure 7.

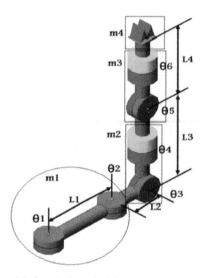

Figure 6. The geometrical model of surgical manipulator

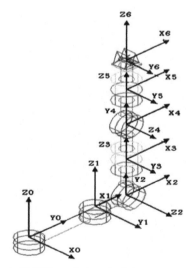

Figure 7. The frame assignment of 6-DOF surgical manipulator

The 6-DOF manipulator kinematic parameters are derived using Denavit Hartemberg formulation shown in Table 2.

Link #	θ_j	d_j	a_j	α_j	T
1	θ_1	0	L_1	0	$^0T_1$
2	θ_2	0	L_2	90	$^1T_2$
3	θ_3	0	0	-90	$^2T_3$
4	θ_4	L_3	0	90	$^3T_4$
5	θ_5	0	0	-90	$^4T_5$
6	θ_6	L_4	0	0	$^5T_6$

Table 2. Full mobility robotic tool: geometry and link parameters

The flowchart representing the sequence of generating the MATLAB CODE of the link transformations matrix is shown in Figure 8.

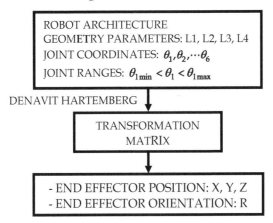

ROBOT ARCHITECTURE
GEOMETRY PARAMETERS: L1, L2, L3, L4
JOINT COORDINATES: $\theta_1, \theta_2, \cdots \theta_6$
JOINT RANGES: $\theta_{1\min} < \theta_1 < \theta_{1\max}$

DENAVIT HARTEMBERG

TRANSFORMATION
MATRIX

- END EFFECTOR POSITION: X, Y, Z
- END EFFECTOR ORIENTATION: R

Figure 8. The flowchart of the link transformations matrix

The general form of the Homogeneous Transformation Matrix is:

$$^{j-1}T_j = \begin{bmatrix} \cos\theta_j & -\sin\theta_j\cos\alpha_j & \sin\theta_j\sin\alpha_j & a_j\cos\theta_j \\ \sin\theta_j & \cos\theta_j\cos\alpha_j & -\cos\theta_j\sin\alpha_j & a_j\sin\theta_j \\ 0 & \sin\alpha_j & \cos\alpha_j & d_j \\ 0 & 0 & 0 & 1 \end{bmatrix} \quad (1)$$

The link transformations matrix can be given as:

$$^0T_1 = \begin{bmatrix} C_1 & -S_1 & 0 & L_1C_1 \\ S_1 & C_1 & 0 & L_1S_1 \\ 0 & 0 & 1 & 0 \\ 0 & 0 & 0 & 1 \end{bmatrix} \quad ^1T_2 = \begin{bmatrix} C_2 & 0 & S_2 & L_2C_2 \\ S_2 & 0 & -C_2 & L_2S_2 \\ 0 & 1 & 0 & 0 \\ 0 & 0 & 0 & 1 \end{bmatrix} \quad ^2T_3 = \begin{bmatrix} C_3 & 0 & -S_3 & 0 \\ S_3 & 0 & C_3 & 0 \\ 0 & -1 & 0 & 0 \\ 0 & 0 & 0 & 1 \end{bmatrix}$$

$$
{}^{3}T_{4} = \begin{bmatrix} C_4 & 0 & -S_4 & 0 \\ S_4 & 0 & C_4 & 0 \\ 0 & -1 & 0 & L_3 \\ 0 & 0 & 0 & 1 \end{bmatrix} \quad
{}^{4}T_{5} = \begin{bmatrix} C_5 & 0 & -S_5 & 0 \\ S_5 & 0 & C_5 & 0 \\ 0 & -1 & 0 & 0 \\ 0 & 0 & 0 & 1 \end{bmatrix} \quad
{}^{5}T_{6} = \begin{bmatrix} C_6 & -S_6 & 0 & 0 \\ S_6 & C_6 & 0 & 0 \\ 0 & 0 & 1 & L_4 \\ 0 & 0 & 0 & 1 \end{bmatrix}
$$

The kinematics equations of the end effectors are manipulated using MATLAB symbolic Toolbox were as follows:

$$
\begin{bmatrix} P_X \\ P_Y \\ P_Z \\ Z \end{bmatrix} = \begin{bmatrix} ((-(C_1*C_2-S_1*S_2)*C_3*C_4-(-C_1*S_2-S_1*C_2)*S_4)*S_5+ \\ (C_1*C_2-S_1*S_2)*S_3*C_5)*L_4-(C_1*C_2-S_1*S_2)*S_3*L_3+ \\ C_1*L_2*C_2-S_1*L_2*S_2+L_1*C_1 \\ \\ ((-(C_1*S_2+S_1*C_2)*C_3*C_4-(C_1*C_2-S_1*S_2)*S_4)*S_5+ \\ (C_1*S_2+S_1*C_2)*S_3*C_5)*L_4-(C_1*S_2+S_1*C_2)*S_3*L_3+ \\ S_1*L_2*C_2+C_1*L_2*S_2+L_1*S_1 \\ \\ (-S_3*C_4*S_5-C_3*C_5)*L_4+C_3*L_3 \\ \\ 1 \end{bmatrix}
$$

2.3. The robot workspace

The workspace of a robot can be defined as the set of points that are reachable by the manipulator (with fixed base). Roughly speaking the workspace is the volume of space which the end effector of the robot can reach. Both shape and total volume are important. Workspace is also called work volume or work envelope.

The workspace depends on the characteristics of the manipulator; physical configurations, size, number of axes, the robot mounted position (overhead gantry, wall-mounted, floor mounted, on tracks, etc), limits of arm and joint configurations. The addition of an end effector can move or offset the entire work volume.

The kinematics design of a manipulator can tailor the workspace to some extent to the operational requirements of the robot.

Some robots will have unusable spaces such as dead zones, singular poses, and wrist-wrap poses inside of the boundaries of their reach. Elbow manipulators tend to have a wider volume of workspace.

1. Dexterous workspace: This is the volume of space which the end-effector of the manipulator can reach with all orientations.
2. Reachable workspace: This is the volume of space which the end-effector of the manipulator can reach with at least one orientation.

The dexterous workspace is obviously a subset of the reachable workspace.

2.3.1. The workspace calculation

The workspace may be found mathematically by writing equations that define the robot's links and joints and including their limitations, such as ranges of motions for each joint. Alternatively, the workspace may be found empirically, by moving each joint through each range of motion and combining all the space in can reach and subtracting what it cannot reach.

The workspace of the surgical manipulator can be represented by solving the inverse kinematic equations and taking into consideration all the physical limits of the joints. Figure 9 represents the flowchart showing the sequence of generating the three dimensional workspace of the robot and end-effector to be manipulated using the MATLAB symbolic Toolbox.

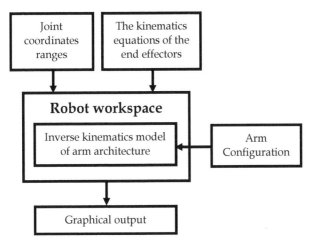

Figure 9. The flowchart of The Robot workspace

Table 3 represent the physical limits of the six joints while Figure10 represent the workspace of end-effector respectively.

Link #	1	2	3	4	5	6
θ_i (degree)	-180°	-90°	0	-180°	-90°	-180°
θ_f (degree)	180°	90°	180°	180°	90°	180°
L (mm)	0	50	15	36	0	39.5

Table 3. Joint coordinates ranges

The workspace of the end-effector depends on the physical limits of the six joints angle, i.e. if the angle range of the robot joints is changes the workspace of the robot changes. So it is important to take into account the accuracy in determining the angle range of the robot joints to get the required workspace which covers the work area.

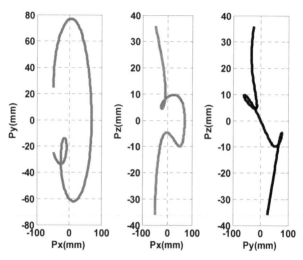

Figure 10. The work space of end effector

2.4. The robot Jacobian

The Jacobian is a representation of the geometry of the elements of mechanism in time. It allows the conversion of differential motions or velocities of individual joints to differential motions or velocities of pints of interest. It also relates the individual joint motion to overall mechanism motions. Jacobian is time related; since the values of θ_i vary in time, and the magnitude of the elements of Jacobian vary in time as well.

2.4.1. The differential motions and velocities equations

Differential motions are small movements of robot parts that can be used to derive velocity relationships between different parts of the robot. To find these relations the following steps, are to be considered:

1. Frames relative to a fixed frame.
2. Robot joint relative to a fixed frame.
3. Jacobian matrix.
4. Robot velocity relationship.

2.4.2. The Jacobian equations

Suppose we have a set of equations Y_i in terms of variables X_j

$$Y_i = f_i(X_1, X_2, X_3 \cdots, X_j)$$ (2)

The differential change in Y_i for a differential change in X_j is:

$$\delta Y_1 = \frac{\partial f_1}{\partial X_1}\delta X_1 + \frac{\partial f_1}{\partial X_2}\delta X_2 + \cdots\cdots\cdots + \frac{\partial f_1}{\partial X_i}\delta X_j$$

$$\delta Y_2 = \frac{\partial f_2}{\partial X_1}\delta X_1 + \frac{\partial f_2}{\partial X_2}\delta X_2 + \cdots\cdots\cdots + \frac{\partial f_2}{\partial X_i}\delta X_j$$

$$\vdots \qquad \vdots \qquad\qquad \vdots \qquad\qquad\qquad \vdots \tag{3}$$

$$\delta Y_i = \frac{\partial f_i}{\partial X_1}\delta X_1 + \frac{\partial f_i}{\partial X_2}\delta X_2 + \cdots\cdots\cdots + \frac{\partial f_i}{\partial X_i}\delta X_j$$

2.4.3. The Jacobian matrix

$$\left[\delta Y_i\right] = \left[\frac{\partial f_i}{\partial X_i}\right]\left[\delta X_j\right] \equiv [D] = [J][D_\theta] \tag{4}$$

2.4.4. The Jacobian relations

The Kinematics equations of the end effectors which are used to calculate the Jacobian matrix of the robot are:

$P_X = f_1 = ((-(C_1*C_2-S_1*S_2)*C_3*C_4-(-C_1*S_2-S_1*C_2)*S_4)*S_5+(C_1*C_2-S_1*S_2)*S_3*C_5)*L_4-$
    $(C_1*C_2-S_1*S_2)*S_3*L_3+C_1*L_2*C_2-S_1*L_2*S_2+L_1*C_1$

$P_Y = f_2 = ((-(C_1*S_2+S_1*C_2)*C_3*C_4-(C_1*C_2-S_1*S_2)*S_4)*S_5+(C_1*S_2+S_1*C_2)*S_3*C_5)*L_4-$
    $(C_1*S_2+S_1*C_2)*S_3*L_3+S_1*L_2*C_2+C_1*L_2*S_2+L_1*S_1$

$$P_Z = f_3 = (-S_3*C_4*S_5-C_3*C_5)*L_4+C_3*L_3$$

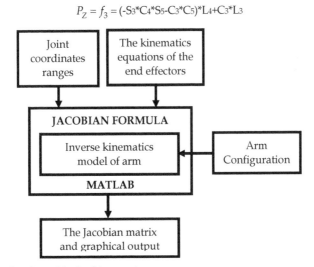

Figure 11. The flowchart of the Jacobian matrix

The Jacobian matrix of the robot can be calculated by MATLAB symbolic Toolbox using the kinematics equations as shown in the Figure 11.

The differential equations of motion of the end effector for the surgical robot are represented by:

$$
\begin{aligned}
dP_x = V_x = &((((C_1{}^*S_2+S_1{}^*C_2)^*C_3{}^*C_4-(-C_1{}^*C_2+S_1{}^*S_2)^*S_4)^*S_5+(-C_1{}^*S_2-S_1{}^*C_2)^*S_3{}^*C5{}^*L_4- \\
&(-C_1{}^*S_2-S_1{}^*C_2)^*S_3{}^*L_3-S_1{}^*L_2{}^*C_2-C_1{}^*L_2{}^*S_2-L_1{}^*S_1)^*d\theta_1+(((((C_1{}^*S_2+S_1{}^*C_2)^*C_3{}^*C_4- \\
&(-C_1{}^*C_2+S_1{}^*S_2)^*S_4)^*S_5+(-C_1{}^*S_2-S_1{}^*C_2)^*S_3{}^*C_5)^*L_4-(-C_1{}^*S_2-S_1{}^*C_2)^*S_3{}^*L_3-S_1{}^*L_2{}^*C_2- \\
&C_1{}^*L_2{}^*S_2)^*d\theta_2+((((C_1{}^*C_2-S_1{}^*S_2)^*S_3{}^*C_4{}^*S_5+(C_1{}^*C_2-S_1{}^*S_2)^*C_3{}^*C_5)^*L_4- \\
&(C_1{}^*C_2-S_1{}^*S_2)^*C_3{}^*L_3)^*d\theta_3+((C_1{}^*C_2-S_1{}^*S_2)^*C_3{}^*S_4-(-C_1{}^*S_2-S_1{}^*C_2)^*C_4)^*S_5{}^*L_4{}^*d\theta_4+ \\
&(((-C_1{}^*C_2+S_1{}^*S_2)^*C_3{}^*C_4-(-C_1{}^*S_2-S_1{}^*C_2)^*S_4)^*C_5-(C_1{}^*C_2-S_1{}^*S_2)^*S_3{}^*S_5)^*L_4{}^*d\theta_5
\end{aligned}
$$

$$
\begin{aligned}
dP_y = V_y = &((((-C_1{}^*C_2+S_1{}^*S_2)^*C_3{}^*C_4-(-C_1{}^*S_2-S_1{}^*C_2)^*S_4)^*S_5+(C_1{}^*C_2-S_1{}^*S_2)^*S_3{}^*C_5)^*L_4- \\
&(C_1{}^*C_2-S_1{}^*S_2)^*S_3{}^*L_3+C_1{}^*L_2{}^*C_2-S_1{}^*L_2{}^*S_2+L_1{}^*C_1)^*d\theta_1+(((((-C_1{}^*C_2+S_1{}^*S_2)^*C_3{}^*C_4- \\
&(-C_1{}^*S_2-S_1{}^*C_2)^*S_4)^*S_5+(C_1{}^*C_2-S_1{}^*S_2)^*S_3{}^*C_5)^*L_4-(C_1{}^*C_2-S_1{}^*S_2)^*S_3{}^*L_3+C_1{}^*L_2{}^*C_2- \\
&S_1{}^*L_2{}^*S_2)^*d\theta_2+((((C_1{}^*S_2+S_1{}^*C_2)^*S_3{}^*C_4{}^*S_5+(C_1{}^*S_2+S_1{}^*C_2)^*C_3{}^*C_5)^*L_4- \\
&(C_1{}^*S_2+S_1{}^*C_2)^*C_3{}^*L_3)^*d\theta_3+((C_1{}^*S_2+S_1{}^*C_2)^*C_3{}^*S_4-(-C_1{}^*C_2-S_1{}^*S_2)^*C_4)^*S_5{}^*L_4{}^*d\theta_4+ \\
&(((-C_1{}^*S_2-S_1{}^*C_2)^*C_3{}^*C_4-(-C_1{}^*C_2-S_1{}^*S_2)^*S_4)^*C_5-(C_1{}^*S_2+S_1{}^*C_2)^*S_3{}^*S_5)^*L_4{}^*d\theta_5
\end{aligned}
$$

$$
dP_z = V_z = ((-C_3{}^*C_4{}^*S_5+S_3{}^*C_5)^*L_4-S_3{}^*L_3)^*d\theta_3+S_3{}^*S_4{}^*S_5{}^*L_4{}^*d\theta_4+(-S_3{}^*C_4{}^*C_5+C_3{}^*S_5)^*L_4{}^*d\theta_5
$$

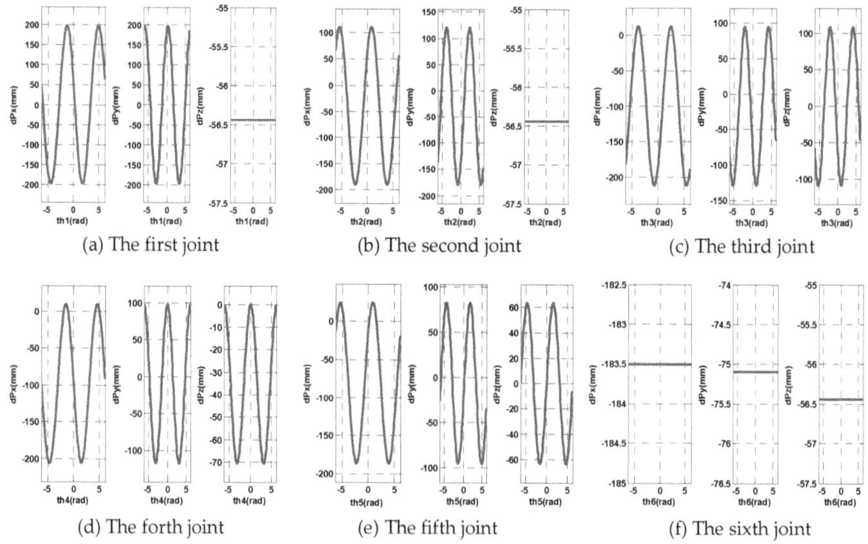

(a) The first joint   (b) The second joint   (c) The third joint

(d) The forth joint   (e) The fifth joint   (f) The sixth joint

Figure 12. The relation between angle of joints and the end effector differential translation

The previous differential equations of motion of the end effector represent the relation between the magnitude of the elements of Jacobian (the elements of end effector motion) and the joints angle. Figures 12 a, b, c, d, e and f represents the relation between angle of joints and the end effector differential translation. This shows six figures is (a, b, c, d, e and f) for six joints. It is to be noted that in Figures 12-a and 12-b for the first and second joints respectively the relation between angle of joint and the end effector differential translation in the Z direction is constant i.e. the motion of the end effector in the Z direction is not affected by the change in angle of the first and second joints. In the same time the motion of the end effector in all directions (X, Y and Z) is not affected by the change in angle of the six joints because the frame of the end effector is in the same directions of the frame of the joint number six. This can clearly be inferred from the geometrical model and the frame of the robot given in Figures 6 and 7 respectively.

The relations between the magnitude of the elements of Jacobian (the elements of end effector motion at all directions) i.e. dP_X, dP_Y and dP_Z give of the path of the robot joints as shown in Figures 13 a, b, c, d, e and f.

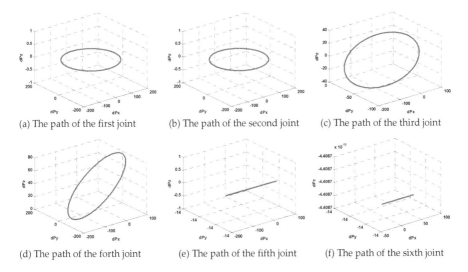

(a) The path of the first joint   (b) The path of the second joint   (c) The path of the third joint

(d) The path of the forth joint   (e) The path of the fifth joint   (f) The path of the sixth joint

Figure 13. The path of the robot joints

3. The trajectory planning

3.1. Introduction to the trajectory planning

Robot study is divided into two parts; they are the kinematics and dynamics. This means that using the equations of motion of the robot, its position can be determined if the joint variables are known. Path and trajectory planning relates the way a robot is moved from one location to another in controlled manner. In this chapter, a study of the sequence of movements is to be made to create a controlled movement between motion segments, in straight-line motion, or in sequential motions. Path and trajectory planning requires the use of both kinematics and dynamics of robots. In practice, precise motion requirements are so intensive that approximations are always necessary [23].

What is the different between the path and the trajectory planning?

A Path is defined as a sequence of robot configurations in particular order without regard to timing of these configurations as shown in Figure 14. A trajectory is concerned about when each part of the path must be obtained thus specifying timing (Velocity and Acceleration). Or a trajectory is a spatial position/time curve that usually represents a desired manipulation motion in either link or Cartesian space as shown in Figure 15.

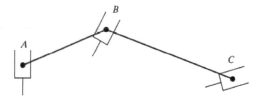

Figure 14. Sequential robot movements in a path [23]

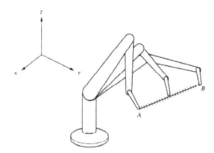

Figure 15. Sequential motions of a robot to follow a straight line [23]

3.2. The methods to calculate trajectory planning

There are four different methods which have been derived to calculate the trajectory planning of the robot using MATLAB code. The trajectory planning in the four methods needs two parameters, namely the joint angle range and the final time required to complete the process. The first one was selected from the workspace needed to complete the process In any case, this dependent on the type of surgical applications and can easily be identified. The final time required is a very important parameter to derive the trajectory planning of the robot. As all the results that have been inferred from the orientation, velocity, acceleration and torque of the robot are based on this parameter. If the time increases the velocity required decreases and acceleration i.e. the inertia of the robot link consequently decreases accidentally irrespective of the methods used. The orientation must be seen carefully examined and the behaviour should be increasing gradually with the time from the initial angle to the final angle. The final time required to complete the process for each method should be optimized and this is called optimal planning. In this work the trajectory planning of the four times is derived and then, comparison of the results at specific joint is made. The proper time which gives satisfactory results is obtained.

3.2.1. Third-Order polynomial trajectory planning

The most common techniques for trajectory planning for industrial robots are the use of polynomial of different orders, such as Cubic and B-splines, linear segments with parabolic blends and the soft motion trajectory [22]. The Linear Segments with Parabolic blends trajectories are faster and more suitable for industrial applications. On the other hand, the higher order polynomials trajectory as well as the soft motion trajectory [24] are easy to design and control especially for the jerk. They are accurate, precise and suitable for medical applications. In this work, the trajectory planning for each joint is designed using third order polynomial as a rest-to-rest manoeuvring where the link starts from rest, accelerates and decelerates at the end of the trajectory. The trajectory is given by [23]:

$$\theta(t) = C_0 + C_1 t + C_2 t^2 + C_3 t^3 \tag{5}$$

In which C_0, C_1, C_2 and C_3 are coefficients to be determined from the initial conditions as follows:

$$\dot{\theta}(t) = C_1 + 2 C_2 t + 3 C_3 t^2 \tag{6}$$

$$\dot{\theta}(t_i) = 0 \text{ and } \dot{\theta}(t_f) = 0 \qquad \text{(Rest to Rest manouvering)}$$

By substituting in to equation (6):

$$\dot{\theta}(t_i) = C_1 = 0$$

$$\dot{\theta}(t_f) = C_1 + 2 C_2 t_f + 3 C_3 t_f^2 = 0 \tag{7}$$

The initial and final location and orientation of robot are known from:

$$\theta(t_i) = \theta_i \text{ and } \theta(t_f) = \theta_f$$

By substituting in to equation (5):

$$\theta(t_i) = C_0 = \theta_i$$

$$\theta(t_f) = C_0 + C_1 t_f + C_2 t_f^2 + C_3 t_f^3 = \theta_f \tag{8}$$

By solving equations (7), (8) simultaneously:

$$C_2 = 3(\theta_f - \theta_i)/t_f^2 \text{ and } C_3 = 2(\theta_f - \theta_i)/t_f^3$$

3.2.2. Fifth-Order polynomial trajectory planning

The third order trajectory only takes into account starting and end velocities. The equations of the fifth order polynomial takes into account starting and end accelerations. In this case, the total number of boundary conditions are six, allowing a fifth.

The initial and final velocities are zero. (Rest to Rest manoeuvring) and the trajectory is given by [23]:

$$\theta(t) = C_0 + C_1 t + C_2 t^2 + C_3 t^3 + C_4 t^4 + C_5 t^5 \tag{9}$$

In which C_0, C_1, C_2, C_3, C_4 and C_5 are coefficients to be determined from the initial and final conditions as follows:

$$\dot{\theta}(t) = C_1 + 2C_2 t + 3C_3 t^2 + 4C_4 t^3 + 5C_5 t^4 \tag{10}$$

$$\ddot{\theta}(t) = 2C_2 + 6C_3 t + 12C_4 t^2 + 20C_5 t^3 \tag{11}$$

$$\dot{\theta}(t_i) = 0 \text{ and } \dot{\theta}(t_f) = 0 \qquad \text{(Rest to Rest manoeuvring)}$$

$$\ddot{\theta}(t_i) = \ddot{\theta}_i \text{ and } \ddot{\theta}(t_f) = \ddot{\theta}_f$$

$$C_0 = \theta_i \ , C_1 = \dot{\theta}_i \ , \ C_2 = \frac{\ddot{\theta}_i}{2}, \ C_3 = \frac{20\theta_f - 20\theta_i - (8\dot{\theta}_f + 12\dot{\theta}_i)\,t_f - (3\ddot{\theta}_i - \ddot{\theta}_f)t_f^2}{2t_f^3},$$

$$C_4 = \frac{30\theta_f - 30\theta_i + (14\dot{\theta}_f + 16\dot{\theta}_i)\,t_f + (3\ddot{\theta}_i - 2\ddot{\theta}_f)t_f^2}{2t_f^4} \text{ and } C_5 = \frac{12\theta_f - 12\theta_i - (6\dot{\theta}_f + 6\dot{\theta}_i)\,t_f + (\ddot{\theta}_i - \ddot{\theta}_f)t_f^2}{2t_f^5}$$

3.2.3. Linear segments with parabolic blends

Linear segments can be blended with parabolic sections at the beginning and the end of the motion segment, creating continuous position and velocity. Acceleration is constant for the parabolic sections, yielding a linear velocity at the common points A and B as shown in the Figure 16.

3.2.3.1. First parabolic blends (t_0 to t_a)

$$\theta(t) = C_0 + C_1 t + \frac{1}{2}\, C_2 t^2 \tag{12}$$

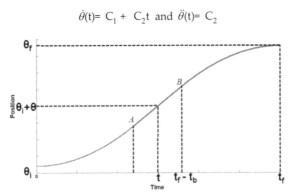

$$\dot\theta(t) = C_1 + C_2 t \text{ and } \ddot\theta(t) = C_2$$

Figure 16. Scheme for linear segments with parabolic blends

The position of the robot at time t0 is known and using the inverse Kinematic equations of the robot, the joint angles at via points and at the end of the motion can be found.

To blend the motion segments together, the boundary conditions at each point are used to calculate the coefficients of the parabolic segments.

3.2.3.2. Straight line (t$_a$ to t$_b$)

$$\theta_A = \theta_B + wt \;, \; \dot\theta_A = \dot\theta_B + w \text{ and } \ddot\theta = 0$$

3.2.3.3. Second parabolic blends (t$_f$ – t$_b$ to t$_f$)

$$\theta(t) = C_f + \frac{w}{2t_b}(t_f - t)^2 \tag{13}$$

$$\dot\theta(t) = \frac{w}{t_b}(t_f - t) \text{ and } \ddot\theta(t) = -\frac{w}{t_b}$$

$$t_b = \frac{(\theta_i - \theta_f + wt_f)}{w} \;, \; C_2 = \frac{w}{t_b} \text{ and } w_{max} = \frac{2(\theta_f - \theta_i)}{t_f}$$

3.2.4. Soft motion trajectory planning

In this method we consider the trajectory planning of points generated by a motion planning technique. The motion planner calculates the trajectory which the end effector must follow in space. However, the temporal characteristics of this movement are independent. One important difference between industrial robotic manipulators and service robot applications is the human interaction, which introduce safety and comfort constraints. In this work, we define soft motions conditions to facilitate this cohabitation. An on-line trajectory planner is proposed here. It generates the necessary references to produce soft motion and a control loop that guarantees the end effector's motion characteristics (jerk, acceleration, velocity and position) in the Cartesian space, by using quaternion feedback. Two visual feedback control loops are proposed: a visual servoing control loop in a shared position - vision schema and a visual guided loop (which is the general case of soft motion trajectory) are given by:

3.2.4.1. The motion with a maximum jerk (J_{max})

$$\theta(t) = \theta_0 + \dot{\theta}_0 t + \frac{1}{2}\ddot{\theta}t^2 + \frac{1}{6}J_{max}t^3$$

(14)

$$\dot{\theta}(t) = \dot{\theta}_0 + \ddot{\theta}_0 t + \frac{1}{2}J_{max}t^2, \ \ddot{\theta}(t) = \ddot{\theta}_0 + J_{max} \ \text{and} \ J(t) = J_{max}$$

3.2.4.2. The motion with a maximum acceleration (A_{max})

$$\theta(t) = \theta_0 + \dot{\theta}_0 t + \frac{1}{2}\ddot{\theta}_{max}t^2$$

(15)

$$\dot{\theta}(t) = \dot{\theta}_0 + \ddot{\theta}_{max}, \ \ddot{\theta}(t) = \ddot{\theta}_{max} \ \text{and} \ J(t) = 0$$

3.2.4.3. Finally, the equations for the motion with a maximum velocity (V_{max})

$$\theta(t) = \theta_0 + \dot{\theta}_{max}t$$

(16)

$$\dot{\theta}(t) = \dot{\theta}_{max}, \ \ddot{\theta}(t) = 0 \ \text{and} \ J(t) = 0$$

The initial conditions are:

$$\ddot{\theta}(0) = 0, \ \dot{\theta}(0) = 0, \ \theta(0) = \theta_0 \ \text{and} \ D = \theta_D - \theta_0$$

Where: D is general traversed angular movement.

The final conditions are:

$$\ddot{\theta}(t_f) = 0, \ \dot{\theta}(t_f) = 0 \text{ and } \theta(t_f) = \theta_D$$

We have two limit conditions to obtain the traversed angular movement:

- **Condition (1):**

Where $\dot{\theta}_{max}$ is reached. It means, $\ddot{\theta}_{max}$ is reached too. Then we have to find the traversed angular (Dthr1). The limit times used to calculate (Dthr1) are:

$$T_j = T_{j_{max}} \ , \ T_a = T_{a_{max}} \ \text{ and } \ T_v = 0$$

The angular movement (Dthr1) becomes:

$$\text{Dthr1} = \frac{\ddot{\theta}_{max}\dot{\theta}_{max}}{J_{max}} + \frac{\dot{\theta}_{max}^{\ 2}}{\ddot{\theta}_{max}}$$

- **Condition (2):**

Where only $\ddot{\theta}_{max}$ is reached. Then we have to find the traversed angular (Dthr2). The limit times used to calculate (Dthr2) are:

$$T_j = T_{j_{max}} \ , \quad T_a = 0 \ \text{ and } \ T_v = 0$$

The angular movement (Dthr2) becomes:

$$\text{Dthr2} = 2\frac{\ddot{\theta}_{max}^{3}}{J^{2}_{max}}, \ T_{j_{max}} = \frac{\ddot{\theta}_{max}}{J_{max}} \ \text{ and } \ T_{a_{max}} = \left(\frac{\dot{\theta}_{max}}{\ddot{\theta}_{max}}\right) - \left(\frac{\ddot{\theta}_{max}}{J_{max}}\right)$$

The soft motion trajectory planning of 6-DOF surgical robot is divided in to three cases depending on the maximum Jerk algorithm as:

- **Case (1) (General case):** If $D \geq \text{Dthr1}$

$$T_j = T_{j_{max}} \ , \quad T_a = T_{a_{max}} \ \text{ and } \ T_v = \frac{D - \text{Dthr1}}{\dot{\theta}_{max}}$$

- **Case (2):** If $\text{Dthr2} > D \geq \text{Dthr2}$

$$T_v = 0, \ T_j = T_{j_{max}} \ \text{ and } \ T_a = \sqrt{\frac{\ddot{\theta}^{2}_{max}}{4J_{max}} + \frac{D}{\ddot{\theta}_{max}}} - \frac{3\ddot{\theta}_{max}}{2J_{max}}$$

- **Case (3):** If $D < \text{Dthr2}$

$$T_v = 0, \ T_a = 0 \ \text{ and } \ T_j = \sqrt[3]{\frac{D}{2J_{max}}}$$

3.3. The robot trajectory planning parameters

In this work, four different methods are applied here to design the joints trajectories third order polynomial, fifth order polynomial, linear segments with parabolic blends and soft motion trajectory. The trajectories have the same initial and final angles and different four duration times (5, 10, 20 and 60 s) are applied to choose the best duration time give the correct dynamic response. As well but they differ in the acceleration and the jerk. After designing the joints trajectories, the hub torques of the robot actuators can be simulated using MATLAB. The parameters of six joints were obtained using inverse kinematics analysis as shown in Table 4.

The flowchart representing the sequence of generating the trajectory planning is shown in the Figure 17.

Link#	1	2	3	4	5	6
θ_i(degree)	-180°	-90º	0	-180°	-90º	-180°
θ_f (degree)	180°	90º	180°	180°	90º	180°
L (mm)	0	50	15	36	0	39.5
$\ddot{\theta}_i$ (degree /s2)	5	5	5	5	5	5
$\ddot{\theta}_f$ (degree /s2)	-5	-5	-5	-5	-5	-5
$\dot{\theta}_{max}$(degree /s)	135	70	70	135	70	135
$\ddot{\theta}_{max}$ (degree /s2)	80	40	40	80	40	80
J_{max} (degree /s3)	160	80	80	160	80	160
t_i (s)	0	0	0	0	0	0
t_f (s)	5	5	5	5	5	5

Table 4. Full robotic mobility information used in trajectory planning

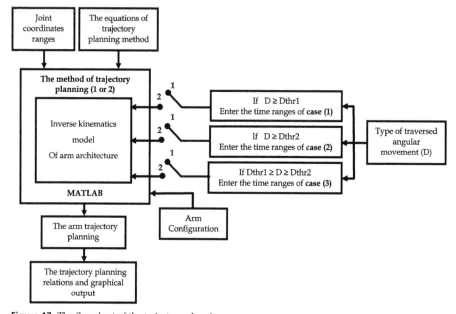

Figure 17. The flowchart of the trajectory planning

Where: Position.1 for first methods of trajectory planning and Position .2 for Soft motion trajectory planning.

4. The dynamic model

4.1. Introduction to the dynamic model of robot

Manipulator dynamics is concerned with the equations of motion, the way in which the manipulator moves in response to torques applied by the actuators, and external forces. The history and mathematics of the dynamics of serial-link manipulators are well covered in the literature. The equations of motion for an n-axis manipulator are given by [25]:

$$Q = M(q)\,\ddot{q} + C(q.\dot{q}\;)\,\dot{q} + G(q) \tag{17}$$

These equations of motion can be derived by six methods, namely the Newton's second law method, D'Alembert method, Lagrange method, Hemilton method, Lagrange-Euler method and Newton-Euler method. But not all previous methods can be used to derive the equations of motion for the robot subject of this work. That is not all methods can easily derived the equations of motion for a robot having multi-degree of freedom.

4.2. Dynamic equations for multiple-degree of freedom robots

As we have stated, the dynamic equation for two-degree of freedom system is much more complicated than a one-degree of freedom system. Similarly, these equations for multiple-degree of freedom robot are cumbersome and complicated, but can be found by calculating the kinetic and potential energies of the links and joints [25]. For the robot considered in this work the robot has 6-DOF and the most appropriate method to derive the equations of motion is likely to be Lagrange-Euler technique.

4.2.1. Derivation of the equations of motion by Lagrange-Euler technique

The Lagrange-Euler technique is utilized here to calculate the kinetic energy, potential energy and to derive the dynamic equations in symbolic form using the MATLAB symbolic toolbox for the six-degree of freedom robot. The equations of motion are given in a concise form similar to that given in [25].

4.2.1.1. The total kinetic energy

The total kinetic energy of multiple-degree of freedom robot is given in a concise form as:

$$K_i = \frac{1}{2}\sum_{i=1}^{n}\sum_{p=1}^{i}\sum_{r=1}^{i} Trace(U_{ip} J_i U_{ir} T)\dot{q}_p \dot{q}_r + \frac{1}{2}\sum_{1}^{n} I_{iact}\dot{q}_i^{\,2} \tag{18}$$

$$U_{ip} = \frac{\partial^0 T_i}{\partial \theta_p} = Q_P{}^0 T_i \;\;,\; U_{ir} = \frac{\partial^0 T_i}{\partial \theta_r} = Q_r{}^0 T_i \;\;,\; U_{ir} = U_{ri}, U_{iP} = U_{Pi} \;\text{ and}$$

$$Q_i(revolute) = \begin{bmatrix} 0 & -1 & 0 & 0 \\ 1 & 0 & 0 & 0 \\ 0 & 0 & 0 & 0 \\ 0 & 0 & 0 & 0 \end{bmatrix} , \; Q_i(prismatic) = \begin{bmatrix} 0 & 0 & 0 & 0 \\ 0 & 0 & 0 & 0 \\ 0 & 0 & 0 & 1 \\ 0 & 0 & 0 & 0 \end{bmatrix}$$

But in our case all joints in the robot arm used in surgical applications are considered revolute joints where $Q_P = Q_r = Q$.

4.2.1.2. The potential energy

The potential energy of multiple-degree of freedom robot may be given in a concise from as:

$$P = \sum_{j=1}^{n} P_i = \sum_{j=1}^{n} [-m_i g^T ({}^0T_j X \overline{r_j})] \tag{19}$$

$$g^T = \begin{bmatrix} g_x & g_y & g_z & 0 \end{bmatrix}$$

4.2.1.3. Robot equations of motion

The equations of motion of multiple-degree of freedom robot be given in a compact form as:

$$T_i = \sum_{j=1}^{n} D_{ij} \ddot{q}_j + I_{i(act)} \ddot{q}_i + \sum_{j=1}^{n} \sum_{k=1}^{n} D_{ijk} \dot{q}_j \dot{q}_k + D_i \tag{20}$$

$$D_{ij} = \sum_{p=\max(i,j)}^{n} Trace(U_{pj} J_p U_{pi}^T), \ D_{ijk} = \sum_{p=\max(i,j,k)}^{n} Trace(U_{pjk} J_p U_{pi}^T),$$

$$D_i = \sum_{p=1}^{n} -m_p g^T U_{pj} \overline{r_p}, \ U_{Pik} = \frac{\partial U_{Pi}}{\partial \theta_k} = U_{Pi} Q_k {}^0T_k$$

$$J_i = \begin{bmatrix} \dfrac{(-I_{XX}+I_{YY}+I_{ZZ})}{2} & I_{XY} & I_{XZ} & m_i \overline{X_i} \\[2ex] I_{XY} & \dfrac{(I_{XX}-I_{YY}+I_{ZZ})}{2} & I_{YZ} & m_i \overline{Y_i} \\[2ex] I_{XZ} & I_{YZ} & \dfrac{(I_{XX}+I_{YY}-I_{ZZ})}{2} & m_i \overline{Z_i} \\[2ex] m_i \overline{X_i} & m_i \overline{Y_i} & m_i \overline{Z_i} & m_i \end{bmatrix}$$

Link #	1	2	3	4	5	6
I_{act} (Nmm)	10000	10000	10000	10000	10000	10000
m (kg)	6.055	6.055	6.055	6.055	6.055	6.055
L (mm)	0	50	15	36	0	39.5
g (m/s2)	9.81	9.81	9.81	9.81	9.81	9.81
R (mm)	75	75	75	75	75	75
I_{xx}			$(1/12)*m_i*(3*(R_2)+(L_i/4)2)$			
I_{yy}			$(1/12)*m_i*(3*(R_2)+(L_i/4)2)$			
I_{zz}			$m_i * R_2$			
I_{xy}			0			
I_{xz}			0			
I_{yz}			0			
X			$L_i/2$			
Y			0			
Z			0			

Table 5. Full robotic mobility parameters

For the MATLAB simulation, the parameters of the robotic arm are given in table 5. The flowchart for the algorithm employed to calculate the torque history for each actuator based on the derived equations of motion (Equation 20) is shown in the Figure 18. The simulated results for the actuators torques change depending on the method of trajectory planning used to calculate the torque. For example the simulated results for the actuators torques calculated by the Third-Order Polynomial trajectory planning are presented in section 3. It can be seen that the torque history over the selected period of time (5, 10, 20 and 60 s) has considerable fluctuations.

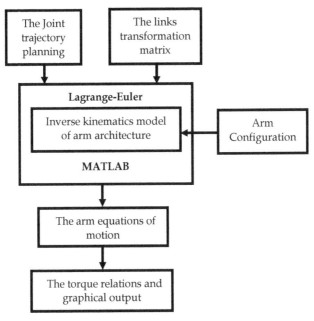

Figure 18. The flowchart of the dynamic model

5. The dynamic response

5.1. Introduction to the dynamic response and dynamic response analysis

The results presented in this chapter are those of chapters IV and V that is the trajectory planning and dynamic modeling respectively as they are very much related to each other. The results are divided into two sections. The first one is for the trajectory planning of the surgical robot which is divided into four parts, each represents a method from four chosen different methods for trajectory planning. As mentioned in chapter IV the joints limits for some of the joints are similar as the joints (1, 4, and 6) and (2, 5). Only the trajectory planning of similar joints will be represented. It should be noted that the results of trajectory planning for all methods were derived using four different times (5, 10, 20 and 60 s) in order to select the best time which gives the best and smooth orientation, velocity, acceleration (i.e. the inertia of the robot link) and torque. The dynamic modeling results are dependent on the trajectory planning results. This requires the results of the dynamic modeling to be represented after the trajectory planning results i.e. after comparison of the results of the trajectory planning and selecting the best time to be used.

Finally, a comparison of the results is held to choose the best method that gives the smooth set trajectory planning and best performance of the robot under investigation.The simulation results were obtained using MATLAB.

5.2. The trajectory planning analysis

As previously stated that trajectory planning was derived using four methods of the trajectory planning to select the best method that gives the smooth set trajectory planning and best performance of the robot under investigation.

The trajectory planning results is presented in two ways. The first one shows the trajectory planning of the first joint of robot derived using four different times and the second one shows the torque history for the first joint and a comparison between the four times of the first joint of robot in terms of the orientation, velocity, acceleration and the torque history to select the best time that can be used to derive the trajectory planning and torque history for all joints of robot model.

5.2.1. Third order Polynomial trajectory planning

Figures 19 and 20 show comparisons between the orientation, velocity, acceleration, torque and four different time ranges (5, 10, 20 and 60 s) of the first joint of the surgical robot. It is clearly shown in Figure 19 that the orientation behaviour increases gradualy with the time from the initial angle to the final angle and as the time increases the velocity required decreases and also the acceleration i.e. the inertia of the robot link decreases. It is also clearly shown in Figure 20 that the original torque history has considerable fluctuations. It is clear that the highest hub torque is for joint one while actuator torque of joint 6 is the lowest.

From Figures 19 and 20 the optimum final time required to complete the process for the robot can be selected. By inspection of Figure 19 for the trajectory planning of the robot we find that for all times the same behaviours i.e. the velocity and acceleration are inversely proportional with the times and the orientation behaviour increases gradualy with the time from the initial angle to the final angle. The largest time i.e. 60s to complete the results of the surgical robot can be selected. Since this time has the lowest acceleration i.e the lowest inertia. In Figure 20 for the torque history in the time 60s we find that the torque decreases with time and the over shooting decreases gradualy near the steady state time 60s.

It is seen from Table 4 that the joints angle ranges are very large. So, it is assured that the robot accelerations will not exceed the maximum permissible limits for robot's capabilities if the robot is satisfying the trajectory in one segment.

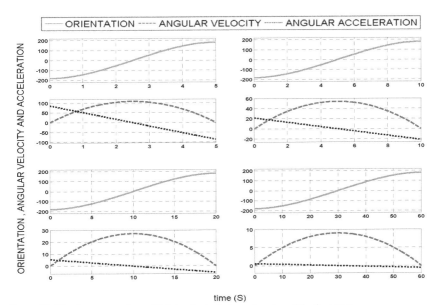

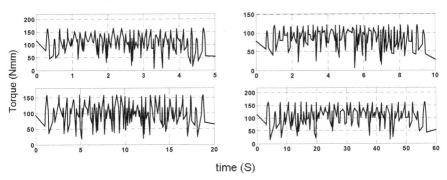

time (S)

Figure 19. The time comparison of third order trajectory planning of the first joint

Figure 20. The comparison between the time and torque of the first joint using third order trajectory planning

For Third-order Polynomial trajectory planning the maximum accelerations for robot's capabilities is given by:

$$\ddot{\theta}_{max} = \left| \frac{6(\theta_f - \theta_i)}{(t_f - t_i)} \right| \tag{21}$$

From Figure 19 the robot acceleration needed at the beginning of the motion is 0.62 (degree/s²) as well as -0.62 (degree/s²) deceleration at the end of the motion.

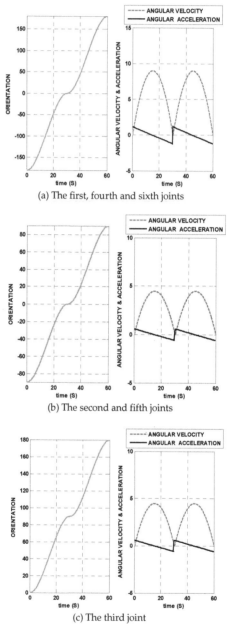

(a) The first, fourth and sixth joints

(b) The second and fifth joints

(c) The third joint

Figure 21. The orientation, angular velocity and angular acceleration for six joint micro-robot using Third order Polynomial trajectory planning

But from the equation 6.1 the maximum permissible accelerations for this robot joints is 0.6 (degree/s^2). So to be ensured that robot joint accelerations will not exceed the maximum accelerations for robot's capabilities the robot should satisfy the trajectory planning in two or more segments.

Figures 21a, b and c show the modified trajectories for the six joints, after dividing the trajectory in to two segments.

The joints angle ranges of the initial and final angles are large compared to the values of the velocity and accelerations. So it is more suitable to represent the angle-Time relation and velocity and acceleration – Time relations in two separate figures.

5.2.2. Fifth order Polynomial trajectory planning

Figures 22 and 23 show comparisons between the orientation, velocity, acceleration, and torque for four different time ranges (5, 10, 20 and 60 s) of the first joint of the robot. As is clearly shown in Figure 22 the orientation behaviour increases gradually with time from the initial angle to the final angle for the times (5, 10 and 20 s) only. But for the time 60s the orientation increases gradually from the initial angle to 40 degree then decreases to -40 degree and then increases reaching the final angle. And if the time increases the velocity required decreases. This is similar as to what is shown in Figure 23 which presents the original torque history that has considerable fluctuations. It is clear that the highest hub torque is for joint one while actuator torque of joint 6 is the lowest.

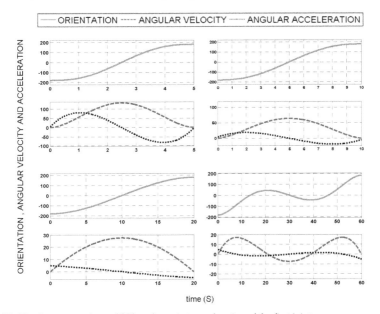

Figure 22. The time comparison of fifth order trajectory planning of the first joint

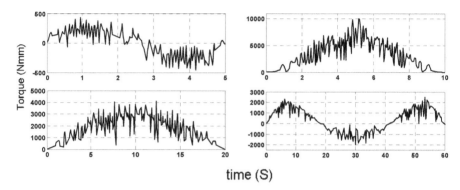

Figure 23. The comparison between the time and torque of the first joint using fifth order trajectory planning

From Figures 22 and 23 the optimum final time required to complete the process for the robot can be selected. It is seen from figures that the trajectory planning of the robot for the times (5, 10 and 20 s) has the same properties i.e. the velocity is inversely proportional with time. The orientation behaviour increased gradualy with the time from the initial angle to the final angle. Where the time 60s is omitted from selected. For figure 23 for the torque history in the time (5, 10, 20 and 60 s) it is found for $t_f = 5$ s, the dominant part in the torque history is the inertia matrix. Increasing the final time to 10, 20 and 60s shifts the dominant term from inertia matrix to Centrifugal and Coriolis matrices. This is due to the vanishing of the acceleration at most of the joint trajectory. Another consequence of increasing the final time is the dramatic increase in the peak value of the joint torque which requires big actuator size for the same task (i.e. the same joint parameters). The time 5s to complete the results of the surgical robot can be selected. Since this time has orientation behaviour was increased gradualy with the time from the initial angle to the final angle and the torque history curves were affected by the inertia of the link of robot.

Figures 24a, b and c show the trajectories for the six joints of the robot using Fifth order Polynomial trajectory planning.

5.2.3. Linear segments with parabolic blends

Figures 25 and 26 show comparisons between the orientation, velocity, acceleration, torque and four different time ranges (5, 10, 20 and 60 s) of the first joint of the surgical robot. It is clearly shown in the Figure 25 that the orientation behaviour increases gradually with the time from the initial angle to the final angle and as the time increases the velocity required decreases and also the acceleration i.e. the inertia of the robot link decreases. It is also clearly shown in the Figure 26 that the original torque history has considerable fluctuations. It is clear that the highest hub torque is for joint one while actuator torque of joint 6 is the lowest.

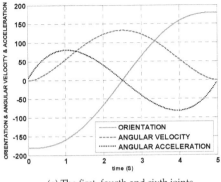

(a) The first, fourth and sixth joints

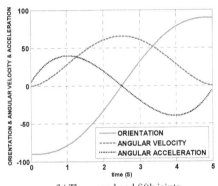

(b) The second and fifth joints

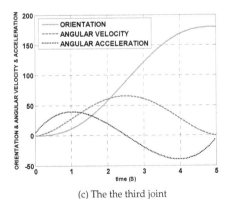

(c) The the third joint

Figure 24. The orientation, angular velocity and angular acceleration for six joint micro-robot using Fifth order Polynomial trajectory planning

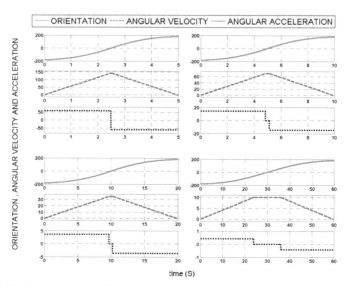

Figure 25. The time comparison of liner segments with parabolic blends trajectory of the first joint

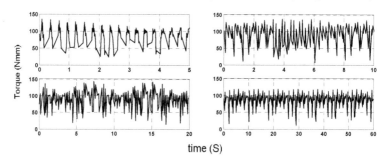

Figure 26. The comparison between the time and torque of the first joint using liner segments with parabolic blends trajectory planning

From Figures 25 and 26 the optimum final time required to complete the process for the robot can be selected. By inspection of Figure 25 the trajectory planning has three segments they are First parabolic blends, Straight line and Second parabolic blends. The straight line segment was very important segment because the velocity in this segment is constant and the acceleration was zero i.e. no inertia of the link of the robot in this segment of time. It is therefore better to have a larger period for this segment. The largest time i.e. 60s to complete the results of the robot can be selected. Since this time has the largest period of straight line segment. By inspection of Figure 26 for the torque history in the time 60s we find that the torque decreases with the time and the shooting decreases gradualy near the steady state time 60s.

Figures 27a, b and c show the trajectories for the six joints of the robot using linear segments with parabolic blends.

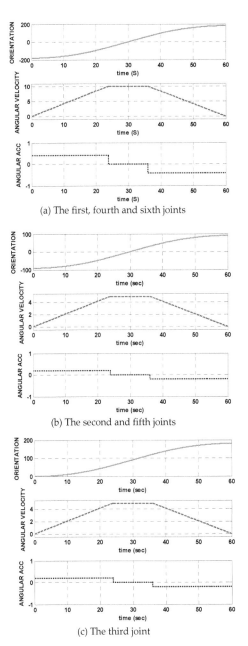

(a) The first, fourth and sixth joints

(b) The second and fifth joints

(c) The third joint

Figure 27. The orientation, angular velocity and angular acceleration for six joint micro-robot using parabolic blends trajectory planning

5.2.4. Soft motion trajectory planning

Figures 28 and 29 show comparisons between the orientation, velocity, acceleration, jerk, torque and four different time ranges (5, 10, 20 and 60 s) of the first joint of the surgical robot. It is clearly shown in the Figure 28 that the orientation behaviour increases gradually with the time from the initial angle to the final angle and as the time increases the velocity required decreases and also the acceleration i.e. the inertia of the robot link decreases. It is also clearly shown in Figure 29 that the original torque history has considerable fluctuations. It is clear that the highest hub torque is for joint one while actuator torque of joint 6 is the lowest.

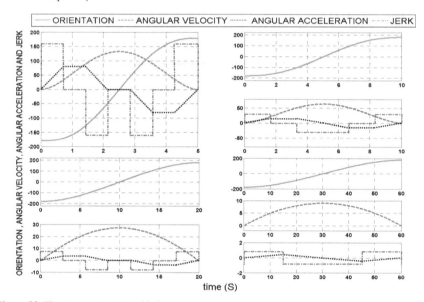

Figure 28. The time comparison of Soft motion trajectory planning of the first joint

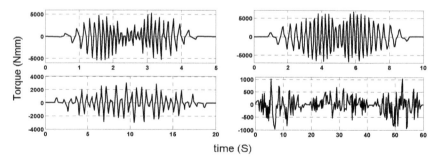

Figure 29. The comparison between the time and torque of the first joint using soft motion trajectory planning

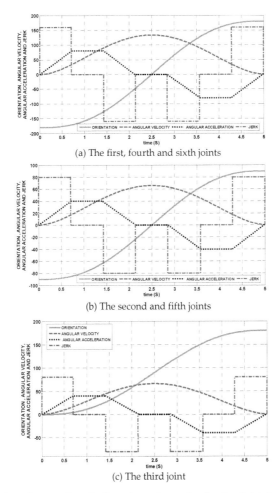

(a) The first, fourth and sixth joints

(b) The second and fifth joints

(c) The third joint

Figure 30. The orientation, angular velocity and angular acceleration for six joint micro-robot using soft motion trajectory planning

From Figures 28 and 29 we can select the optimum final time required to complete the process for the robot. By inspection of Figure 28 we find the trajectory planning three segments they are maximum jerk, maximum acceleration and maximum velocity. The maximum acceleration and maximum velocity segments were very important segments because the velocity in the maximum velocity segment is constant and the acceleration was zero i.e. no inertia of the link of the robot in this segment of time and the acceleration in the maximum acceleration segment is constant and the jerk of the link of the robot was zero. It is therefore better to have a larger period for this segment. It is seen from figures that the segments were released from time 60s but the the maximum velocity segment only was released from time 10s. Where the times (10 and 60 s) is omitted from selected i.e. the times (10 and 60 s) have properties were not satisfactory for trajectory of robot. And by inspection of Figure 29 for the torque history in the times (5 and 20 s) we find for $t_f = 5$ s, the dominant part in the torque history is the inertia matrix. Increasing the final time to 20s, shift the dominant term from inertia matrix to Centrifugal and Coriolis matrices since the effect of angular velocity will be obviously high. This is due to the vanishing of the acceleration at most of the joint trajectory. Another consequence is of increasing the final time is the dramatic change in the peak value of the joint torque which requires big actuator size for the same task. So we can select the time 5s to complete the results of the robot because the torque history curve was affected by the inertia and it has the important segment i.e. maximum acceleration and maximum velocity segments.

Figures 30a, b and c show the trajectories for the six joints of the robot using soft motion trajectory planning.

5.3. The dynamic response analysis

As previously stated that the dynamic analysis of the surgical robot was derived using Lagrange-Euler technique and the results of the dynamic analysis were depended on the method of trajectory planning. In the trajectory planning results were derived using four different methods. The dynamic analysis results of surgical robot are divided into four parts each part in for each special method of the four different methods which have been derived from the trajectory planning.

Figures 31 to 34 show the original torque history which clearly shown considerable fluctuations. It is clear that the highest hub torque is experienced at joint one while actuator torque of joint 6 is the lowest.

5.3.1. The dynamic analysis results using Third order Polynomial trajectory planning

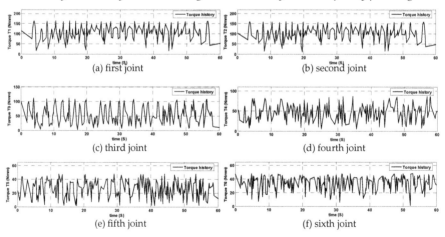

(a) first joint   (b) second joint

(c) third joint   (d) fourth joint

(e) fifth joint   (f) sixth joint

Figure 31. Torque history for Third order Polynomial trajectory planning

5.3.2. The dynamic analysis results using Fifth order Polynomial trajectory planning

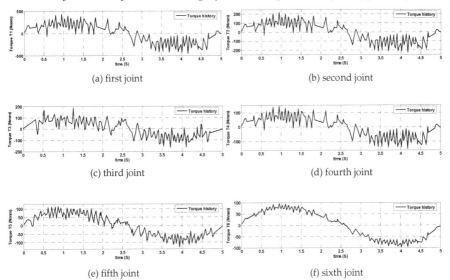

(a) first joint   (b) second joint

(c) third joint   (d) fourth joint

(e) fifth joint   (f) sixth joint

Figure 32. Torque history for Fifth order Polynomial trajectory planning

5.3.3. The dynamic analysis results using Linear segments with parabolic blends trajectory planning

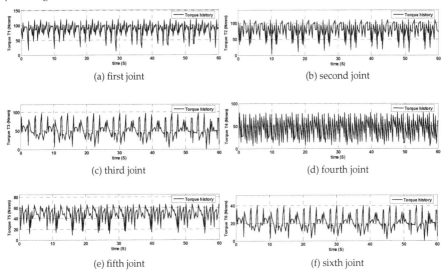

(a) first joint   (b) second joint

(c) third joint   (d) fourth joint

(e) fifth joint   (f) sixth joint

Figure 33. Torque history for Linear segments with parabolic blends trajectory planning

5.3.4. The dynamic analysis results using Soft motion trajectory planning

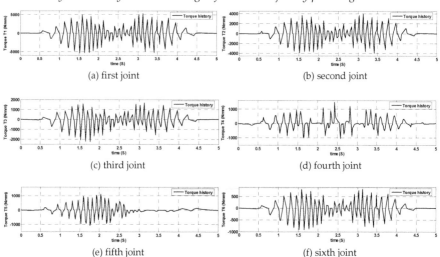

(a) first joint   (b) second joint

(c) third joint   (d) fourth joint

(e) fifth joint   (f) sixth joint

Figure 34. Torque history for Soft motion trajectory planning

6. Conclusions

A kinematic and dynamic analysis for a six-degree-of-freedom surgical robot were presented in this work. The kinematic model is based on Denavit-Hartenberg representation and the workspace of the end-effector is defined by solving the inverse kinematics problem. Four different methods were used to derive the trajectory planning for the six joints and were designed and employed to calculate the torque history for the six actuators. The dynamic equations of motion in symbolic form were derived using the   Lagrange-Euler technique and the torque history was obtained using MATLAB for each joint. The proposed algorithm is flexible and can be extended to any robot configuration provided that the Denavit-Hartenberg presentation was available and the physical limits of joints are defined. The original torque history has considerable fluctuations. It was shown that the highest hub torque was of joint 1 while actuator torque of joint 6 was the lowest. It should be also noted that changing the final time for the joint trajectory changes the torque history considerably. The final time required to complete the process was selected depending on the method used to derive the trajectory planning as previously stated.

It was clearly shown in this work that the best method of trajectory planning that gives the smooth set trajectory planning and best performance of the robot under investigation was the soft motion trajectory planning because the most important reason for this selection was the torque history that has the lowest number ever of shooting and the shooting was distributed regularly over the period of time unlike the other methods which have a long number of shootings and were distributed randomly. Also the reason for selecting this method was the disappearance of the shooting quite before the final time of trajectory i.e. the steady state time. T

Author details

Wael A. Al-Tabey
*Department of Mechanical Engineering Faculty of Engineering,
Alexandria University, Alexandria, Egypt*

Appendix

Appendix (A): Notation

C_j	$\cos \theta_j$
S_j	$\sin \theta_j$
j	the total number of joints
i	the total number of coordinates
n	the total number of links
k and p	coefficient (1, 2, 3... n)
x, y, z	local joint coordinates
X, Y, Z	global joint coordinates
Y_i	the Kinematics equations of the end effectors
X_j	the joint variables (θ_1, θ_2, θ_3, θ_4, θ_5, θ_6)
D	the end effector differential translation matrix
D_θ	the joint differential motion matrix
J	the robot Jacobian matrix (i x j)
θ_i	the initial values of each joint angle
θ_f	the final values of each joint angle
t_f	the time duration
$\theta(t)$, $\dot{\theta}(t)$, $\ddot{\theta}(t)$, $J(t)$	the orientation, angular velocity, angular acceleration and angular jerk respectively
$\ddot{\theta}_0, \dot{\theta}_0, \theta_0$	the initial conditions
T_{jpa}	Jerk positive initial time
T_{aca}	Acceleration constant initial time
T_{jna}	Jerk negative initial time
T_{vc}	Velocity constant time
T_{jnb}	Jerk negative final time
T_{acb}	Acceleration constant final time
T_{jpb}	Jerk positive final time
q	the vector of generalized joint coordinates
$\dot{q}$	the vector of joint velocities
$\ddot{q}$	the vector of joint accelerations
M	the inertia matrix

C	the Coriolis and centrifugal matrix
G	the gravity matrix
Q	the vector of generalized force associated
g^T	he gravity matrix (1x4)
g_x, g_y and g_z	the gravity components in x, y and z direction respectively
$\bar{r}_j$	the location of the center of mass of link relative to the frame representing the link
T_j	the torque on joint (j)
J_i	the inertia matrix
I_{XX}, I_{YY} and I_{ZZ}	the principal moments of inertia for the link
I_{XY}, I_{XZ} and I_{YZ}	the parallel moments of inertia for the link
m_i	the mass of the link
$\bar{X}_i$, $\bar{Y}_i$ and $\bar{Z}_i$	the distance between the X, Y and Z axis to the center of the link mass respectively

Appendix (B): MATLAB Code

```
%*********************************************************************************
%                            Micro-Robot Management
%                        Complete MATLAB Code for kinematic
%*********************************************************************************
syms th1 th2 th3 th4 th5 th6 L1 L2 L3 L4
%***********************THE INPUTS OF ROBOT ************************************
L1=input('please enter The length of Link NO(1) (mm)=');
L2=input('please enter The length of Link NO(2) (mm)=');
L3=input('please enter The length of Link NO(3) (mm)=');
L4=input('please enter The length of Link NO(4) (mm)=');
th1min=input('please enter minth1 (degree)=');
th1max=input('please enter maxth1 (degree)=');
th2min=input('please enter minth2 (degree)=');
th2max=input('please enter maxth2 (degree)=');
th3min=input('please enter minth3 (degree)=');
th3max=input('please enter maxth3 (degree)=');
th4min=input('please enter minth4 (degree)=');
th4max=input('please enter maxth4 (degree)=');
th5min=input('please enter minth5 (degree)=');
th5max=input('please enter maxth5 (degree)=');
th6min=input('please enter minth6 (degree)=');
th6max=input('please enter maxth6 (degree)=');
%*********************************************************************************

th1=th1min:2:th1max;th2=th2min:th2max;th3=th3min:th3max;
th4=th4min:2:th4max;th5=th5min:th5max;th6=th6min:2:th6max;
%*********************************************************************************
```

c1=cos(th1);c2=cos(th2);c3=cos(th3);c4=cos(th4);c5=cos(th5);c6=cos(th6);
s1=sin(th1);s2=sin(th2);s3=sin(th3);s4=sin(th4);s5=sin(th5);s6=sin(th6);
%*********************D.H matrix**

A1=[c1,-s1,0,L1*c1;s1,c1,0,L1*s1;0,0,1,0;0,0,0,1];A2=[c2,0,s2,L2*c2;s2,0,-c2,L2*s2;0,1,0,0;0,0,0,1];
A3=[c3,0,-s3,0;s3,0,c3,0;0,-1,0,0;0,0,0,1];A4=[c4,0,-s4,0;s4,0,c4,0;0,-1,0,L3;0,0,0,1];
A5=[c5,0,-s5,0;s5,0,c5,0;0,-1,0,0;0,0,0,1];A6=[c6,-s6,0,0;s6,c6,0,0;0,0,1,L4;0,0,0,1];
A01=A1;A02=A1*A2;A03=A1*A2*A3;A04=A1*A2*A3*A4;A05=A1*A2*A3*A4*A5;
A06=A1*A2*A3*A4*A5*A6;
%***********The Kinematics equations of the end effectors**

px= A06(4,1),py= A06(4,2),pz=A06(4,3)
subplot(1,3,1);plot(xa,ya);
xlabel('Px');ylabel('Py');grid on
subplot(1,3,2);plot(xa,z);
xlabel('Px');ylabel('Pz');grid on
subplot(1,3,3);plot(ya,z);
xlabel('Py');ylabel('Pz');grid on
%**THE end***
%*****************CREATED BY DR/WAEL A. AL-TABEY**********************************

7. References

[1]   Frumento, C. (2005). Development of micro tools for surgical applications. A Ph. D. Co-Tutorship Thesis, University' Degli Studi De Genova/ Uiversite Piere et Marie Currie Paris.

[2]   Venita, C. Sanjeev, D. and Craig, T. (2006). Surgical robotics and image guided therapy in pediatric surgery: Emerging and converging minimal access technologies, Seminars in Pediatric Surgery, Volume 14, pp. 267– 275.

[3]   Tsai, T. and Hsu, Y. (2004). Development of a parallel surgical robot with automatic bone drilling carriage for stereotactic neurosurgery, IEEE SMC, International Conference on Systems, Man and Cybernetics, Hague, Netherlands, October 10-13, 2004.

[4]   Miller, A. and Christensen, H. (2003). Implementation of Multi-rigid-body Dynamics within a Robotic Grasping Simulator, Proceedings of International Conference, Volume 2, pp. 2262, 14-19 Sept. 2003.

[5]   Featherstone, R. and Orin, D. (2000). Robot Dynamics: Equations and Algorithms, Proc. IEEE Int. Conf. on Robotics and Automation, pp. 826-834.

[6]   Wang, S. (2008). Conceptual design and dimensional synthesis of Micro-Hand, Mechanism and Machine Theory, Volume 43, Issue 9, pp. 1186-1197.

[7]   Alıcı, G. and Shirinzadeh, B. (2004). Loci of singular configurations of 3-DOF spherical parallel manipulator, Robotics and Autonomous Systems, Volume 48, pp. 77–91.

[8]   Ben-Horin, R. (1998). kinematics, dynamics and construction of a planarly actuated parallel robot, Robotics and computer –integrated Manufacturing, Volume 14, pp. 163–172.

[9]   Bonnifait, P. and Garcia, G. (1999). 6-DOF dynamic localization of an outdoor mobile robot, Control Engineering Practice, Volume 7, pp. 383–390.

[10] Abdellatif, H. and Heimann, B. (2008). Computational efficient inverse dynamics of 6-DOF fully parallel manipulators by using the Lagrangian formalism, Mechanism and Machine Theory, Volume 7, pp. 383–390.

[11] Zhu, Z. (2005). Kinematic and dynamic modelling for real-time control of Tau parallel robot, Mechanism and Machine Theory, Volume 40, pp. 1051–1067.

[12] Gouliaev, V. and Zavrazhina, T. (2001). Dynamics of a flexible multi-link cosmic robot-manipulator, Journal of Sound and vibration, Volume 243(4), pp. 641-65.

[13] Carrera, E. and Serna, M. (1996). Inverse dynamics of flexible robots, Mathematics and Computers in Simulation, Volume 41, pp. 485–508.

[14] Martins, F. (2008). An adaptive dynamic controller for autonomous mobile robot trajectory tracking, Control Engineering Practice, Volume 16, pp. 1354–1363.

[15] Valero, F. (2006). Trajectory planning in workspaces with obstacles taking into account the dynamic robot behaviour, Mechanism and Machine Theory, Volume 41, pp. 525–536.

[16] Geng, T. (2005). Dynamics and trajectory planning of a planar flipping robot, Mechanics Research Communications, Volume 32, pp. 636–644.

[17] Alessandro, G and Vanni, Z. (2008). A technique for time-jerk optimal planning of robot trajectories, Robotics and Computer-Integrated Manufacturing, Volume 24, pp. 415–426.

[18] Pires, S. (2007). Manipulator trajectory planning using a MOEA, Applied Soft Computing, Volume 7, pp. 659–667.

[19] Chettibi, T. (2004). Minimum cost trajectory planning for industrial robots, European Journal of Mechanics A/Solids, Volume 23, pp. 703-715.

[20] Alessandro, G. and Vanni, Z. (2007). A new method for smooth trajectory planning of robot manipulators, Mechanism and Machine Theory, Volume 42, pp. 455–471, 2007.

[21] Corke, P. (1996). A Robotics Toolbox for MATLAB, IEEE Robotics and Automation Magazine, 3(1):pp.24–32.

[22] Ata, A. (2007). Optimal Trajectory Planning for Manipulators: A Review, Journal of Engineering Science and Technology, Volume 2, No. 1, pp. 32-54.

[23] Niku, S. (2001). Introduction to Robotics Analysis, Systems, Applications, London, International (UK) Limited, pp. 147-159.

[24] Herrera, I. and Sidobre, D. (2006). Soft Motion and Visual Control of Service Robot, The Fifth International Symposium in Robotics and Automation, August 2006.

[25] Niku, S. (2001). Introduction to Robotics Analysis, Systems, Applications, London, International (UK) Limited, pp. 128-138.

[26] Al-Tabey, W. (2010). Effect of Trajectory Planning on Dynamic Response of Micro-Robot for Surgical Application, 9th WSEAS International Conference on System Science and Simulation in Engineering (ICOSSSE '10), ISBN: 978-960-474-230-1, Iwate Prefectural University, Japan, October 4-6, 2010.

[27] Tawfik, K. Ata, A. Al-Tabey, W. (2009). Kinematics and dynamics analysis of micro-robot for surgical applications, World Journal of Modelling and Simulation, Vol. 5, No. 1, pp. 22-29, ISSN 1 746-7233.

Chapter 2

Model-Based Simulation of an Intelligent Microprocessor-Based Standalone Solar Tracking System

C.S. Chin

Additional information is available at the end of the chapter

1. Introduction

Renewable energy resources will be an increasingly important part of power generation in the new millennium. Besides assisting in the reduction of the emission of greenhouse gases, they add the much- needed flexibility to the energy resource mix by decreasing the dependence on fossil fuels [1]. Among the renewable-energy resources, solar energy is the most essential and prerequisite resource of sustainable energy because of its ubiquity, abundance, and sustainability. Regardless of the intermittency of sunlight, solar energy is widely available and completely free of cost. Recently, photovoltaic (PV) system is well recognized and widely utilized to convert the solar energy for electric power applications. It can generate direct current (DC) electricity without environmental impact and emission by way of solar radiation. The DC power is converted to AC power with an inverter, to power local loads or fed back to the utility [2]. Being a semiconductor device, the PV systems are suitable for most operation at lower maintenance costs.

The PV applications could be grouped according to the scheme of interaction with utility grid: grid connected, stand alone, and hybrid. PV systems consist of a PV generator (cell, module, and array), energy storage devices (such as batteries), AC and DC consumers and elements for power conditioning. The most common method uses the PV cells in the grid network. However, to understand the performance and to maximize the efficiency of the irradiation of the PV cells, the standalone PV cells have spurred some interest, especially, in the area of the solar tracker system.

Over the years, test and researchers had proven that development of smart solar tracker maximizes the energy generation. In this competitive world of advanced scientific discoveries, the introductions of automated systems improve existing power generation methods. Before the introduction of solar tracking methods, fixed solar panels were positioned within a reasonable tilted direction based on the location. The tilt angle depending on whether a slight winter or summer bias is preferred in the system. The PV systems would face "true north" in the northern hemisphere and "true south" in the southern hemisphere. Solar tracking is best achieved when the tilt angle of the tracking PV systems is synchronized with the seasonal changes of the sun's altitude. Several methods of sun tracking systems have been surveyed and evaluated to keep the PV cells perpendicular to the sun beam. An ideal tracker would allow the PV cells to point towards the sun, compensating for both changes in the altitude angle of the sun (throughout the day), latitudinal offset of the sun (during seasonal changes) and changes in azimuth angle. In the light of this, two main types of sun trackers exist: passive (mechanical) and active (electrical) trackers. The detailed literatures review can be found in [3].

One class of the passive solar trackers is the fixed solar panel. It is placed horizontally on the fixed ground and face upwards to the sky. But most of the passive solar trackers are based on manual adjustment of the panel[4], thermal expansion of a shape memory alloy[5]or two bimetallic strips made of aluminum and steel[6]. Usually this kind of tracker is composed of a couple of actuators working against each other, which are, by equal illumination, balanced. By differential illumination of actuators, unbalanced forces are used for orientation of the apparatus in such direction where equal illumination of actuators and balance of forces is restored. Another passive tracking technology is based on the mass imbalance [6] between both ends of the panel. This kind of trackers does not use any kind of electronic control or motor. Two identical cylindrical tubes are filled with a fluid under partial pressure. The sun heats the fluid causing evaporation and transfer from one cylinder to another, which creates the mass imbalance. Passive solar trackers, compared to active trackers, are less complex but works in low efficiency. Although passive trackers are often less expensive, they have not yet been widely accepted by consumers.

On the other hands, major active trackers can be categorized as a microprocessor based, computer-controlled date and time based, auxiliary bifacial solar cell based and a combination of these three systems. In the microprocessor based solar tracker systems [7-11], a controller is connected to DC motors. Once the location is selected, the azimuth elevation range is determined, and the angular steps are calculated. Usually for monitoring the power generation, they also connected this tracking device to a PC by a code written in Assembly or C++ languages. In this solar tracker design, sensors were often used. For example, a photo-resistor [12-13] was put in a dark box with a small holes on the top to detect the illumination, and a light sensor or photosensor called light-dependent resistor (LDR) [11,14] to indicate the intensity of the radiation (that changes its electrical resistance from several thousand Ohms in the dark to only a few hundred Ohms when light falls upon it). The signals were then captured by the microcontroller that provides a signal to the motors to rotate the panel.

Whilst in the auxiliary bifacial solar cell [15] systems, the bifacial solar cell senses and drives the tracker system to the desired position. Auxiliary solar cells (panels) connected directly to a permanent magnet DC motor are fixed to a rotary axle of the tracker and can both sense and provide energy for tracking. In this design, unreliable and expensive components like batteries and driving electronics were completely eliminated. Hence, it is a very simple, reliable solar tracker for space and terrestrial applications. On the other hands, the computer-controlled date and time based system calculates the sun positions with respect to date and time with algorithms and creates signals for the system control via motor to the panel. In the solar tracking system that was designed by [16-17], the required position was calculated in advance and was programmed into Programmable Logic Control (PLC) that in term controls the motor to adjust the panel to maintain position perpendicular to the sun.

In another method that uses the combination of microprocessor with sensor and date/time based system [18-19], the sensors such as pyrheliometers (that measure the direct beam of sun irradiance) and/or light sensors send the signal to the microprocessor. Using the real-time clock (RTC), the tracker computes the position of the sun based on the date/time information of its clock. The data gathered during the day are analyzed, and a new improved set of parameters for the installation errors is computed. These data are used in the next day to compute more accurate positions of the sun, and the cycle continues.

Hence, the main difference between the active trackers is the ability to reduce the pointing error using external sensors, thereby increasing the daily irradiation the solar cells receive and the electric energy that they produced. A comparative study[3] shows that, the power consumption by the tracking device is only 2-3 % of the increased energy. The annual energy available to the two axis tracker was 72% higher than a fixed surface and 30% for single axis East-to-West tracker. However, the two or more axes trackers are more complex and costly to maintain as compared to the single-axis tracker. Furthermore, as Singapore is near to the equinoxes, the sun rises directly in East and set directly West regardless of the latitude, the single axis solar tracker becomes more favorable in this region. Based on the above-mentioned tracking systems, we have suggested that the active based single-axis tracker system is less complex to design and maintain. Additionally, for the system to work solely based on light-sensor tracking technology is not practical due to Singapore's unexpected changes in weather conditions. We have therefore come about with the idea to integrate a time-based tracking technology with the light-sensor tracking technology in the tracker system. With high numbers of high-rise buildings in Singapore, the ideas of having a wall-mounted design for each household usage become an attractive option.

In the new solar tracking system installed with sensor feedback, and real-time clock control was capable of performing both automatic and preset mode of operation. The system's ability to switch between the modes proves to be an important feature. The position and "status" of the sun is detected by two light-dependent resistor (LDR) sensors that are located at the both ends of the surface of the photovoltaic panel. In the automatic modes, the resultant signals from the sensors are fed into an electronic control system that operates a low- speed DC motor to rotate the panel via a speed-reduction system. In this mode, the Sun is not constantly tracked to prevent energy consumed by the motor, and the system will be in 'sleep' mode when the night falls. In the preset mode, the solar tracker rotates at a pre-determined angle from the sunrise to the sunset. The increment of the angle is determined through the data collected on the day and is analyzed and re-programmed for a better tracking ability on the next day. Whilst in the manual mode, the solar tracker is set to a desired angle by manually increasing or decreasing the angle via the input to the PIC microcontroller. In all modes, a night return algorithm repositioned the panel to its initial home position facing the East (at sunrise).

Besides, the ability to operate as a solar tracker, computer models of the PV panel and the electro-mechanical systems are modeled using MATLAB™/Simulink™ environment. In literature [20], a simple visual C++ program was used to provide an excellent graphic user interface (GUI) and control normal DC power supply output using the computer printer port to exactly simulate solar panel characteristics. As seen in [21-23], MATLAB ™/Simulink ™ was used to model and analyze the PV model characteristics. However, there are only a few attempts [24] to model the entire PV standalone system, including the electro-mechanical subsystem such as DC motor, drive transmission, microcontroller output, battery and charging module. Whether like or not, this is essential as they are parts of the PV systems and the influence on the overall performance such as efficiency and power output can be compromise if the electro-mechanical system is poorly design for the active solar tracker and when it is subjected to external disturbances such as wind and raindrops. With that in mind, the PV standalone system model consists of a PV panel, a servo motor, a battery, a charger, two LDR sensors, external disturbances and the microcontroller are modeled using MATLAB™/Simulink™. It was chosen due to its easy to program language supported by ready toolboxes and graphic block diagrams can be designed for complicated systems simulation. With the completed system model, it is used to determine the power and its efficiency over the fixed solar panel before actual implementation.

In summary, the book chapter presents the modeling and simulation of the solar tracker system consisting of the photovoltaic system under a constant load using MATLAB™ and Simulink™. The chapter is organized as follows. The overview of the electro-mechanical design of the single-axis solar tracker is described in Section 2. This is followed by the description of the proposed MATLAB™ and Simulink™ models in Section 3. The experiments and testing are described in Section 4. Lastly, conclusions are drawn in Section 5.

2. Solar tracker system descriptions

2.1. Mechanical structure

After the solar panels and other components were selected, the overall structural design of the solar tracker as seen in Fig.1 was fabricated. The solar tracker weight 3 kg and has an overall dimension of 340mm x 270mm x 500mm. The compactness of the proposed solar tracker enables it to be mounted on the wall. It consists of the PV panel, the pulley-chain transmission system; the motor and electronics boards support and the vertical pillar with base plate support. The entire structure was fabricated using the aluminum rods and plates. The pillar holding panel is aligned to the center of the panel for better flexibility during the panel rotation. The tracker is designed to have a single-axis rotation (East to West), and the motor is mounted in such a way that the tracker systems have only a single-axis freedom of rotation. The fixture to hold the sensors are then assembled and aligned at both ends of the PV panel to sense the sun irradiance.

The PV panel frame support (as seen in Fig. 1) has a support rod that runs across the PV panel width. The pulley on the rod supported by two bearings is directly connected to the motor shaft via the pulley transmission system. The two mechanical stoppers at each ends were incorporated to limit the rotation of the panel. As shown in Fig. 1, the components were arranged along the vertical pillar mounted on the base plate support.

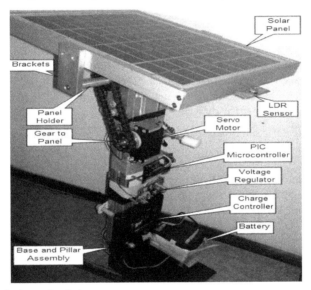

Figure 1. Actual solar tracker design

2.2. Electrical system

The overall mechanical and electrical subsystems were integrated into the solar tracker system as shown in Fig. 2. The detailed design of the circuitry could be found in [24]. The block diagram of the solar tracker system consists of mostly electrical components. The solar tracker consists of the PV cells, the charge controller and the lead-acid battery. Other subsystems such as the LDR sensors, the voltage regulator, and the microcontroller-PIC18F4520 target board were also used. The LDR sensors sense the sunlight intensity and send the signal to the microcontroller to rotate the PV panel via the servo motor. The electrical energy is then stored in the lead-acid battery that is later used to power the respective components.

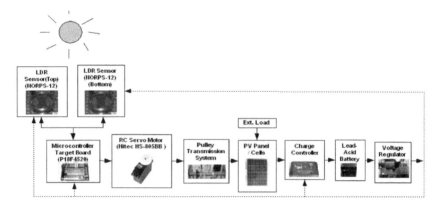

Figure 2. Schematic diagram of the standalone solar tracker system

The PV cells are a device that helps to convert the solar energy into electrical energy. The solar panel selected is capable of generating 10W power. As per the vendor specification, it weighs about 1.3kg with a dimension of 341mm x 269 mm x 28mm. Charge controller was supplied together with the solar panel's unit. It requires 12V supply and is capable of handling a maximum of 5A. The charge controller prevents the over-charging of the battery.

The LDR sensors (NORPS-12) are basically resistors that vary their resistance according to the sunlight intensity when exposed to irradiance. The output of the sensor circuit is an analogue voltage that is used as an input to the PIC microcontroller. To determine the value of resistor R, various values of different resistors were examined to finalize an appropriate resistor. The desired resistor value should provide a voltage that covers the sunny and cloudy conditions. The following resistor values as shown in Table 1 were tested. From the test result, it was found that varying the value of resistors in the voltage divider circuit helps to improve the sensitivity of the output. The resistor of 100Ω was found to be suitable to differentiate between the sunny and cloudy day.

Fixed Resistor (Ω)	V_{out} on sunny day	V_{out} on cloudy day	ΔV_{out}
50	2.14	0.82	1.32
100	*3.95*	*0.90*	*3.05*
200	4.56	1.35	3.21
500	4.78	1.41	3.37
1000	5.02	1.9	3.12

Table 1. Recorded Voltage variation at different resistor values

The driving mechanism includes the servo motor and the pulley system. The servo motor was controlled using the microcontroller. The controller uses the PWM (Pulse Width Modulation) signal to drive the servo motor at a controlled speed correspond to a maximum voltage of 6V. The PWM wave is a continuous square wave signal that changes between 0V and 6V. The duration or width of the pulse determines the angle of the shaft's rotation. A voltage regulator circuit was used to bring the supply voltage down to a level suitable for use in the microcontroller, the charge controller and the LDR sensors. The microcontroller target board in the system was used to control the servo motor. It receives the signals from the LDR sensors. The analogue voltage is converted into digital signal (logic 1 or 0) for processing. The processor was a PIC18F4520 from Microchip Inc. The PICKIT2 programmer was then used to interface MPLAB Integrated Development Environment to the target board. To program the microcontroller target board, MPLAB C18 Compiler software that runs on the Microsoft Window as a 32-bit application was used. The C program was then compiled into assembly language before downloading into the target board.

2.3. Modes of operation

There are three modes of operation in the solar tracker. They are namely: automatic, preset and manual mode. In the automatic mode, the PIC microcontroller rotates the PV panel to balance the light intensity at both LDR sensors. In the case when both sensors receive a low voltage due to cloudy conditions, the PV panel is programmed to wait for 15minutes and automatically switched to preset mode (using internal real-time clock). In this mode, the PV panel is programmed to rotate 2° towards west in every 15 minutes. If the extreme position towards the west is sensed (at sunset), the night return algorithm repositioned the panel to its initial home position facing the East (at sunrise). In the manual mode, it allows the panel to rotate to the desired angle by manually increasing or decreasing the angle via the input to the PIC microcontroller. Once the PV panel is positioned to the desired angle, it switches back to the automatic mode.

In summary, the operation modes for the control of solar tracker and the features in these user options are shown below.

- When the SW1 switch is pressed, it rotates the panel to the home position and waits for the user to select the automatic mode (SW2), the preset mode (SW3) or manual mode (SW4).
- When the SW2 switch is pressed, it starts the tracking in "automatic mode". In this mode, the rotation of the PV panel depends on the LDR sensors.
- When the SW3 switch is pressed, it starts the tracking in "preset mode". In this case, it rotates the panel in a pre-determined angle till the sunset.
- When the SW4 switch is pressed; the panel is allowed to rotate manually to a desired position. Once it is positioned, it switches back to the automatic mode.

3. Standalone solar tracker system modeling

In this section, the main aim is to simulate the single axis solar tracking system during the automatic mode using MATLAB™ /Simulink™ (see Fig. 3). To obtain a more realistic model, the solar tracker is subjected to external disturbances such as wind and raindrop. It should be similar to the real prototype made in section 2 such that comparisons could be made fairly. All the data for building the simulation models were obtained from either the components' datasheets or the experiments conducted. The simulation run was performed in every second of the entire 10 hours or 36000 seconds of experimental setup. The rapid accelerator mode has been chosen to reduce the simulation time to about 180-seconds real time (one-second second simulation time is equivalent to 180-seconds real time). The rapid accelerator mode gives the best speed improvement compared to normal mode when simulation execution time exceeds the time required for code generation. For this reason, the rapid accelerator mode generally performs better than normal mode when simulation execution times are several minutes or more. The ODE45 solver type of variable step size was used throughout the simulations. Solar tracker model developed in Simulink could detect the sun irradiance to produce the required current. The simulation model is implemented in such a way that when the sun irradiance falls on the sensors, the servo motor moves the PV panel in an incremental way until the sunset.

The PV tracking panel with two LDR sensors, namely: V_LDR_B and V_LDR_T are the bottom and top voltage outputs based on the corresponding sun irradiance data. The irradiance from the sun model was obtained by dividing the power obtained from the tracker by the surface area of the PV cells. The outputs were used as inputs to the microcontroller. The servo motor rotates the panel at an angle based on the microcontroller PWM signal. This process repeats again until the sunset. During the process, the PV panel generates direct current that keeps the 12V battery charged. The battery gets charged or discharged depending on the state of the charger. The external load was modeled by a pure resistor to simulate the loading on the motor shaft. The wind and rain droplet were modeled as additional current load (that is by deducting the actual current generated from the solar cells) on the solar tracker. The efficiency of the proposed solar tracking system over the fixed panel can be compared. With the model, it is used to determine the types of PV systems that could be successfully combined to give a required level of efficiency before actual implementation.

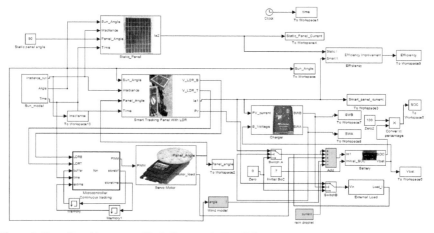

Figure 3. Overall tracking system block diagrams in Simulink

3.1. PV panel model

The simplest equivalent circuit of a solar cell is a current source in parallel with a diode as shown in Fig. 4. The current source represents the current generated by the PV cell due to the photons received by it, and is constant under constant sun irradiance and temperature. During darkness, the solar cell is not an active device; it works as a diode. It produces neither a current nor a voltage. However, if it is connected to an external supply (large voltage) it generates a saturation current or dark current. The key parameters for a PV cell are short circuit current (*Isc* or the current from the solar cell when the voltage across the cell is zero), open circuit voltage (*Voc*) and sun irradiance value. Usually these values are given by the manufacturer in the data sheet.

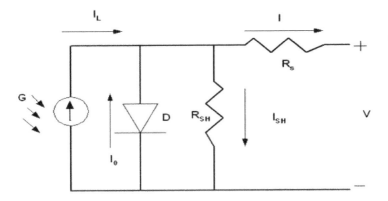

Figure 4. Circuit diagram of a PV cell model

Normally a single PV cell produces a rather small voltage that have less practical use. The real PV panel always uses many cells to generate a large voltage. For example the Kamtex-10W PV module used for our project comprises of 36 cells to generate a large enough voltage to charge a 12 volt battery. The data sheet for Kamtex-10W is given in Table 2.

Parameter	Value
Maximum Power (P_{max})	10W
Voltage at P_{max}	17.6V
Current at P_{max}	0.57A
Short-circuit current (I_{sc})	0.6A
Open-circuit voltage (V_{oc})	21.6V
Temperature coefficient of open-circuit voltage	-(10+/-1)mV/degree Celsius
Temperature coefficient of short-circuit current	(0.065+/-0.015)%/degree Celsius
Nominal Operating Cell Temperature (NOCT)	30+/-3degree Celsius

Table 2. Electrical characteristics of PV Module-Kamtex (KMX-10W)

The following parameters were used in the calculation of the net current of a PV cell.

- Saturation current of the diode, I_0.
- Net current from the PV panel I.
- Light-generated current inside the cell I_L.
- Series resistance R_s, which is internal resistance of the PV panel;
- Shunt resistance R_{sh}, in parallel with the diode, R_{sh} is very large unless many PV modules are connected in a large system;
- Diode quality factor, n;

In an ideal cell R_s is 0 and R_{sh} is infinite. The net current of the PV cells is the difference between the output current [25-26] from the PV cells and the diode current is given by.

$$I = I_L - I_o \left[e^{\frac{q(V + IR_s)}{nkT}} - 1 \right] \tag{1}$$

where V is the voltage across the PV cell, k is the Boltzmann's constant (=1.381×10^{-23} J/K), T is the junction temperature in Kelvin, q is the electron charge (=1.602×10^{-19}C), n is the diode ideality factor ($\approx$1.62).

$$I_L = I_L(T_1) + K_0(T_{ref} - T_1) \tag{2}$$

$$I_L(T_1) = I_{sc}(T_1).G(T_{ref}) \tag{3}$$

$$K_0 = \frac{I_{sc}(T_2) - I_{sc}(T_1)}{T_2 - T_1} \tag{4}$$

Here, T_{ref} equals to 298K is the reference temperature of the PV cell, G (T_{ref}) equals to 1000W/m^2. K_0 is the temperature coefficient are used. Then,

$$I_0 = I_0(T_{ref}) \times \left(\frac{T}{T_{ref}} \right)^{\frac{3}{n}} e^{\frac{-qV_g}{nk}\left(\frac{1}{T_{ref}} - \frac{1}{T_1} \right)} \tag{5}$$

$$I_0(T_{ref}) = \frac{I_{sc}(T_1)}{e^{\frac{qV_{oc}(T_1)}{nkT_1}} - 1}; \quad V_0(T_1) = \frac{nkT_1}{q} \ln\left(\frac{I_L}{I_0} \right) \tag{6}$$

where V_g is the band gap energy (=1.12eV). It is the energy needed to break a bond in the crystal, V_{oc} is the open circuit voltage corresponds to the photocurrent I_L. The resistance within each cell in the connection between cells is the series resistance, R_s

$$R_s = \frac{dV}{dI_{Voc}} - \frac{1}{X_v} \tag{7}$$

$$X_v = I_0(T_1)\frac{q}{nkT_1}e^{\frac{qV_{oc}(T_1)}{nkT_1}} - \frac{1}{X_v} \tag{8}$$

By Newton's method,

$$x_{n+1} = x_n - f(x_n)/f'(x_n) \tag{9}$$

where $f'(x)$ is the derivative of the function $f(x) = 0$, x_n is a present value, and x_{n+1} is the next value. So,

$$f(I) = I_L - I - I_0\left[e^{\frac{q(V+IR_s)}{nkT}} - 1\right] = 0 \tag{10}$$

Then using Newton's equation:

$$I_{n+1} = I_n - \frac{I_L - I_n - I_0\left[e^{\frac{q(V+IR_s)}{nkT}} - 1\right]}{-1 - I_0 qR_s \cdot e^{\frac{q(V+IR_s)}{nkT}}} \tag{11}$$

By using MATLAB™, the above function can be computed numerically to obtain the net output current from the PV cells.

The fixed PV panel was modeled as shown in Fig.5 using the equations as seen in (11). The output voltage of the battery is 12V. The temperature (T_{aC}) obtained during the experiment and the sun irradiance data (G) that represents the intensity (or the power of sunlight falling per unit area) were used. The solar irradiance data were taken hourly, and the averages in each hour were then tabulated. The PV Cells Array block diagram computes the net current from the PV cells using the embedded MATLAB function. The plot for the actual and simulated net output current is shown in Fig. 6. The deviation in the plot may due to the averaging done during each hour and the power consumed before noon was actually higher than expected. This is reasonable as the sunlight is stronger during the day.

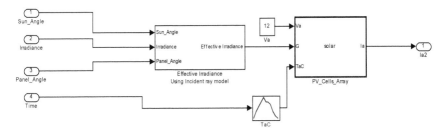

Figure 5. Fixed PV panel model

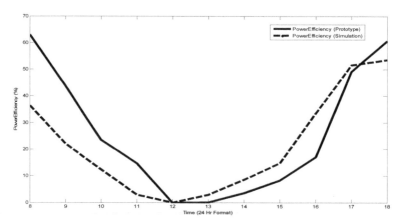

Figure 6. Actual and simulated net output current value of fixed panel

To simulate the sun irradiance at different PV panel's angle, the effective irradiance was used. Details of the effective irradiance block diagram can be seen in Fig. 7. The block diagram defined the angle between sun's incident ray and PV panel. For a static panel, it is always parallel to the ground that is at 90 degrees (0 degree for sunrise and 180 degrees for sun set). A simple program was written to obtain the relationship of the effective sun irradiance when the difference between the sun angle and panel angle is more than +/-90 degrees. To limit the angle to 90 degrees, the cosine trigonometric function was introduced in the model to create the zero sun irradiance when such a situation occurs.

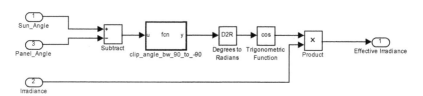

Figure 7. Effective sun irradiance model

3.1.1. Smart tracker PV panel

The smart tracker panel was installed with two LDR sensors. Assuming both sensors are placed in parallel with the PV panel, the effective irradiance is similar. As the results, the smart tracker is unable to perform the proposed sun tracking algorithm. To circumvent this, the top and bottom sensors were positioned at 45 degrees and 135 degrees respectively as seen in Fig. 8. When the sunlight falls onto the PV panel, the LDR sensors generate different voltages (that is V_LDR_B and V_LDR_T according to the changes in the sun irradiance) to move the PV panel.

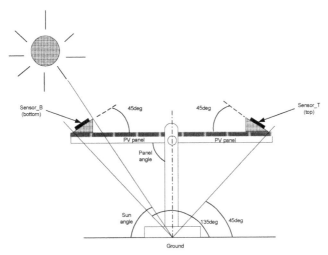

Figure 8. PV panel and LDR sensor angle position

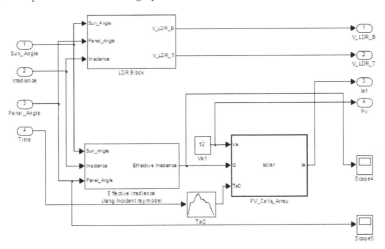

Figure 9. Smart tracker PV panel Model

3.2. Sun model

At each time instant, the actual sun irradiance data obtained from the experiment was used. In the sun model, the sun is assumed to travel from the 0 degree (sunrise) to 180 degrees (sunset) from 7am to 5pm. During these 10 hours, the PV panel rotates 180 degrees. As shown in Fig. 10, the initial sun's angle is at 30 degrees and with the angle changes at 15 degrees per hour or 0.004147 per simulated time in second; the corresponding sun angle (with respect to the base) is obtained.

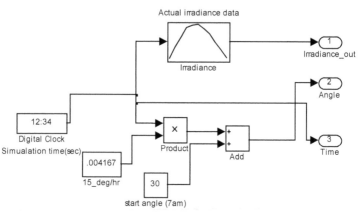

Figure 10. Sun's model

3.3. LDR sensor model

The LDR sensor is a variable resistor that changes the resistance according to the intensity of incident ray illuminated onto it. As the intensity of sunlight changes, the resistance and the voltage of LDR sensors change. The output voltage across the resistor (resistance value of 100Ω) is converted into digital signal at the input of the microcontroller. Based on the TTL input, the servo motor rotates clockwise (CW) or anticlockwise (CCW). In the LDR sensor model as shown in Fig. 11, the difference between the panel angle and the assumed sun position was calculated. The angles were limited to +/- 90 degrees. When 90 degrees is reached, the LDR sensor output a zero irradiance that corresponds to a certain voltage as shown in Table 1. Recalled, V_LDR_B and V_LDR_T are the voltage output from the bottom and top sensors.

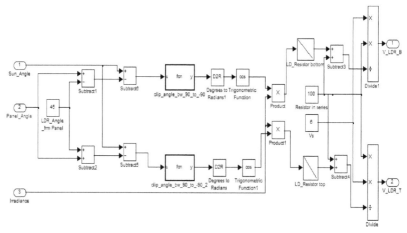

Figure 11. LDR sensor model

3.4. Microcontroller model

As shown in Fig. 12, the microcontroller model is modeled using the embedded MATLAB™ function. The inputs to this function are LDR_B and LDR_T, a real-time clock and initial buffer value of 1.5. One of the inputs (named Extime) is used to compare the current time with the previous time when the PWM value changes. The microcontroller generates output duration of 1.5ms to rotate the PV panel if the voltage difference of the LDR sensors is less than 0.07V and are both less than 0.75V (very low irradiance). If LDR sensor's voltages are both greater than 0.75V but the voltage difference is less than 0.07V, the PV panel remains in the current position. When the LDR sensor values is greater than 0.07V, the motor turns the PV panel by adjusting its PWM value until the sensors' voltages are equal. The delay time of 0.7 seconds and increment steps were found using the trial-and-error method during the simulation.

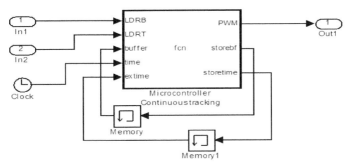

Figure 12. Microcontroller model

3.5. Charger model

A charger is essential to protect the battery from over-charged and fully drained. In an ideal case, the battery charge remains between 20% and 100% based on a PSpice photovoltaic model [27]. This charger model (see Fig. 13) includes two switches namely: Switch A and B to control the battery voltage flow. Switch A remains deactivated for any value of battery charge above 12.95V (100% charged). Switch B deactivates once the battery charge drops to 11.6V (20% charge left). The truth table for the charge control is given in Table 3.

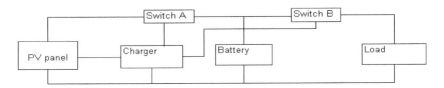

Figure 13. Block diagram of charge control

The Switch A is connected to the PV module on one side and the battery on the other side. When the net output current from the PV panel is positive, it begins to charge the battery until the maximum charge of 12.95V is reached. When there is no current from PV panel, the switch remains activated, the current required is obtained from the battery. After the battery is fully charged, the switch disconnects. The switch is activated again if the battery voltage drops below to 12.2 V.

The Switch B is connected when the battery is in charging mode (greater than 12.25V). When the battery voltage drops below 11.6 V, the battery is draining, and hence it is important to cut off the loads in order not to damage the motor. The conditions for the switching are given in Table 3 and the corresponding values of Switch A and Switch B (previous states and current states) are given by X, Y, M and N respectively. The value '1' represents the closed switch and '0' represents the open switch.

Voltage range of battery	X	Y		Voltage range of battery	M	N
V>=12.95	0	0		V<=11.6	0	0
V>=12.95	1	0		V<=11.6	1	0
12.2<V<12.95	0	0		11.6<V<=12.25	0	0
12.2<V<12.95	1	1		11.6<V<=12.25	1	1
V<=12.2	0	1		V>=12.25	0	1
V<=12.2	1	1		V>=12.25	1	1

Table 3. Truth table used for discharging (left) and charging (right) condition

The Simulink model of the charger can be seen in Fig. 14. The Compare block diagrams were used to compare the various conditions as shown in Table 3. The logic gate after the comparisons serves as the truth table for operating the Switch A and B.

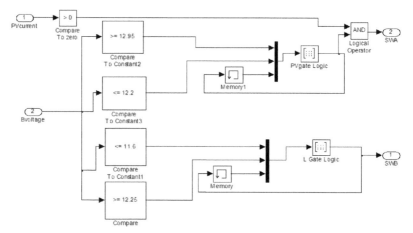

Figure 14. Charger model in Simulink

3.6. Battery model

The lead-acid battery model was implemented based on a PSpice model [27] for a lead acid battery. It has two modes of operation – charging and discharging modes. When the current to the battery is positive (negative), the battery is in the charging (discharging) mode. The following parameters were used for modeling the battery.

- SOC_i is the initial state of charge,
- SOC (%) is the available charge.
- SOC_m is the maximum state of charge.
- n_s is the number of 2V cells in series.
- D (h^{-1}) is the self-discharge rate of battery.
- K_b (no unit) is the charging and discharging battery efficiency.

As SOC varies linearly with V_{ocb} (open circuit voltage of the battery), the relationship between open circuit battery voltage and state of charge can be determined using the Table 4.

Voltage	State of Charge (%)
12.63	100
12.54	90
12.45	80
12.39	75
12.27	60
12.18	50
11.97	25
11.76	Completely discharged

Table 4. State of charge with respect to Voc

The terminal voltage for the battery is given by:

$$V_{bat} = V_1 + I_{bat}R_1 \tag{12}$$

Here V_1 and R_1 both depend on the mode of battery operation and have different equations. Battery current; I_{bat} is positive when battery is in charge (ch) mode and negative when in discharge (dch) mode.

In charging mode, we can write the resistance and voltage as follows:

$$R_1 = R_{ch} = \left(0.758 + \frac{0.139}{[1.06 - SOC(t)]n_s}\right)\frac{1}{SOC_m} \tag{13}$$

$$V_1 = V_{ch} = [2 + 0.148 \cdot SOC(t)]n_s \tag{14}$$

where $SOC\,(t)$ represents the current state of charge (%), $SOC\,(t)$ is defined by a set of equations later. In discharging mode, the resistance and voltage are written as follows:

$$R_1 = R_{dch} = \left(0.19 + \frac{0.1037}{[SOC(t) - 0.14]n_s}\right)\frac{1}{SOC_m} \tag{15}$$

$$V_1 = V_{dch} = [1.926 + 0.124 \cdot SOC(t)]n_s \tag{16}$$

To estimate the value of $SOC\,(t)$, the following equations have been used to describe them in the PSpice model[27].

$$SOC(t + dt) = SOC(t)\left(1 - \frac{D\ dt}{3600}\right) + \frac{K_b\left(V_{bat}I_{bat} - R_1I_{bat}^2\right)\ dt}{3600} \tag{17}$$

In equation (17), the time is assumed in seconds, so some terms must be divided by 3600 such that SOC is in Wh. By substituting V_{bat} as a function of V_1, the value of $SOC\,(t)$ can be determined as shown.

$$SOC(t) = SOC(t - 1) + \frac{1}{3600}\int_{t-1}^{t}\left[\frac{K_bV_1I_{bat}}{SOC_m} - SOC(t - 1)D\right]dt \tag{18}$$

The Simulink model in Fig. 15 is used to model the charging and discharging conditions during the process. The left-hand side of the Fig. 15 shows the respective functions used. There are namely: V_{ch}, V_{dch}, R_{ch} and R_{dch}. The input to the battery is the net current output from the PV panel and the output is the battery voltage, V_{bat}. In order to obtain 12V, six 2V cells denoted by n_s were used. The maximum state of charge, SOC_m was set to 84. The discharge rate, D and the efficiency, K_b are set as 1.5×10^{-5} and 0.8 respectively. As the battery is in charging or discharging mode, it allows only one value for R_1 and V_1 to the equations.

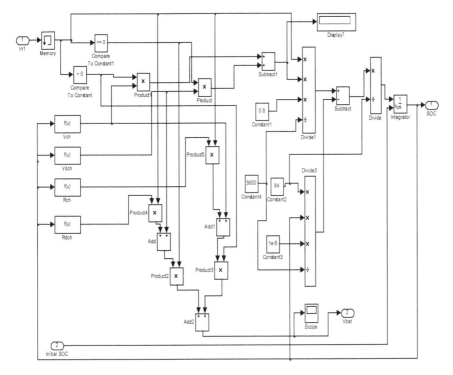

Figure 15. Battery model in Simulink

3.7. PWM servo motor model

The solar panel is designed to drive the PV panel in a small angle, between 0 to 180 degrees at a low speed. PWM is used to control the motor. The PWM is a continuous square wave with a period of 20ms. With the PWM signal, the output shaft of the servo motor changes the angular position of the PV panel. The following parameters are used for the servo motor.

- Moment of inertia $(J) = 0.01 \text{ kg.m}^2/\text{s}^2$;
- Damping ratio $(b) = 0.1$ Nms;
- Electromotive force constant $(K_t) = 0.01$Nm/Amp;
- Back electromotive force constant $(K_e) = 0.01$s.s/rad;
- Electric resistance $(R_m) = 1$ ohm;
- Electric inductance $(L_m) = 0.5$H;
- Input Voltage (V_m);
- Output angle (θ);

For the PWM servo motor, the transfer function between the output rotational angle and the input voltage is written as follows.

$$\frac{\theta(s)}{V_m(s)} = \frac{15}{(s+1)(s+1)+14} = \frac{15}{s^2+2s+15} \tag{19}$$

Based on this transfer function, the servo motor model can be modeled in Simulink (as seen in Fig. 16) using the look-up tables. The look-up table uses the PWM as an input to rotate the motor to a pre-determined angle. When pulse width changes from 1.25ms to 1.75ms, the panel angle changes from the 0 degree to 180 degrees in a linear manner. The second look-up table on the feedback path provides the actual pulse width results. The actual and the desired pulse-width are then compared to obtain the error signal for the Proportional-Integral-Derivative (PID) controller (using the controller gains: $K_p = 60, K_I = 30, K_D = 3$) to drive the motor to the desired angle. The embedded MATLAB™ function block is used to deactivate the motor load when it is not turning. An external load was added to show whether the motor is able to drive the PV panel. The weight could vary due to the modeling error. In this case, the external load is modeled as a pure resistance value ($\approx 40\Omega$).

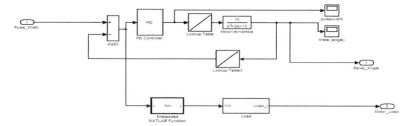

Figure 16. PWM Servo motor model in Simulink

3.8. Wind model

Tracking the sun irradiance in an ideal condition would involve no disturbances on the system. But in practice, factors such as external force like wind and rain (as seen in Fig. 17) moves the tracker away from its position. It is therefore vital for the solar tracker to be able to track the sun throughout the daytime. Two types of disturbances are considered: wind and raindrop as depicted in Fig. 17 schematically.

The drag force due to the wind comprises of two main forms: (a) friction drag is present when the panels are near to horizontal position; (b) Pressure drag is prominent when the tracker is positioned near to vertical position. As a preliminary model, the drag coefficient is modeled as a flat plate and the area of the solar tracker varies with angle, θ. The seventh power law [28], as shown below can estimate the air velocity over the tracker.

$$\frac{u}{U_0} = \left(\frac{y}{d}\right)^{1/7} \tag{20}$$

where u is air velocity at height y; U_0 is air velocity at boundary layer; y is height above surface; d is height of boundary layer (taken from ground).

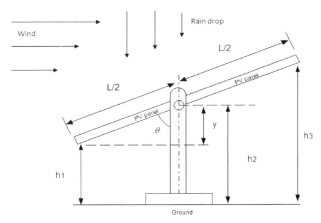

Figure 17. Schematic diagram of disturbances acting on solar tracker

Taking small changes on both sides,

$$du = \frac{U_o}{d^{1/7}}(dy)^{1/7} \quad (21)$$

For a certain velocity at any height above the ground, the drag force acting on a tilted plate is written as:

$$F_D = \frac{1}{2}C_d\rho_a A_a U^2 \quad (22)$$

Using (21) and (22), the wind drag force must be integrated over the area of the tilted solar tracker facing the wind. The resulting moment or torque about the central axis becomes:

$$dM = \frac{1}{2}C_d\rho_a A_a \cos\theta \left(\frac{U_o}{d^{1/7}}\right)^2 \left[\left(\int_{h_2}^{h_1} \left(y-h_2\right)^{7/2} dy\right)^{1/7} - \left(\int_{h_3}^{h_2} (h_2-y)^{7/2} dy\right)^{1/7}\right]^2 \quad (23)$$

where h_1 and h_3 are heights of each side of the solar tracker; h_2 is height of centre axis of rotation as shown in Fig. 17. This moment differential about the central axis, due to the wind force, can be modeled using MATLAB/Simulink as a continual force that consumes the current obtained from the irradiance.

The Simulink model is shown in Fig.18. Equation (23) was modeled in Simulink. The integral terms in (23) are modeled as a summation in the difference between the lower vertical height ($y-h_2$) acting in counter-clockwise direction and its upper vertical height (h_2-y) acting in the clockwise direction. The values for the parameters as shown in Fig. 18 are as follows: h_1=0.415m, h_2=0.500m, h_3=0.585m, L= 0.34m, ρ_a = 1.165 kg/m³ (at outdoor temperature of 30ºC), A = 0.092m², U_o=0.8m/s (around 1.56 knots) , C_d=1.0 and d=1m.

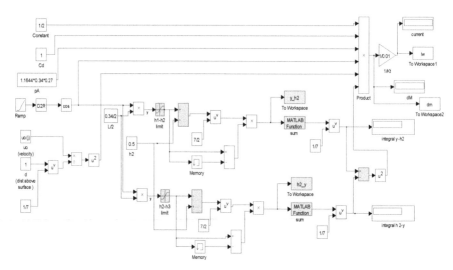

Figure 18. Simulink model for wind force

As shown in Fig. 19, the increases in the wind speed causes the current consumption (or moment) acting on the tilted solar tracker to increases. It could be observed that the wind loading is cyclic in nature as the moment acting on the solar tracker changes as time increases. As an increase in the torque required implies an increase in the current (as shown in the relationship K_t=0.01Nm/A) needed to drive the tilted solar tracker, this causes an increase in the current drawn from the battery. For a wind speed of 0.8m/s (or 1.56 knots), the estimated moment acting on the tilted solar tracker is estimated to be around 0.0022Nm and the corresponding current consumed is computed to be approximately 0.22A.

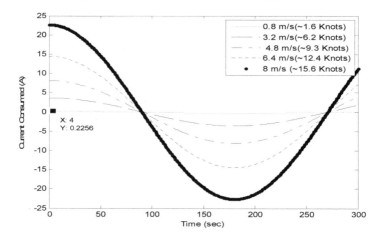

Figure 19. Current consumed due to wind force over time

3.9. Raindrop

Raindrop is driven along by the gravitational force. The movements can be evaluated by considering the equation of motion of the particles in horizontal along-wind, cross-wind and vertical directions. In this paper, we considered the raindrop that is not driven by the wind. Instead, we consider the mass of rain droplet (m) acting on the surface of the solar tracker. As the volume of the rain droplet is spherical in shape, the mass can be computed by multiplying it by the water density. The total force acting on the surface of the solar tracker can be computed as:

$$F_R = \frac{4}{3}\pi r_r^3 \rho_w g \tag{24}$$

where ρ_w is the water density, r_r is the radius of the raindrop and g is the gravitational constant.

In the simulation, the total force, F_r acting on the surface of the solar tracker could be easily modeled. The point force acting on the surface is translated into the torque acting about the central axis by multiplying the value by $L/2$ (that is half of the width of the solar panel). The radius of the rain droplet r_r is assumed to be small, that is 0.25mm instead of large raindrop. The current consumed as a result of the rain droplet is around 0.011 mA.

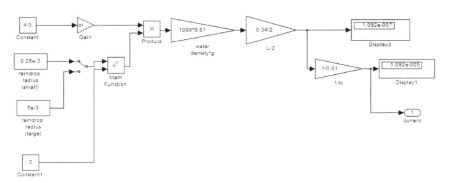

Figure 20. Rain droplet model on surface of solar tracker

4. Experimental and simulation results

In order to validate the proposed modeling, it was necessary to compare the experiment results for the fixed panel with the smart solar tracker system. To obtain this data, simple experiments were performed. The experiment setup for both fixed, and tracker system can be seen in Fig. 21. The setups were installed on building roof top that was 40m above the ground. The temperatures during the experiment were recorded using the Type-K thermocouple sensor. The open-circuit voltage and the current readings were recorded using a multi-meter connected to the solar cells. The climatic condition considered for experimental was sunny during the entire test period. The average temperature recorded was around 30°C and the local wind speed was broadcasted to be around 0.8m/s (or 1.6knots) during the tests.

Figure 21. Experiment Setup for fixed (left) and smart tracker (right) system

The simulation results of the solar tracker using the Simulink are shown in Fig. 22. As observed from the plots, the solar tracker is able to follow the sun angle. In the plot, the smart solar tracker produces a higher current output as compared to the static PV panel. The other part of the graph shows the state of the charge during the simulation. As seen in the battery voltage, the Switch A was deactivated when the maximum allowable voltage of 12.95V reached. The switch B was always connected during the entire duration (in charging mode).

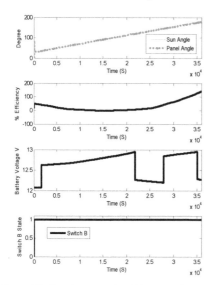 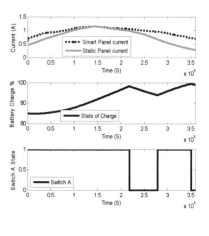

Figure 22. Simulation results of the standalone smart solar tracker

In Fig. 23, the simulated power output (or current) over the day was quite close to the actual results obtained. There was some slight deviation during the noon and evening period due to the modeling of the actual irradiance obtained from the experiment. Furthermore, the current consumed during the actual test was different as the wind loading and other disturbances were not modeled in the simulation.

Power Output

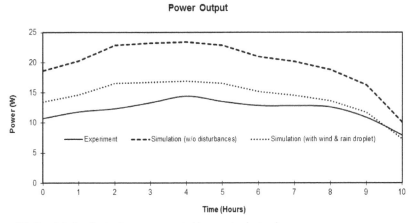

Figure 23. Simulated and actual power generated by smart solar tracker

The output power of the smart tracker was compared with the fixed panel design in order to determine the efficiency of the solar tracker system. As expected the overall power (or the efficiency) generated by the tracking panel is higher than that of the static panel. However, with the disturbances acting on the simulated models (see Fig. 23), the simulated curve exhibits closer behavior to the actual response obtained from experiment. Here, the efficiency refers to the ratio of difference between the sum of smart tracker and the fixed panel power to the sum of fixed panel power over the period of interest. The efficiency (obtain from experiment results) is around 20%. As compared to various the solar trackers as seen in [3], the average efficiency is around 12-15% and hence, the proposed design is slightly higher and comparable to the existing design. The solar tracker was efficient during most of the day except during the noon time where the sun irradiance was found to be the highest. The fixed panel that lies horizontally on the ground is therefore, quite comparable to the solar tracker system and hence zero efficiency was obtained. This explained why it is common to use a fixed panel in a sunny day where it experienced the maximum sun irradiance during the noon time.

For the cost and benefit of the proposed solar tracker system, it has some special features such as the initial expenditure on the equipment is usually high but there is no fuel cost involved, and the maintenance cost is low. The accumulated data [29] show that at present a PV system is competitive where small amounts of energy are required at a place that is far away from an electric grid or any other source of energy. For the economic evaluation of a system, the parameters that are usually considered are the life-cycle cost (LCC), payback period (PP) and rate of return (RR). LCC is the sum of all the costs of a system over its lifetime, expressed in today's money. In case of the analysis of a PV system, the lifetime of the modules is usually taken as 20 years. The calculations were made on the basis of the approach described in [29-30]. Our estimates of the electricity cost matched with those reported in [29] for the PV, diesel generator and grid-extension systems. Our analysis shows that the cost of electricity from a PV system is approximately equal to that from a diesel generator and cheaper than a grid extension. This PV system may be used for domestic applications, especially in remote areas. Keeping in view the environmental impact and economic assessments of the designed PV system it is evident to the listed data that the PV system even at present is a competitive choice for small power requirements. With the expectation that the cost of a solar module will reduce from around $ 3/Wp to somewhere below $2/Wp in the near future (see one of the quarterly report from Solarbuzz.com), a PV system may as well become an economic and more attractive option for higher loads.

5. Conclusions

The design, modeling and testing of an active single axis solar tracker were presented. In the proposed design and operation of the solar tracker system, the sun was not constantly tracked based on the simulated irradiation. This helps to prevent unnecessary energy to be consumed by the devices and the system stops moving when the night falls. Hence, the proposed control structure provides the flexibility to accommodate different weather conditions, and also different user preference. The completed MATLAB™/Simulink™ model of the solar tracker with external disturbances is first used to provide a computer-aided design tool to determine the efficiency over the fixed solar panel, net current output, power generated and the types of PV systems that can be combined to give a required level of efficiency before actual implementation. The experimental results show a similar behavior in the power, the efficiency and the current output over the fixed solar panel when compared them with the simulation results. The external disturbances such as wind loading and raindrop model provide an insight to the impact of the current consumption on the model of the solar tracker before actual implementation.

Author details

C.S. Chin
Faculty of Science Agriculture and Engineerin,Newcastle University,
Newcastle upon Tyne , United Kingdom

6. References

[1] Lopes L A C, Lienhardt A M, (2003) A Simplified Nonlinear Power Source for Simulating PV Panels. IEEE 34th Annual Conference on Power Electronics Specialist: 1729- 1734.
[2] Kroposki B, DeBlasio R (2000) Technologies for the New Millennium: Photovoltaics as a Distributed Resource. IEEE Power Engineering Society Summer Meeting: 1798 – 1801.

[3]   Mousazadeh H, Keyhani A, Javadi A, Mobli H, Abrinia K, Sharifi A (2009) A Review of Principle and Sun-Tracking Methods for Maximizing Solar Systems Output. Renewable and Sustainable Energy Reviews 13:1800-1818.

[4]   Mwithiga G, Kigo S N (2006) Performance of a Solar Dryer with Limited Sun Tracking Capability. Journal of Food Engineering 74: 247-252.

[5]   Poulek V (1994) Testing the New Solar Tracker with Shape Memory Alloy Actors. IEEE Photovoltaic Specialists Conference 1: 1131–1133.

[6]   Clifford M J, Eastwood D (2004) Design of a Novel Passive Solar Tracker. Solar Energy 77: 269-280.

[7]   Bingol O, Altintas A O (2006) Microcontroller Based Solar-Tracking System and Its Implementation. Journal of Engineering Sciences 12:243-248.

[8]   Koyuncu B, Balasubramanian K (1991) A Microprocessor Controlled Automatic Sun Tracker. IEEE Transactions on Consumer Electronics 37: 913-917.

[9]   Zeroual A, Raoufi M, Ankrim M, Wilkinson A J (1998) Design and Construction of a Closed Loop Sun-Tracker with Microprocessor Management. Solar Energy 19: 263-274.

[10] Jinayim T, Arunrungrasmi S, Tanitteerapan T, Mungkung N (2007) Highly Efficient Low Power Consumption Tracking Solar Cells for White LED-Based Lighting System. International Journal of Electrical Computer and Systems Engineering 1: 1307-5179.

[11] Hatfield P (2006) Low Cost Solar Tracker, Bachelor of Electrical Engineering Thesis, Department of Electrical and Computer Engineering, Curtin University of Technology.

[12] Rumala S (1986) A Shadow Method for Automatic Tracking. Solar Energy 37: 245-247.

[13] Palavras I, Bakos G C (2006) Development of a Low-Cost Dish Solar Concentrator and its Application in Zeolite Desorption. Renewable Energy 3: 2422-2431.

[14] Kalogirou S A (1996) Design and Construction of a One-Axis Sun-Tracking. Solar Energy 57: 465-469.

[15] Poulek V, Libra M (2000) A Very Simple Solar Tracker for Space and Terrestrial Applications. Solar Energy Materials and Solar Cells 60: 99-103.

[16] Mohamad A (2004) Efficiency Improvements of Photo-Voltaic Panels using a Sun Tracking System. Applied Energy 79: 345-354.

[17] Khader M, Badran O, Abdallah S (2008) Evaluating Multi-Axes Sun-Tracking System at Different Modes of Operation in Jordan. Renewable and Sustainable Energy Reviews 12: 864-873.

[18] Roth P, Georgiev A, Boudinov H (2004) Design and Construction of a System for Sun Tracking. Renewable Energy 29: 393-402.

[19] Hession P J, Bonwick W J (1984) Experience with a Sun Tracker. Solar Energy 32: 3-11.

[20] Kulkarni S S, Thean C Y, Kong A W (2003) A Novel PC Based Solar Electric Panel Simulator. The Fifth International Conference on Power Electronics and Drive Systems: 848 – 852.

[21] Yu T C, Chien T S (2009) Analysis and Simulation of Characteristics and Maximum Power Point Tracking for Photovoltaic Systems. International Conference on Power Electronics and Drive Systems: 1339-1344.

[22] Tsai H L (2010) Insolation-Oriented Model of Photovoltaic Module using Matlab/Simulink. Solar Energy 84: 1318-1326.

[23] Tsai H L, Tu C S, Su Y J (2008) Development of Generalized Photovoltaic Model Using MATLAB/Simulink, Proceedings of the World Congress on Engineering and Computer Science, San Francisco, USA:1-6.

[24] Chin C S, Babu A, McBride W (2011). Design, Modeling and Testing of a Standalone Single-Axis Active Solar Tracker using MATLAB/Simulink. Renewable Energy 36(11): 3075-3090.

[25] Enrique J M, Duran E, Sidrach-de-Cardona M, Andu J M (2007) Theoretical Assessment of the Maximum Power Point Tracking Efficiency of Photovoltaic Facilities. Solar Energy 81: 31–38.

[26] Villalva M G, Gazoli J R, Filho E R (2009) Comprehensive Approach to Modeling and Simulation of Photovoltaic Arrays. IEEE Transactions on Power Electronics 5: 1198–1208.

[27] Luis C, Silvestre S (2002) Modelling Photovoltaic Systems Using PSpice, John Wiley and Sons, Chichester.

[28] White F M (1999) Fluid Mechanics, fourth ed. McGraw-Hill.

[29] Karimov K S, Saqib M A, Akhter P, Ahmed M M, Chattha J A, Yousafzai S A (2005) A Simple Photo-Voltaic Tracking System. Solar Energy Materials and Solar Cells 87: 49-59.

[30] Markvart T (2000) Solar Electricity, Wiley, New York.

Chapter 3

Remote Process Control and Monitoring Using Matlab

Vedran Vajnberger, Semir Silajdžić and Nedim Osmić

Additional information is available at the end of the chapter

1. Introduction

Remote control is one of the best solutions for managing inaccessible systems. Many researches have been made in the field of the remote control [1-4]. These researches have improved certain aspects of industry, medicine, military, etc. The benefits of remote control are numerous such as: operating in hazard environment, telemedicine, missile guidance, etc. The most important characteristic of remote control is operating in real-time as shown in papers form references [5-7].

Many applications in the field of medicine and industry use different kind of motor-based systems especially stepper motors because of their wide-range of sufficient characteristics like the fact that they can be used as constant power devices with accurate positioning and fast response [8-12].

In today's society, robots are used in various areas especially in those where high precision is required. Some of the examples where robotic arms found their appliance are: in vehicle construction where efficiency and reliability are required, in chemical industry where environment is not suitable for human, in medicine where robotic arm precision is used in operations, etc [13]. Robots have improved life standards and we are upgrading their performances in order to make our lives easier and more comfortable.

This chapter describes implementation of the proposed remote control of the stepper motor and robotic arm with five DOF via web server and VNC server [14, 15]. VNC server was used to receive visual feedback from robotic arm. The quality of image was important and it couldn't be sent via MATLAB server because real time characteristic would be lost. The decision to use microcontroller was based on its characteristics. Developing such system is cheaper than developing on other platforms such as PLC or FPGA.

The realized system exhibits the following:

1. implementation based on PIC16F877a microcontroller,
2. adjustment
    a. of the velocity, number of steps and rotation direction of the stepper motor,
    b. of the rotation direction of the DC motors inside each joint of the robotic arm
3. precise control over RS-232 serial communication,
4. extension to remote control the whole system,
5. feedback
    a. data acquisition and transmission to confirm the proper operation of the stepper motor
    b. visual feedback and contact sensors to confirm the proper operation of the robotic arm
6. realized GUI.

Both systems consist of all previously mentioned characteristics, where character 'a)' refers to stepper motor and character 'b)' to robotic arm.

This chapter is structured as follows: In section 2. whole data analysis of the realization of the system in accordance with previously specified requirements is described. Section 3. provides hardware description that was realized manually. Section 4. explains hardware programming.

2. Problem analysis

The problem of realizied systems that remotely control stepper motor and robotic arm can be divided into several interconnected units, as it will be described in the following text and shown on Figure 1. and Figure 2. To understand the problem and its solution, a brief description of each part will be provided in the rest of this section.

a. Control via microcontroller

The Microchip microcontroller PIC16F877a © generates impulses on four pins that are used to stimulate the movement of the stepper motor gear as shown in Figure 2. Stepper motor consists of multiple "toothed" electromagnets ranged around a coil of iron. Those electromagnets need to be stimulated by some kind of external control unit, in our case a microcontroller. The microcontroller provides electrical impulses which stimulate the gear's teeth to magnetically be attracted to electromagnet's teeth. When the gear's teeth are thus aligned to the first electromagnet, they are slightly offset from the next electromagnet. When the next electromagnet is turned on and the first is turned off, the gear rotates slightly to align with the next one, and from there the process is repeated. Each of those slight rotations is called a "step," with an integer number of steps making a full rotation. In that way, the motor can be turned by a precise angle [16].

The impulses (U1÷U4) and response on Figure 2. show the movement of the stepper in one direction by four steps. Each step corresponds with one triggering impulse.

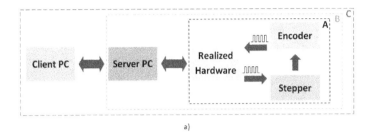

a)

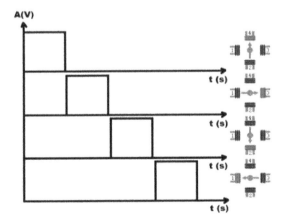

b)

Figure 1. a) Interconnected units of stepper motor system; b) Interconnected units of robotic arm system

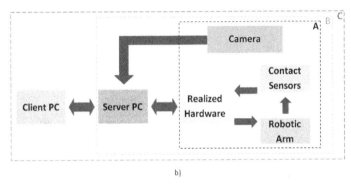

Figure 2. Triggering impulses and gear response

If triggering impulses are reversed (U4÷U1) movement of the motor is in the opposite direction. The length of the triggering impulses depends on desired velocity. The width between those impulses is infinitesimal. The shorter the length of the triggering impulses is, the higher velocity becomes; i.e. to reach 60 [rpm], the length of each triggering impulse needs to be 5 [ms], to reach 120 [rpm] length should be 2.5 [ms]. As earlier mentioned, besides velocity control, there was the urge for exact positioning. This task was realized by sending a certain amount of triggering impulses in the correct order.

Even though stepper motors are used in open-looped systems because of their characteristics, in this case an additional encoder was installed on the system. Its purpose is to check if the stepper responses accurately to the given commands i.e. combination of impulses.

Similar to the robotic arm (Figure 1.b), Microchip microcontroller PIC16F877A© generates impulses on ten pins (PORT D and two pins from PORT C) which are triggering relays. Signals from relays are used to stimulate the movement of the DC motors implemented inside joins of the robotic arm.

For every degree of freedom (DOF) two pins of microcontroller and two relays are assigned (pins RD0 and RD1 for base, RD2 and RD3 for shoulder, RD4 and RD5 for elbow, RD6 and RD7 for wrist and RC0 and RC1 for fist).

Depending on the state of two pins, there are four situations:

- if both pins are low, two relays controlled by them are open and motor of the appropriate DOF is not running,
- if one pin is high and another is low, current flows in one direction and motor is running in appropriate direction,
- for opposite state of pins, motor is running in opposite direction,
- 'forbidden combination' is when both pins are high, because then both relays are active and source is short circuited.

Figure 3. explains the movement of robotic arm.

b.   Control via RS-232

In this chapter, the advantages of a microcontroller were used to establish a communication with the server PC. The used communication is the serial communication RS-232. Serial communication is the most common low-level protocol for communicating between two or more devices [17, 18]. Texas Instruments' MAX232 is used to make adjustment between microcontroller's TTL logic level (5V÷0V) and logic level for RS232 standard (-12V÷12V). An example of the conversion is shown in Figure 4.

The communication was established through MATLAB using three m-files. One m-file was written to create serial port object and to configure its properties. The communication between the server PC and the microcontroller is realized by using second m-function called "send". It has five input arguments: *send(s1, message1, message2, message3, message4)*. The first input argument is the name of a created serial port object. Other arguments are one-byte values that are sent to the microcontroller. Those values represent desired mode of operation (velocity or positional mode), direction of rotation, velocity and number of steps (available only in positional mode). The first bit of message1 is start bit (1 for start of rotation and 0 for stop). The second bit represents desired mode of operation (1 for velocity and 0 for positional mode). The third bit determines direction of rotation. The last five bits of message1, together with message2, represent desired velocity (13 bits for velocity). Message3 and message4 are low and high bytes of desired number of steps. The last m-file ends the serial port session.

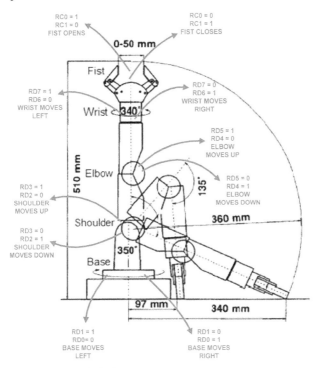

Figure 3. Movement description of robotic arm

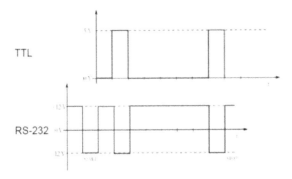

Figure 4. Conversion TTL logic level into RS232 logic level

For the robotic arm system, communication was established through MATLAB using two m-files. First m-file creates serial port and configures its properties. The communication between the server PC and the microcontroller is realized using second m-file. In this m-file, function was created to collect data set by user inside GUI.

c.   Remote control via web server

Because MATLAB was used to send control commands to the microcontroller, an additional toolbox called TCP/UDP/IP was installed. This toolbox establishes a connection between two computers (server and client) using the TCP/IP protocol as shown in Figure 5.

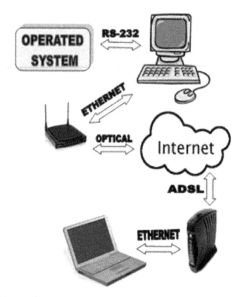

Figure 5. Established connection

One of the computers is used as the server, while the other one is used as a client. The web server is established on the server computer. All commands that control the stepper and robotic arm are sent from the client computer. On the other hand, all feedback needed for acknowledgment of the proper remote control, i.e. did the stepper reached the desired velocity or did robotic arm reached assigned position, is send from the server to the client via established connection. All that was needed to establish a connection was provided in the additional toolbox using the created m-files such as pnet, pnet_putvar and pnet_getvar. Using the pnet m-file a handler called 'con' was created. This handler was used in combination with m-files pnet_putvar and pnet_getvar to send the necessary data to the connection and to collect that data from connection respectively. To access the visual information of the robotic arm acquired by the camera, VNC server was used. The camera is connected to the server computer and by using VNC server we can gain access to the server from a remote desktop.

Two m-files were created (for host and client) using previously mentioned m-files. The required toolbox can be found in the references along with all explanations for each m-file [19].

3. Hardware structure

Figure 6. shows detailed hardware structure of the implemented distributed systems. It is a product of fully independent work.

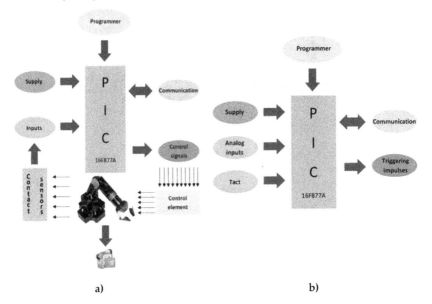

a)   b)

Figure 6. a) Block structure of stepper motor system; b) Block structure of robotic arm system

Production implied the implementation of the entire hardware circuit and construction of work algorithm. The structure consists of a microcontroller and controlling elements for both systems.

The stepper motor system is operated with commands from host PC which are sent through serial connection. Microcontroller interpretates those commands and generates trigger impulses on PORT D. These impulses are sent to unipolar transistors which are combined to form a power amplifier. This power amplifier is directly connected to the step motor. The step motor has an encoder disc mounted to its shaft. The encoder recognizes alterations from encoder disc and sends them as impulses to the analog input on PIC. These impulses are used to determine proper work of the stepper motor. Figure 7. shows the most important components used in this hardware realization.

The robotic arm, shown in Figure 3., has five degrees of freedom modeled after the human arm. The controlling element consists of ten relays (Figure 8.), all assembled in accordance with scheme on Figure 9.

Figure 7. Realized system for stepper motor control

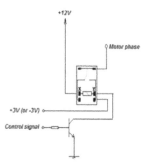

Figure 8. Relay scheme

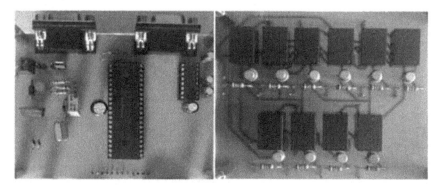

Figure 9. Microcontroller sheme and controlling elements – relays

The operating princip of the relay is simple. When current flows between pins X and Y, it leads to the creation of a magentic field. The influence of the magnetic field causes a change in the position of the switch inside the relay. Control signals from microcontroller are sent to the controlling element. Those control signals need to enable the flow of current which is necessary to trigger the DC motors placed inside the joints of the robotic arm. The system is operated from the client's computer GUI. The commands from server are sent through serial connection. Microcontroller interpretates those commands and generates the control signals. These signals are sent to the controlling element made of relays. The controlling element is directly connected to the robotic arm. The proper work of the robotic arm is monitored via camera. There are also contact sensors on each joint of the arm used to prevent movements that could cause a malfunction. Those signals are transmitted back to the microcontroller and, in the case of a possible malfunction, the movement of the affected joint will be stopped immediately. Figure 9. shows the individual parts of the realized structure and Figure 10. shows the final structure.

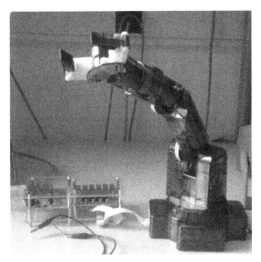

Figure 10. Final structure of the robotic arm system

4. Hardware programming

a.   Stepper motor

After making the hardware, the next step was to program the circuit itself. The code is written in CCSC Compiler, version 4, from manufacturer Custom Computer Services Inc. [20]. The user chooses mode of operation, desired direction of rotation, velocity and number of steps using GUI. That information is collected into four 8-bits values and sent to server PC via ETHERNET. Server PC forwards those messages to microcontroller using RS-232. Microcontroller analyses received messages and sets/resets appropriate bits according to chosen mode, direction, velocity and number of steps. In the main program, if START bit is set, microcontroller generates appropriate sequence of triggering impulses based on chosen direction and velocity. The width of one impulse is given by:

$$T_{width} = \frac{60\,000}{RPM \cdot 200}\,[ms] \tag{1}$$

Timer1 is set to appropriate value so it overflows every 100 ms and an interrupt is generated. In Timer1 Interrupt Service Routine microcontroller sends number of steps made in last 100 ms to server PC via RS-232. Timer0 is used as counter. Output of encoder is led to pin RA4/T0CKI. Timer0 increments on every step. Client PC uses received information about number of steps made, calculate the velocity and shows it in GUI (Figure 11.).

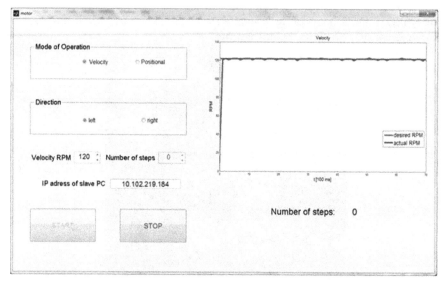

Figure 11. Graphical User Interface for stepper motor system

How hardware is programmed for stepper motor is shown on Figure 12.

b.   Robotic arm

After making the hardware, the next step was to program the circuit itself. The code is written in MPLAB IDE v7.5 [21]. Figure 13. shows how hardware is programmed.

To establish communication via ETHERNET, Real VNC program [22] and MATLAB Server are used. Real VNC program is used to obtain visual feedback by camera, and MATLAB Server is used for transmission of control messages from client PC to server PC. VNC Server was installed on server PC (PC connected to realized hardware structure), while VNC Viewer was used by client PC. By running the VNC Viewer and entering IP address of server PC, connection between two computers is established.

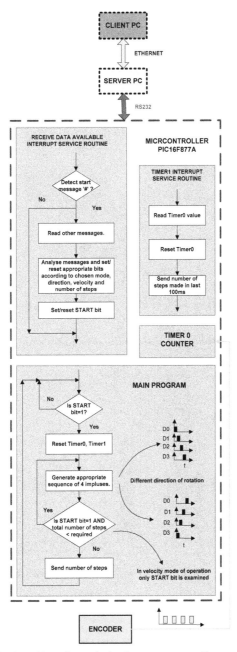

Figure 12. Schematic display of the software for hardware structure with stepper motor

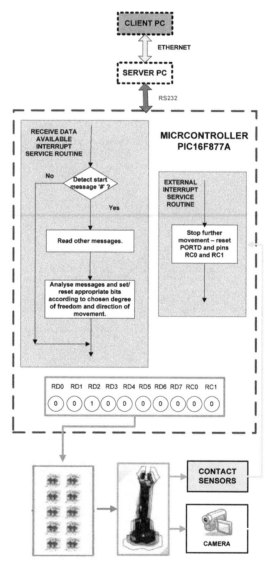

Figure 13. Schematic display of the software for hardware structure with robotic arm

When user chose degree of freedom and direction of movement, function from MATLAB is called. This function codes user's requirement into a short message which is sent to server and then to microcontroller via RS-232. Depending on the content of received message, microcontroller generates appropriate value to the PORT C or PORTD which is described in subchapter 2. section A.

Using the GUI (Figure 14.) the user chooses degree of freedom to manipulate with and the direction of movement.

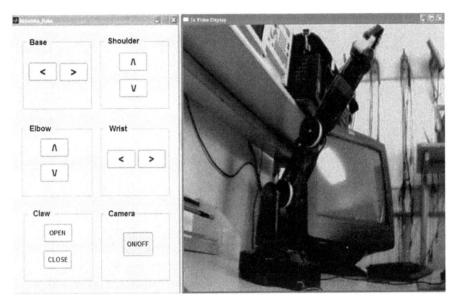

Figure 14. Graphical User Interface for robotic arm system

The user monitor movement of robot arm by camera. Beside this visual feedback, for every DOF contact micro-sensor is implemented to avoid possible damage of the arm. When DOF reaches its final position, the micro-sensor becomes active and further movement is stopped.

5. Testing results

The effectiveness of a stepper motor is rated by the response of a single phase to the provided trigger impulse. The experimental results obtained by applying one impulse are shown on Figure 15., Figure 17. and Figure 19. The responses to certain defined velocities are shown on Figure 16., Figure 18. and Figure 20.

The responses are almost instant as shown on Figure 15., Figure 17. and Figure 19. The small deviation is the result of mechanical characteristics of stepper motor. The noise seen in those figures is caused by imperfection of the encoder and its disc. The response signal collected from encoder is raised by 0.5 (V) because of the encoder's saturation, which represents a nonlinear acting.

Figure 16., Figure 18. and Figure 20. show various measurements of desired and actual velocity. It can be seen that the actual velocity follows the desired one. At certain moments there are deviations of actual velocity. These deviations are caused by restrictions of the used encoder. The shape of those deviations is the result of linear approximation of the characteristic.

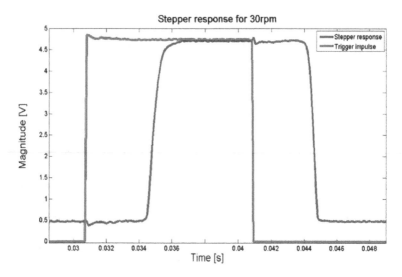

Figure 15. Response to one step for velocity of 30 RPM

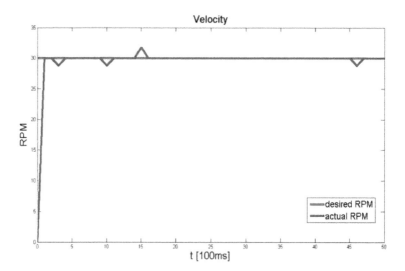

Figure 16. Desired and actual velocity of 30 RPM

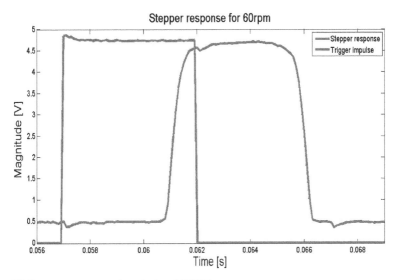

Figure 17. Response to one step for velocity of 60 RPM

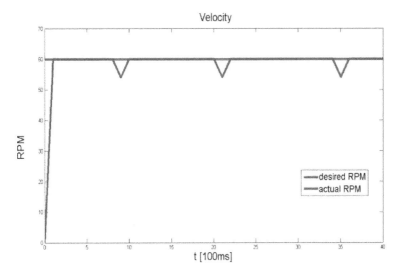

Figure 18. Desired and actual velocity of 60 RPM

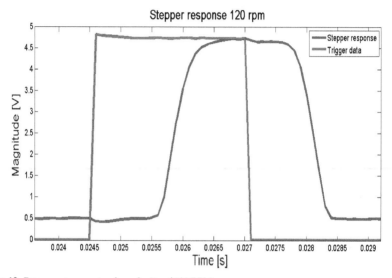

Figure 19. Response to one step for velocity of 120 RPM

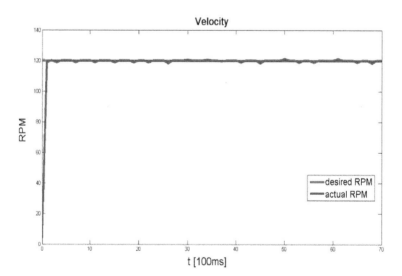

Figure 20. Desired and actual velocity of 120 RPM

6. Conclusion

This paper presented the design of a remotely controlled stepper motor and robotic arm via web server. Operating algorithms and GUI were realized for both systems. Through the GUI for the stepper motor user can operate the motor in two modes: velocity and positional. The feedback received from the encoder is sent through the established connection from server to the client. Experimental results demonstrate the effectiveness of the remotely controlled stepper motor. Using the GUI for the robotic arm, user can operate each joint of robotic arm separately. The feedback received from the camera is sent through the established connection from server to the client. Experimental results are not shown in this paper, because as stated before, this model of robotic arm does not possess encoders. That is the reason why camera was used as visual feedback. The system operates in real time and visual feedback provides us information about current state of robotic arm. System is based on microcontroller and its development is not expensive, unlike the systems which are based on other technologies i.e. PLC. These systems are used in environments which are dangerous for humans.

Author details

Vedran Vajnberger, Semir Silajdžić and Nedim Osmić
Faculty of Electrical Engineering,
Department of Automatic Control and Electronics, Sarajevo, Bosnia and Herzegovina

7. References

[1] T. B. Sheridan (1993) Space teleoperation through time delay review and prognosis, *IEEE Transaction on Robotics and Automation*, vol. 9, pp. 592-606.

[2] C. Sayers (1996) Remote Control Robotics, New York: Springer Verlag.

[3] Velagic, J., Coralic, M. and Hebibovic, M. (2004) The Remote Control of Robot Manipulator for Precise Time-Limited Complex Path Tracking, Proceedings of the IEEE International Conference on Mechatronics and Robotics (MechRob2004), Volume 2, September 13-15, Aachen, Germany, pp. 841-846

[4] D. Lee, and M.W. Spong (2006) Passive Bilateral Teleoperation with Constant Time Delay, *IEEE Transactions on Robotics and Automation*, vol. 22, no.2, pp. 269-281.

[5] Vladimir Lucan, Petr Simacek, Jari Seppälä, Hannu Koivisto, "Bluetooth and Wireless LAN Applicability for Real-time Control"

[6] Xin Liu , Yongtian Wang , Yue Liu , Dongdong Weng, Xiaoming Hu (2009) A Remote Control System Based on Real-Time Image Processing, 2009 Fifth International Conference on Image and Graphics

[7] Chui Yew Leong and Abdul Rahman Ramli, Intelligent Systems and Robotics Laboratory (ISRL), Institute Of Advanced Technology, Universiti Putra Malaysia. 43400 Serdang, Selangor. "Development of a real-time embedded remote triggering and monitoring system with SC12"

[8] G.Srinivasarao, S.Sao, "Security system based on stepper motor control using microcontroller"

[9] Ahmet Altintas, Department of Electrical Education Dumlupinar University, Faculty of Technical Education, 43500 Simav, Kütahya, Turkey, "A graphical user interface for programming stepper motors used at different kinds of applications", Mathematical and Computational Applications, Vol. 14, No. 2

[10] Betin, F. Pinchon, D. Capolino, (2000) "Fuzzy logic applied to speed control of a stepping motor drive", G.-A. Dept. of Electr. Eng., Univ. of Picardie Jules Verne, Cuffies , , Industrial Electronics, IEEE, Jun 2000.

[11] Jan B.A. Habraken, Kora de Bruin, Morgan Shehata, Jan Booij, Roel Bennink, Berthe L.F. van Eck Smit and Ellinor Busemann Sokole, "Evaluation of High-Resolution Pinhole SPECT Using a Small Rotating Animal", Departments of Nuclear Medicine, Radiology, and Medical Technological Development, Academic Medical Center, University of Amsterdam, Amsterdam, The Netherlands, , Basic Science Investigations.

[12] Fang Liu, Zhenlin Hu, Lei Qiu, Chun Hui, Chao Li, Pei Zhong and Junping Zhang (2010) "Boosting high-intensity focused ultrasound-induced anti-tumor immunity using a sparse-scan strategy that can more effectively promote dendritic cell maturation", *Journal of Translational Medicine*

[13] Salcudean, S. E., Ku, S., and Bell, G., 1997, "Performance Measurement in Scaled Teleoperation for Microsurgery," Proceedings of the First Joint Conference in Computer Vision, Virtual Reality and Robotics in Medicine and Medial Robotics and Computer-Assisted Surgery (CVRMed-MRCA '97), Grenoble, France, pp. 789–798.

[14] Jasmin Velagić, Nedim Osmić, Semir Silajdžić, Tarik Terzimehić and Vedran Vajnberger (2010) Remote Control of Stepper Motor via Web Server, Conference on Control and Fault – Tolerant Systems (SysTol'10), Nice, France, 10/2010.

[15] Vedran Vajnberger, Tarik Terzimehić, Semir Silajdžić and Nedim Osmić (2011) Remote Control of Robot Arm with Five DOF, International symposium for information and communication technologies, electronics and microelectronics – MIPRO 2011, Opatija, Croatia

[16] Liptak, Bela G. (2005). *Instrument Engineers' Handbook: Process Control and Optimization*. CRC Press. pp. 2464.

[17] Yidong Wang, Kaiguo Yan, Guozi Sun, Peihuang Lou, "Serial Communication in DNC Information Systems", The CIMS Center of NUAA, Nanjing 210016, China, Published by Moxa Technologies)

[18] Yidong Wang, Kaiguo Yan, Guozi Sun, Peihuang Lou, "Serial Communication in DNC Information Systems", The CIMS Center of NUAA, Nanjing 210016, China, Published by Moxa Technologies)

[19] Peter Rydesaeter, TCP/UDP/IP toolbox 2.0.6. user guide, March 2001.

[20] htttp://www.ccsinfo.com, User guidance

[21] MPLAB® IDE USER'S GUIDE, 2005 Microchip Technology Inc.,

[22] Personal Edition VNC Server 4.4 User Guide, 2008.,

MATLAB/Simulink-Based Grid Power Inverter for Renewable Energy Sources Integration

Marian Gaiceanu

Additional information is available at the end of the chapter

1. Introduction

The main objective of the chapter is the development of technological knowledge, based on Matlab/Simulink programming language, related to grid connected power systems for energy production by using Renewable Energy Sources (RES), as clean and efficient sources for meeting both the environment requirements and the technical necessities of the grid connected power inverters. Another objective is to promote the knowledge regarding RES; consequently, it is necessary to bring contribution to the development of some technologies that allow the integration of RES in a power inverter with high energy quality and security. By using these energetic systems, the user is not only a consumer, but also a producer of energy. This fact will have a direct impact from technical, economic and social point of view, and it will contribute to the increasing of life quality.

The chapter intends to integrate itself into the general frame of the EU energy policies by imposing the global objectives of reducing the impact upon the environment, and promoting the RES for the energy production. At the same time, the chapter is strategically oriented towards the compatibility with the priority requirements from some European programmes: the wide-spread implementation of the distributed energy sources, of the energy storage technologies and of the grid connected systems.

The chapter strategy follows two directions: the first, is thedevelopment of knowledge (a study and implementation of a high performance grid-power inverter; the fuel cells technology as RES; the control methods; specific modelling and simulation methods); the second focuses upon the applicative research (a real time implementation with dSPACE platform is provided).

The interdisciplinary of the chapter consists of using specific knowledge from the fields of: energy conversion, power converters, Matlab/Simulink simulation software, real time implementation based on dSPACE platform, electrotechnics, and advanced control techniques.

2. The grid power converter

The increased power demand, the depletion of the fossil fuel resources and the growth of the environmental pollution have led the world to think seriously of other alternative sources of energy: solar, wind, biogas/biomass, tidal, geothermal, fuel cell, hydrogen energy, gas micro turbines and small hydropower farms.

The number of distributed generation (DG) units, including both renewable and nonrenewable sources, for small rural communities not connected to the grid and for small power resources (up to 1000 kW) connected to the utility network has grown in the last years. There has been an increase in the number of sources that are natural DC sources, for instance fuel cells and photovoltaic arrays, or whose AC frequency is either not constant or is much higher than the grid frequency, for instance micro gas-turbines. These generators necessarily require an DC/AC converter to be connected to the grid. Although some generators can be connected directly to the electric power grid, such as wind power driven asynchronous induction generators, there is a trend to adopt power electronics based interfaces which convert the power firstly to DC and then use an inverter to deliver the power to the 50Hz AC grid.

At the international level, SMA Technologies AG (www.sma.de) promotes the innovative technology based on the renewable sources. The following results can be mentioned: the stand-alone or grid connected systems by using either a single type of source (Sunny Boy 5000 Multi-String inverter based on the modular concept, Hydro-Boy and Windy Boy) or combined (Sunny Island) including the interconnection of wind turbines, photovoltaics, micro-hydro and diesel generators. It is well-known that for systems efficiency increasing, the inverter is the answer of the problem. With this respect, Sunways (www.sunways.de) adopted the HERIC concept (from the Fraunhofer Solar and Energetic Systems Institute), by using a tranformerless inverter, obtaining a 97,33% high efficiency of the inverter for low powers (www.ise.fraunhofer.de). The Master-Slave and Team concepts are embedded in SunnyTeam and Fronius inverters in order to increase the efficiency in the partial load conditions. At world level, the implementation of energetic policies (with respect to renewable sources) has been carried out by performing systems based on a single renewable source. There are such examples in countries all over the world: in Europe, Dewind, Vestas, Enercon, Fronius International GmbH, SMA Technologies AG; Renco SpA, Ansaldo Fuel Cells SpA; in North America-Nyserda, Beacon Power, Magnetek Inc., Sustainable Energy Technology, Logan Energy Corp., IdaTech; Australia-Conergy Pty Ltd, Rainbow Power Company Ltd; and Asia-Nitol Solar, Shenzen Xinhonghua Solar-Energy Co Ltd).

In EU, the implementation of the energetic policies is based upon a legal document, Norm 2001/77/EC regarding the promotion of the electrical energy produced from renewable sources on the Energy Single Market. The objectives of the Norm provide that till 2020, a contribution of 20% of the total energy consumption shall be covered by energy produced from renewable sources. The monitoring of this Norm implementation is managed by the EU Energy General Directorship which presents periodical reports on the European researching and development stages. Considering these reports, under the conditions of implementing the DER concept (Distributed/Descentralized Energy Resources), it is obvious that the futurer research activities will be based upon the hybrid systems (wind-Photovoltaic, wind-biomass, wind-diesel generator) having the target of the energetic security by removing the disadvantages of using a single renewable source.

The consolidation of the objectives proposed by Norm 2001/77/EC and the extension in more geographical areas are possible only by using hybrid systems.

The EU gives a great importance to the improvement of the energy efficiency and to the promotion of the renewable sources. Related to the above mentioned issues, the objectives of the EU are to produce at least 20% ofthe gross energy consumption from renewable sources until 2020 (COM, 2006) and to increase the energy efficiency by 20% until 2020 (EREC, 2011). As far as the energy efficiency is concerned, an EU norm aims at a reduction of 9% of the energy losses until 2020 (EREC, 2008)

2.1. A generic topology of the RES integration

In the context of the international scientific studies related to the development of new alternative solutions for electrical energy production by using renewable energy sources (RES), the aim of this chapter is to contribute to these studies by evaluating and working out the possible concepts for stand-alone and grid connected operating interface of these hybrid systems and the efficient and ecologic technologies to ensure an optimal use of the sources (solar energy, wind energy, hydrogen energy by using fuel cells, hydro-energy, biomass) in industry and residential buildings.The battery and the fuel cells are also meant to be reserve sources (which ensure the additional energy requirements of the consumers and the supply ofboth the residential critical loads and the critical loads of the hybrid system-auxiliary circuits for fuel cell start-up and operating), increasing the safety of the system. The fuel cell integration is provided by using a unidirectional DC/DC converter (to obtain regulated high voltage DC), an inverter and a filter in order to accommodate the DC voltage to the required AC voltage (single phase or three phase). The bidirectional DC/DC converter (double arrow, Fig.1) is used in order to charge/discharge the batteries (placed in order to increase the energy supply security and to improve load dynamics). The unidirectional DC-DC converter prevents the negative current going into the fuel cell stack. Due to the negative current, the cell reversal could occur and damage the fuel cell stack. The ripple current seen by the fuel cell stack due to the switching of the boost converter (unidirectional DC/DC converter) has to be low.

2.2. Three-phase versus single phase

Firstly,the problem of choosing the number of phase for the front end converter is a matter of power. In this case, the three-phase line should be used for a 37kVA power converter.

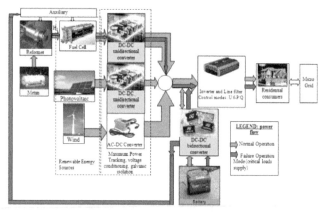

Figure 1. A generic topology of the RES integration

Secondly, in case of using balanced three phase AC loads, the possibility that low frequency components to occur in the fuel cell input current is reduced.

2.3. System description

The proposed way of the efficient integration of RES is illustrated in Fig.1. With this respect only one inverter is used in DC-AC conversion for interfacing the stand-alone or grid-connected consumer (Gaiceanu, *et al.,* 2007b). By its control, the inverter can ensure the efficient operation and the accomplishment of the energy quality requirements related to the harmonics level. The hybrid system can ensure two operation modes: the normal one, and the emergency one (as backup system).

2.3.1. Operation modes

There are four modes of operation:

- *Direct Supply from Utility*: consists of direct supply of the residential consumers from Utility via the Static Switch;
- *Precharge Operation*: The DC capacitors in the inverter part of the Power *Conditioning* System (PCS) can be precharged from the AC busutility. After the DC capacitors are charged, the inverter can be switched on. As soon as it is running, the inverter by itself will keep the DC capacitors charged to a DC level higher than the No-Load level of the Solid Oxide Fuel Cell (SOFC). During the precharge operation, the residential consumers will still be supplied from Utility;
- *Normal Operation*: The PCS converts the DC energy from the SOFC into AC and feeds the Utility and the eventual residential consumers.
- *Island Operation*(failure operation mode): If the Utility goes out of tolerance during normal operation, the PCS will change to island operation. The PCS converts the DC from SOFC and battery and supplies the critical loads.

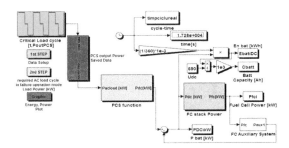

Figure 2. The simplified steady state model of the SOFC Power System for Island Operation Mode

For the sake of simplicity and for chapter length limit reason, only the grid-connected hybrid system with fuel cell generator and battery pack will be investigated.

2.3.1.1 The failure operation mode (Island Operation)

In this operation mode, the power system must assure the power supply for the critical loads (as alarms, auxiliary power systems for fuel cell, reformer and so on, depending on the consumer requirements). In the first stage, the power supply is assured from the battery pack, followed by the SOFC. Therefore, by knowing the critical load power, an adequate Simulink file is designed (Fig.2).A simple and effective energetic model has been considered. This model puts in evidence the inverter power losses at critical load conditions. A repeating table block from the Simulink tool is used in order to implement the load cycle of the residential consummer (critical load cycle, Fig.4). The available acquisition time for the load cycle was at 10 s for each sample, and two days as time interval length. By knowing the critical load power cycle, it is possible to size the required battery pack. Therefore the output inverter power, $P_{out,inv}$, is the same with the critical load power ($P_{acload} = P_{critical\_load}$, Fig.2).

The losses of the Power Conditioning System (PlossPCS=P$_{loss,inv}$) are modelled by using a quadratic function(Metwally, 2005), which is the most used one. The power loss function requires three parameters extracted from the experimental data by the least-squaresmethod.

$$P_{loss,inv} = p_0 + p_1 P_{critical\_load} + p_2 P^2_{critical\_load} \qquad (1)$$

The first parameter, p_0, takes into account the load independent losses[W]. The second parameter, p_1, represents the voltage drops in semiconductors as load linear proportional losses. The last term, p_2, includes the magnetic losses [1/W], known as load ohmic losses. The PCS model has been implemented in Simulink (Fig.3) based on the following function:

$$f(u) = p2 * u^2 + p1 * u + p0 \qquad (2)$$

in which the coefficients of the approximated function are as follows: p0 = 0.0035*Prated, p1=0.005, p2=0.01/Prated.

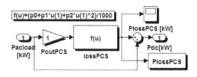

Figure 3. The energetic model of the PCS

In the Fig.3. the energetic component of the PCS block is presented. By knowing the total inverter losses at critical power, $P_{loss,inv}^{tot}$, the corresponding DC power can be obtained:

$$P_{DC} = P_{out,inv} + P_{loss,inv}^{tot} \tag{3}$$

The input and the output inverter powers are related to the inverter efficiency:

$$\eta_{inv} = \frac{P_{out,inv}}{P_{DC}} \tag{4}$$

By taking into account the power requirements of the auxiliary circuits, which are supported only by the battery pack in critical load case during the fuel cell start-up, the corresponding DC power is (Fig.4):

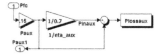

Figure 4. The power losses of the auxiliary power circuits

$$P_{DCi} = P_{DC} + P_{aux} \Rightarrow P_{DCi} = P_{DC} + 0.15 P_{FC}^{critical} \tag{5}$$

The necessary energy of the battery pack is obtained as:

$$W_{batt} = \int_0^t P_{DCi} d\tau \tag{6}$$

The blowers have been considered as main auxiliary loads; the value of $\eta_{aux} = 0.7$ for the equivalent efficiency of the auxiliary power circuits has been considered. In the Fig.4c, the power losses of the auxiliary power circuits have been deducted.

$$\Delta P_{loss,aux} = P_{out,aux} \left(\frac{1}{\eta_{aux}} - 1 \right) \tag{7}$$

PCU Matlab/Simulink simulator results

Based on the PCUMatlab/Simulink simulator (Fig.2, Fig. 5a), the required capacity and energy of the battery have been obtained (Fig. 5b)

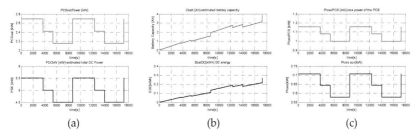

(a)   (b)   (c)

Figure 5. (a) The load power PCSoutPower [kW], the estimated total DC power PDC[kW], including the auxiliary power loss; (b) the required capacity and energy of the battery, respectively; (c) the losses of the PCS and the auxiliary power losses.

2.3.1.2 The Normal operation mode

A. The Fuel Cell Power Conditioning System

The fuel cell power conditioning system consists of fuel cell stack and DC power converter.the fuel cell is an electrochemical device which produces DC power directly, without any intermediate stage. It has high power density and zero emission of green house gases. Fuel cell stacks were connected in series/parallel combination to achieve the desired rating. The main issue for the fuel cell power converter design is the fuel cell current ripple reduction. The secondary issue is to maintain a constant DC bus voltage. The former is solved by introducing an internal current loop in the DC/DC power converter control. The latter design requirement is solved by DC voltage control.

A.1 The Fuel cell stack Matlab/Simulink based model

The polarization curve of the SOFC is based on Tafel equation. The output voltage of the SOFC is built taking into account the Nernst instantaneous voltage equation $E_0 + a\,ln\left(P_{H_2} P_{O_2}^{1/2}\right)$, the activation overvoltage $b\,ln(i)$, the voltage variation due to the mass transport losses $c\,ln\left(1 - \dfrac{i}{i_{lim}}\right)$ and the ohmic voltage drop Ri (Candusso D., et al. 2002). The first three terms are multiplied by No, number of series cells, in order to obtain the fuel cell stack mathematical model.

The parameters of the Tafel equation are the load current, the temperature and the pressures of the hydrogen and oxygen. The demanded current of the fuel cell system is limited between $\pm I_{fc}^{limit}$ at a certain hydrogen flow $q_{H_2}^{in}$ value (Padulles, et al., 2000):

$$\frac{0.8q_{H_2}^{in}}{2K_r} \leq I_{fc}^{in} \leq \frac{0.9q_{H_2}^{in}}{2K_r} \tag{8}$$

The Simulink model of the FC Power System before starting must be initialized (based on *Ifc_init.m* file, Fig.6) from the Fuel Cell data initialization block (Fig.5). In order to obtain the demanded current between certain limits, an adequate Matlab function has been created(Fcn).

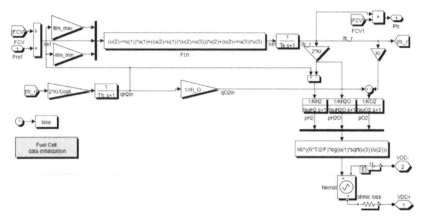

Figure 6. The Simulink model of the solid oxide fuel cell stack

Ifc_init.m

prate=80000; % [W]   Rated power. **Pref**=80000; % [W]   Real power reference

T=1273; % [K]   Absolute temperature. **F**=96487; % [C/mol]   Faraday's constant

R=8314; % [J/(k.mol K)] Universal gas constant. **E0**=1.18; % [V]   Ideal stand potential

N0=384; %   Number of cells in series inside the stack. **Kr**=0.995*10^(-5); % kmol/(sA). Constant, Kr = N0/4F

Umax=0.9; % Maximum fuel utilization. **Umin**=0.8; % Minimum fuel utilization **Uopt**=0.85; % Optimal fuel utilization,

%Value molar constants:

KH2=8.43*10^(-4); % kmol/(s atm) - for hydrogen

KH2O=2.81*10^(-4); % kmol/(s atm) - for water

KO2=2.52*10^(-3); % kmol/(s atm) - for oxygen

tauH2=26.1; % s   - Response time for hydrogen flow

tauH2O=78.3; % s   - Response time for water flow

tauO2=2.91; % s   - Response time for oxygen flow

r=0.126; % ohm   - Ohmic loss

Te=0.8; % s   - Electrical response time

Tfc=5; % s   - Fuel processor response time

rH_O=1.145; % %   - Ratio of hydrogen to oxygen

PF=1.0; % %   - Power factor

% demanded current limits of the fuel cell system, Iref, fuel cell

Ilim_max=Umax/2/Kr;

Ilim_min=Umin/2/Kr;

Figure 7. SOFC Initial data (Padulles; Zhu)

A.2 Simulation results

By using the implemented Simulink model (Fig.5), the output voltage and the output power have been obtained, as shown in Figure 7.

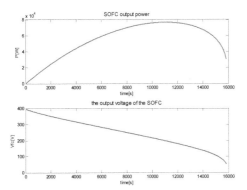

Figure 8. The solid oxide fuel cell characteristics: the power and the output voltage

A.3 Mathematical modeling of the DC-DC power converters for fuel cells and energy storage elements integration: Boost and Buck-Boost power converters

In order to obtain a constant DC voltage, a boost power converter has been taken into consideration (Figure 9), operating in continuous conduction mode (CCM).

The method of the time averaged commutation device is applied to the unitary modeling of the power converters presented in Fig. 9 (Ionescu, 1997).

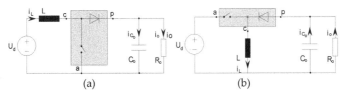

(a)   (b)

Figure 9. DC-DC non-isolated converters: (a)boost; (b) buck-boost

During the DT_s period, the active device is ON and the passive device is OFF. During the $(1-D)T_s$ period, the active device is OFF and the passive device is ON, while the passive terminal p is connected to the common terminal c. The duty factor is denoted D and T_s is the switching period. Taking into consideration the above mentioned hypotheses, the following instantaneous currents can be deduced:

$$i_a(t) = \begin{cases} i_a(t) & \text{during } DT_s \\ 0 & \text{during } (1-D)T_s \end{cases}, i_p(t) = \begin{cases} 0 & \text{during } DT_s \\ i_c(t) & \text{during } (1-D)T_s \end{cases} \qquad (9)$$

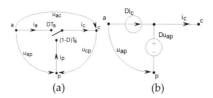

Figure 10. (a) The equivalent three-pole for the commutation device; (b) the equivalent diagram of a time averaged model over a switching period(Ionescu, 1997)

In the similar manner, the specific instantaneous voltages are obtained:

$$u_{cp}(t) = \begin{cases} u_{ap}(t) & \text{during } DT_s \\ 0 & \text{during } (1-D)T_s \end{cases}, u_{ac}(t) = \begin{cases} 0 & \text{during } DT_s \\ u_{ap}(t) & \text{during } (1-D)T_s \end{cases} \tag{10}$$

If averaging is carried out over a period of switching time, equations (9) - (10) will assume the equivalent form of the currents

$$\begin{cases} i_a = D i_c \\ i_p = (1-D) i_c \end{cases} \tag{11}$$

and of voltages, respectively:

$$\begin{cases} u_{cp} = D u_{ap} \\ u_{ac} = (1-D) u_{ap} \end{cases} \tag{12}$$

where, for the sake of convenience , values such as i_a are still considered as time averaged values for a period of switching time.

To demonstrate the validity of the time-averaged commutation device model, the mathematical models for DC –DC converters, boost and boost-buck are considered.

A.4 The Boost converter

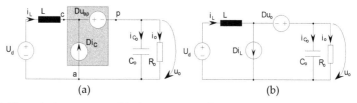

Figure 11. The equivalent structure of the boost converter (Ionescu, 1997)

- From the Fig.11a, the following equivalent relations are obtained:

$$\begin{cases} i_c = -i_L \\ u_{ap} = -u_o \end{cases} \tag{13}$$

- By applying the first Kirchhoff's theorem to the Fig.11b, the first differential equation that characterizes the output voltage dynamic state $\dot{v}_0$ is obtained:

$$(1-D)i_L = C_o \frac{du_o}{dt} + \frac{u_o}{R_o} \text{ or, in the final form } \frac{du_o}{dt} = \frac{1}{C_o}\left[(1-D)i_L - \frac{u_o}{R_o}\right]$$

- By applying the second Kirchhoff's theorem, the second differential equation that characterizes the inductor current dynamic state, i_L, is obtained:

$$U_d + Du_o = L\frac{di_L}{dt} + u_o \text{ or, in the form } \frac{di_L}{dt} = \frac{1}{L}\left[U_d - (1-D)u_o\right]$$

The commutation mathematical model in state space form will be as following:

$$\begin{bmatrix} \dot{i}_L \\ \dot{u}_0 \end{bmatrix} = \begin{bmatrix} 0 & -(1-D)\frac{1}{L} \\ (1-D)\frac{1}{C_o} & -\frac{1}{RC_o} \end{bmatrix} \begin{bmatrix} i_L \\ u_0 \end{bmatrix} + \begin{bmatrix} \frac{1}{L} \\ 0 \end{bmatrix} U_d \tag{14}$$

The voltage u_0 is considered controlled output.

- By vanishing the differential terms, the steady-state regime is obtained from the above deducted dynamic state-vector $\dot{x} = \begin{bmatrix} \dot{i}_L & \dot{u}_0 \end{bmatrix}^T$,:

$$\begin{cases} U_0 = U_d \frac{1}{1-D} \\ I_o = (1-D)I_L = \frac{U_o}{R_o} \end{cases} \tag{15}$$

B. Battery Power Conditioning System

The Battery Power Conditioning Systemconsists of a battery pack and a DC-DC power converter. The NiMH battery produces a variable DC power. The battery pack has as main task to deliver the critical load power (Fig.1).

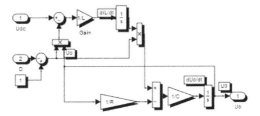

Figure 12. The Simulink diagram of the boost converter

Therefore, individual batteries are connected in series/parallel combination to achieve the desired rating. The Matlab/Simulink battery model from the Mathworks has been used. The main issue for the battery power converter is to charge/discharge battery according to the available flow power. The problem is solved by introducing an internal current loop (Fig.12) in the DC/DC power converter control (Fig.13).

B1. Simulink implementation of the SMC control diagram for DC-DC Boost Power Converter

In (Gulderin Hanifi, 2005) it is shown that the existence condition of the SMC is that the output voltage must be greater than the input one.

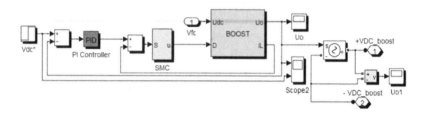

Figure 13. Control of the boost converter: Cascaded DC link voltage loop and current control

The DC-link voltage control is based on the Proportional Integral (PI) controller having $k_p=0.00001$ and $k_i=0.01$ as parameters. The circuit parameters of the boost converter are $L_{boost}=80*1e-6$ [H], $C_{boost}=3240*1e-6$ [F], $R_{boost}=20[\Omega]$.

The current loop is based on the sliding mode control (Fig.14); theMatlab Simulink implementation is shown in Fig.13.

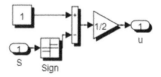

Figure 14. Sliding mode current control

The sliding mode surface S consists of the current error:

$$S = i_L^* - i_L,$$
(16)

which vanishes (S=0) in order to force the system to enter the sliding surface. The sliding mode controller has two functions: the control function and the modulator one. Therefore, the output control of the SMC is the duty cycle, D, of the boost power converter.

$$D = \frac{1}{2}\left(1 - sign(S)\right) \tag{17}$$

In order to follow the current reference, the output DC voltage must be greater than the following limit:

$$U_0 \geq \frac{3}{2}\sqrt{\left(V_{grid}^{max}\right)^2 + \left(L_{inv}\omega I_{grid}^{max}\right)^2} \tag{18}$$

where the RMS grid voltage is V_{grid}^{max}, the maximal grid current is I_{grid}^{max}, ω is the frequency (rad/s), and L_{inv} is the phase inductance (Candusso D, et al., 2002).

After the simulation, results have confirmed the benefits of SMC control (Fig.15a). The output voltage of the converter reaches and stabilizes at the reference value of 690 V at a time of $2 \cdot 10^{-2}$ s (Fig.15b), a very short time in comparison with other control methods, while the error voltage is zero (Fig.15c).

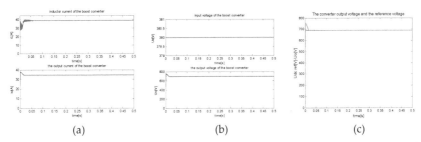

(a)   (b)   (c)

Figure 15. a) The converter output voltage and the reference voltage; b) Input voltage variation; c) The current and the voltage at converter output

The fundamental purpose of using this converter is to raise the voltage from the fuel cell generator. Thus, the battery pack delivers 380Vdc, being the input voltage of the boost converter; the output voltage must be compatible with that of the three-phase voltage source inverter input, i.e. 690Vdc.

The advantages of this type of control are: stability, robustness and a good dynamics.

B1. The mathematical model of the Buck-Boost power converter

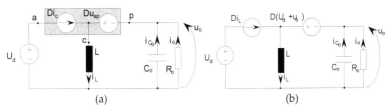

(a)   (b)

Figure 16. Equivalent structure of the boost-boost converter (Ionescu, 1997)

- From the Fig.16a, the following equivalent relations are obtained:

$$\begin{cases} i_c = i_L \\ u_{ap} = U_d + u_o \end{cases} \tag{19}$$

- Following the above procedure applied to the boost power converter, the dynamic model of the buck boost converter is deducted :

$$\begin{cases} \dfrac{di_L}{dt} = \dfrac{1}{L}\left[DU_d - (1-D)u_o \right] \\ \dfrac{du_o}{dt} = \dfrac{1}{C_o}\left[(1-D)i_L - \dfrac{u_o}{R_o} \right] \end{cases} \tag{20}$$

and the steady state regime, respectively:

$$\begin{cases} U_0 = U_d \dfrac{D}{1-D} \\ I_o = (1-D)I_L = \dfrac{U_o}{R_o} \end{cases} \tag{21}$$

B.2. The Simulink model of the Buck Boost power converter

Both the buck boost power converter and the current controller have been implemented and simulated in Simulink (Fig.17).

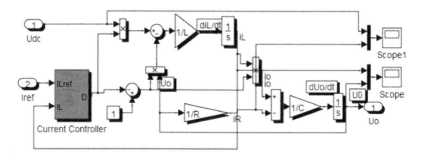

Figure 17. Simulink diagram of the buck-boost converter

B.2.1 The Current Controller

By imposing the inductor current reference (ILref, Fig.18), the current controller will assure the fast reference tracking at the same time with delivering the appropriate duty cycles (D). By introducing an anti-parallel diode for each active power device, a bidirectional buck-boost converter is obtained.

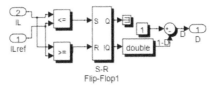

Figure 18. Buck-boost current controller

The buck-boost converter is necessary to connect the battery stack ($U_d=U_{dc}$) to the power inverter system and it comes into operation when the electrical power demanded by consumers is higher than the electrical power obtained from the fuel cell generator. Another reason for the use of the buck-boost converter is to recharge the batteries from the other available sources. The circuit parameters of the buck boost power converter are L=100*1e-5[H], C=500*1e-8[F], R=50[Ω].

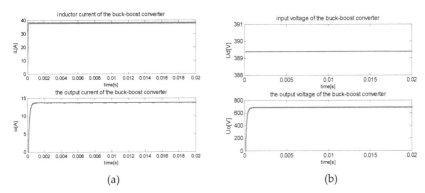

(a)   (b)

Figure 19. The simulation results of the buck-boost power converter

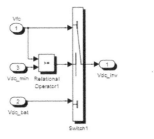

Figure 20. The Power Source Selector

Thanks to the buck boost current controller, the actual inductor current follows the reference current. In the output current a delay of 0.001 s could be found (Fig.19a). The input voltage of the buck-boost converter, U_d, is about 390 Vdc and it is delivered from the battery stack, while the output voltage, U_o, is boosted at 690 Vdc (Fig.19b).

C. Power Source Management (PSM) (Fig.20)

The purpose of the PSM is to assure an adequate DC-link voltage to the power inverter from both power source generators: the solid oxide fuel cell stack and the battery pack.

The final DC link voltage (VDC_inverter, Fig.21) is delivered to the Voltage Source Inverter (VSI) by the Power Source Management block (Fig.20).

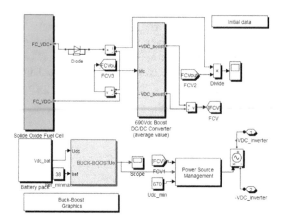

Figure 21. The power sources interconnection

3. Inverter modelling and control

The fundamental types of control can be classified into two categories: current control and voltage control. When the inverter is connected to the network, the network controls the amplitude and frequency of the inverter output and the inverter operates in current control mode. The classical current control can lead to other control methods can be obtained such as active and reactive power control/voltage control. If the network being power injected is not available due to improper network parameters, the inverter will autonomously supply the load; consequently it adequately supplies the alternative voltage in amplitude and frequency and it is not affected by network black outs. In this case, the inverter will control the voltage. The 50 Hz frequency is assured by a phase-locked loop (PLL) control. The grid converter is a full-bridge IGBT transistor-based converter and it normally operates in inverter mode such that the energy is transferred from the hybrid source to the utility grid and/or to the load. When the system is operating in **grid-connected mode**, the PLL tracks the grid voltage to ensure synchronization; but when the system enters in **islanding mode of operation**, the VSI can no longer track the grid characteristics. As seen in Fig. 22, the PLL for the VSI changes the frequency which is sent to the pure integrator for angle calculation by switching between the frequency from the filter and that from another fixed reference. In the islanding mode of operation the VSI needs to have an external frequency reference provided, ω_{fixed} (Fig.22). The PLL for the VSI is the main catalyst for the re-synchronization and re-closure of the system to the Utility once disturbances have passed. The frequency from the filter is used during the grid-connected mode.

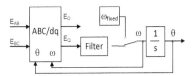

Figure 22. VSI PLL showing switched reference frequency

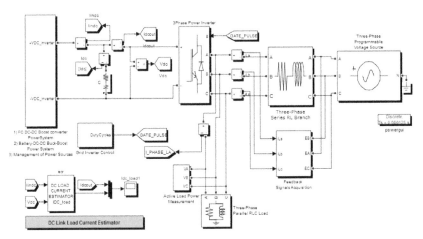

Figure 23. The Simulink model of the Grid Power Inverter for Renewable Energy Sources Integration with DC link Load Current Estimator

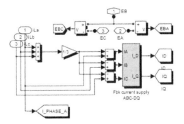

Figure 24. Feedback Signals Acquisition measurement block

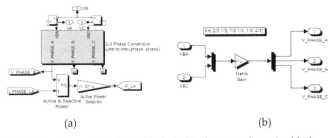

(a)   (b)

Figure 25. (a)Active Load Power Calculation block; (b) 2/3 phase transformation block

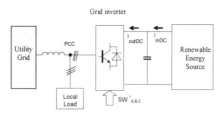

Figure 26. Block diagram of RES, Grid inverter, Local Load and grid interconnection

The Grid Power Inverter for Renewable Energy Sources Integration is of 37kVA and delivers the power to the grid (simulated as three-phase programmable voltage source in Fig. 23) and the necessary power to the consumers (simulated as three-phase parallel RLC load in Fig. 23). There is an adequate boost inductor (three-phase series RL branch, Fig. 23) between the grid and the inverter. In order to calculate the dq components of the grid current, (ID, IQ), the Feedback Signals Acquisition block is used (Fig. 24). Through the implemented Simulink blocks (Figs.25a, 25b), the active power of the load is known.

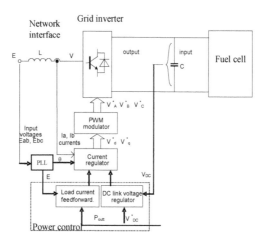

Figure 27. Proposed control system for grid inverter

3.1. The grid inverter control

The grid inverter control block delivers the corresponding duty-cycles to the Power Inverter (Gate_Pulses in Fig.23 or SW*$_{ABC}$ in Fig. 26). To achieve full control of the utility-grid current, the DC-link voltage must be boosted to a level higher than the amplitude of the grid line-line voltage. The power flow of the grid side inverter is controlled in order to keep the DC-link voltage constant. The structure of the DC/AC converter control system is shown in Fig. 27. The control structure of the power inverter is of vector control type and it uses the power balance concept (Sul and Lipo, 1990). Therefore, the load current feedforward component was introduced in order to increase the dynamic response of the bus voltage to load changes.

On the basis of the DC voltage reference V^*_{DC}, DC voltage feedback signal (V_{DC}), AC input voltages (E_{ab} and E_{bc}), current feedback signals (I_a, I_b), and the load power signal (got through a load power estimator) (Gaiceanu, 2004a), the Digital Signal Processor-based software operates the control of the power inverter (DC link voltage and current loops) system and generates the firing gate signals to the PWM modulator (Fig.27). The grid connected PWM inverter supplies currents into the utility line by maintaining the system power balance. By controlling the power flow in power conditioning system, the unidirectional DC-link voltage can be kept at a constant value. Using the synchronous rotating frame the active power is controlled independently by the q-axis current whereas the reactive power can be controlled by the d-axis current.

The control of the grid inverter is based on the minor current loop in a synchronous rotating-frame with a feedforward load current component added in the reference, completed with the DC voltage control loop in a cascaded manner. The outer loop controller consists of two parts: the phase-locked loop (PLL) and the DC link voltage controller. The former, the PLL, is used to extract the fundamental frequency component of the grid voltages and it also generates the corresponding quadrature signals in d-q synchronous reference frame, E_d-E_q, which are necessary to calculate the active and reactive power of the grid. The latter monitors the power control loop. The power control of the PWM inverter, is based on the power detection feedforward control loop and the DC-voltage feedback control loop (Fig.27). The main task of the voltage controller is to maintain the DC link voltage to a certain value. Another task is to control the grid converter power flow. The task of the DC link voltage and of the current regulation has been accomplished by means of the Proportional-Integral (PI) controller type, because of its good steady-state and dynamic behavior with the power inverter. It is important to underline that the PI controller performances are parameters sensitive, because of its design procedure, based on the DC bus capacitor and inductor values. However, in these specific applications, the system parameters values are known with reasonable accuracy. The design of the linear control systems can be carried out in either the time or the frequency domain. The relative stability is measured in terms of **gain margin,** and **phase margin.** These are typical frequency-domain specifications and should be used in conjunction with such tools as Bode plot.

The transfer function of the PI controller (Gaiceanu, 2007b) has the form:

$$C_{PIc}(s) = K_{pc}\left(1 + \frac{1}{T_{ic}s}\right) \tag{22}$$

The calculation of the PI controller coefficients, K_{pc} (proportional gain) and T_{ic} (integral time), is done imposing the phase margin ϕ_{mc} (in radian) and the bandwidth, ω_c, (in radian per second). Imposing these two conditions, the following relations for K_{pc} and T_{ic} are obtained (Gaiceanu, 2007b):

$$\begin{cases} T_{ic} = \dfrac{1}{\omega_c \cdot tan\left(-\dfrac{\pi}{2} - \phi_{mc}\right)} \\[3ex] K_{pc} = \dfrac{-T_{ic} \cdot \omega_c^2 \cdot L}{\sqrt{1 + \left(T_{ic} \cdot \omega_c\right)^2}} \end{cases} \tag{23}$$

3.2. The Phase Locked Loop (PLL)

A phase locked loop (PLL) ensures the synchronization of the reference frame with the source phase voltages by maintaining their d component at zero (E_d=0) through a PI controller; the grid frequency is delivered by knowing the line-line grid voltages (EBA, EBC), as in Figs.28, 29.

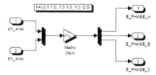

(a) line-line to three phase

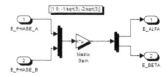

(b) (A,B,C)-(alfa, beta)

Figure 28. The transformation of the coordinates

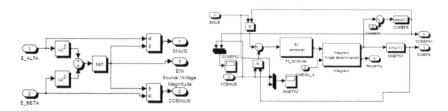

Figure 29. (a) Calculus of the required PLL's input trigonometric functions (b) PLL

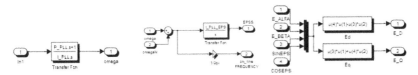

Figure 30. (a) The PI regulator of the PLL (b) The integrator for angle calculation (c) dq grid voltage components: ED, EQ

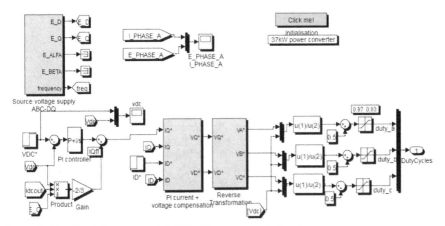

Figure 31. The Simulink structure of the DC/AC converter control system

3.3. The current controllers

By using a decoupling of the nonlinear terms, the cross coupling (due to boost input inductance) between the d and q axes was compensated. To decouple current loops, the proper utility voltage components have been added (Gaiceanu, 2004b) (Fig 32).

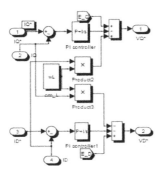

Figure 32. Voltage decoupling control

Fig.33 shows the Simulink implementation of the reverse transformation from synchronous reference frame (d,q) tofixed reference frame (A,B,C) through the (alfa,beta) transformations.

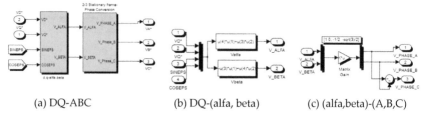

(a) DQ-ABC   (b) DQ-(alfa, beta)   (c) (alfa,beta)-(A,B,C)

Figure 33. Reverse voltage transformation

4. The DClink current estimator

The load power ($P_{load}=P_{out}$) is calculated from the load inverter terminals. Another method is to estimate the load power from the DC link, indirectly, through a first or second order DC load current estimator (Gaiceanu, 2004a). The power feedforward control (Uhrin, 1994) allows the calculus of the input current reference based on the generated power, and it satisfies the power balance in a feedforward manner. By using the load feedforward control, the input reference of the current is changed with load, thus it is obtained a better transient response. The increase in the power response of the DC-AC inverter leads to the possibility of reduction the size of the DC link capacitor by maintaining the stability of thesystem.

The block diagram of the second degree estimator is presented in the Fig. 34, where the input needs the measure of the DC link voltage $V_{dc}(p)$ and the calculus of the input ac load current component I_q. The output of the estimator is the estimated DC link load power $P'_{dcout}(p)$.

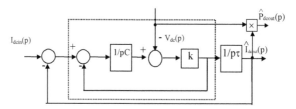

Figure 34. The second order dc link load power estimator

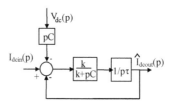

Figure 35. The redrawing estimator

The estimator (Fig. 34), after some manipulations (Fig.35), gets the form presented in the Fig. 36.

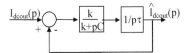

Figure 36. The simplified diagram of the DC load

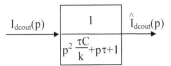

Figure 37. The final second order estimator

Using Laplace transform the DC link voltage equation gets the form

$$pCV_{dc}(p) = I_{dcin}(p) - I_{dcout}(p) \qquad (24)$$

or:

$$I_{dcin}(p) - pCV_{dc}(p) = I_{dcout}(p) \qquad (25)$$

This means that the block diagram from Fig.35 can be redrawing as in Fig. 36.

4.1. Calculus of the estimator parameters

The problem consists of the calculation of the parameters k and τ such that the error between the estimated DC load current $I^{\wedge}_{dcout}(p)$ and the actual DC load current $I_{dcout}(p)$ to be insignificant. The closed loop transfer function of the estimator, (Fig.37), derived from Fig.36, is given by:

$$G(p) = \frac{\overset{\wedge}{I_{dcout}}(p)}{I_{dcout}(p)} = \frac{1}{p^2 \dfrac{\tau C}{k} + p\tau + 1} \qquad (26)$$

Considering a step variation for the $I_{dcout}(p)$, by setting:

$$I_{dcout}(p) = \frac{I_{dcout}}{p} \qquad (27)$$

the estimated DC load current gets the form

$$\overset{\wedge}{I_{dcout}}(p) = I_{dcout} \frac{1}{p(p^2 \dfrac{\tau C}{k} + p\tau + 1)} \qquad (28)$$

The usual form of the equation (28) is given by

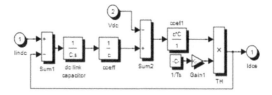

Figure 38. Simulink implementation of the DC link load current estimator

$$\hat{I}_{dcout}(p) = I_{dcout}\,\frac{1}{p(T_0^2 p^2 + 2\xi T_0 p + 1)} \tag{29}$$

where the damping factor is

$$\xi = \frac{\tau \cdot \omega_0}{2} \tag{30}$$

and the pulsation factor

$$\omega_0^2 = \frac{1}{T_0^2} = \frac{\tau}{k \cdot C} \tag{31}$$

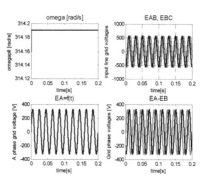

Figure 39. The frequency of the line voltage. The acquisition of the grid line voltages (EAB,EBC) and the phase transformation (EA, EB).

The parameters k and τ are chosen such that the response $I^{\wedge}_{dcout}(p)$ to have an acceptable overshoot

$$\sigma = e^{-\frac{\pi\xi}{\sqrt{1-\xi^2}}}, \tag{32}$$

a small step time response

$$t_a = \frac{ln(0.05\sqrt{1-\xi^2})}{-\xi \cdot \omega_0}, \qquad (33)$$

and a minimum output noise.

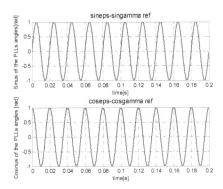

Figure 40. The input and the output signals of the PLL circuit

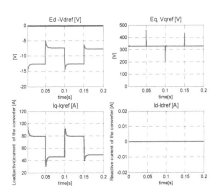

Figure 41. The comparison of the grid voltage and the converter voltage (Ed,Vdref), (Eq, Vqref) and the performances of the current controllers

An advantage of the estimated method is that there is no ripple presence in the feed-forward reference current of the source side. The small reference current ripple is delivered from the output of the DC link voltage controller.

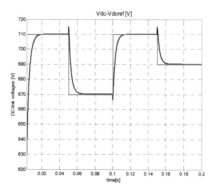

Figure 42. DC link voltage reference, Actual DC link voltage.

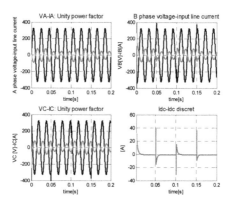

Figure 43. Waveforms showing the unity power factor operation: A, B, C phase grid voltages and the corresponding IA, IB, IC line currents. Simulation results. Idc- the current through the DC link capacitor

4.2. Simulation results

Fig. 41 shows the comparison of the grid voltage and the converter voltage (Ed,Vdref): the Ed component is 0 and the voltage Vdref is calculated as Vdref =om*Lin*IqN+Ed in steady state regime (Gaiceanu, 2007a). The voltages Eqref and Vqref have the same value of 326.55[V].

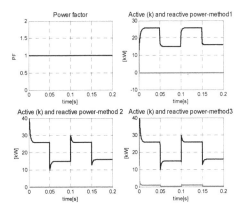

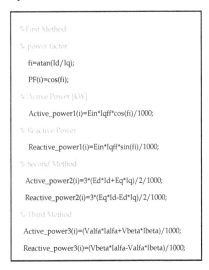

Figure 44. The unitary power factor operation and comparison results of the three methods of active and reactive power deduction

The reference and actual d axis current waveforms (Id-Idref) are shown in Fig.41 proving the cancellation of the reactive power.

```
% First Method

%  power factor

    fi=atan(Id/Iq);

    PF(i)=cos(fi);

%  Active Power [kW]

    Active_power1(i)=Ein*Iqff*cos(fi)/1000;

%  Reactive Power

    Reactive_power1(i)=Ein*Iqff*sin(fi)/1000;

%  Second Method

    Active_power2(i)=3*(Ed*Id+Eq*Iq)/2/1000;

    Reactive_power2(i)=3*(Eq*Id-Ed*Iq)/2/1000;

%  Third Method

    Active_power3(i)=(Valfa*Ialfa+Vbeta*Ibeta)/1000;

    Reactive_power3(i)=(Vbeta*Ialfa-Valfa*Ibeta)/1000;
```

The DC link voltage step response was obtained by using a DC link voltage test generator (Fig.42) under a load current variation between [0.65, 1.15]×I$_N$ (Fig.41), I$_N$ being the rated value of the line current.

The performances of the active current inverter control are shown in Fig.41. The actual active current, I_q, accurately follows the reference I_{qref} (Fig.41). In Fig. 42 the performances of DC-link voltage controllers are shown. The trace of the A phase of the line current is in phase with A phase of the grid voltage, which clearly demonstrates the unity power factor operation (Fig. 43). Comparative waveforms showing unity power factor operation during regeneration obtained from DC-AC power converter are shown in Fig. 43. For all three methods of active and reactive power deduction (Fig.44) the steady state values are the same, however the first method is more accurate in transient regime (Fig.44) (Gaiceanu, 2004b).

The 2nd degree DC link current estimator was implemented for a 37kVA power inverter. The dynamic performances of the DC load current estimator are presented (Gaiceanu, 2004a).

By an adequate choice of the estimator parameters an acceptable step response can be obtained (Fig.45).

Through simulation (Figs. 45-46) the real and the estimated DC link currents are obtained.

The power semiconductor active devices operate with a switching time T_s=125μs, and a 2μs dead time. The converter specifications are given as follows: Supply voltage (line-to-line): 400V; Main frequency: 50Hz, Line current: 69A, Line inductance: 0.5 mH, DC bus capacitor: 1000 μF, Ambient temperature 40⁰C,DC voltage reference: 690V.

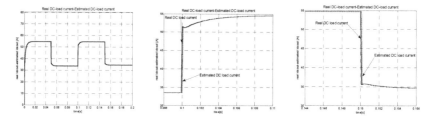

Figure 45. Simulation results. The real DC load current I_{dcout}, the estimated DC link current $I^{\hat{}}_{dcout}$.

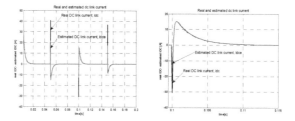

Figure 46. Simulation results. The real DC link current I_{dc}, the estimated DC link current $I^{\hat{}}_{dc}$

5. dSpace implementation

The PI Current Control in Synchronously Reference Frame is shown in Fig.47. The current regulators have two tasks: the error cancelling, and the modulation (the appropriate switching states are provided).

For an adequate tuning of the current regulators, the actual load current, iA, accurately follows its reference i*A (Fig. 49), despite of an inappropriate tuning of the current controllers (Fig.48).

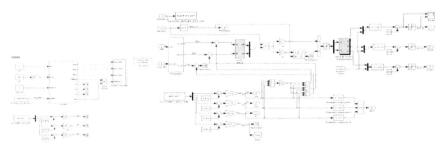

Figure 47. Real time implementation of the current control by using dSpace 1103 platform

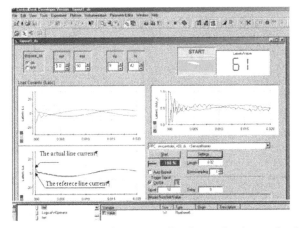

Figure 48. The three phase load currents, the corresponding duty cycles, the actual and the reference line currents for the inaccurate tuning of the current regulator parameters: Kp=9, Ki=42

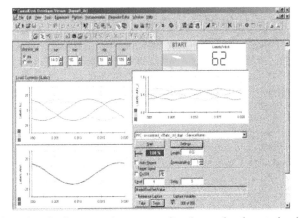

Figure 49. The three phase load currents, the corresponding duty cycles, the actual and the reference line currents for the accurate tuning of the current regulator parameters: Kp=18, Ki=105

6. Conclusions

The main outcomes of the chapter:

- The chapter pursuits to increase the awareness of public regarding the renewable energy technologies through the open access, and to determine the researchers to implement renewable energy projects.
- The chapter will contribute the promotion of RES through the formation of experts so that these experts can later carry out RES projects with outstanding results.

The implicit longer term outcomes are related to:

1. Accurate models for fuel cells power systems.
2. New design of the adequate controllers for integrated systems, which will enable the efficient operation of such power inverters connected to the grid, with high stability in service and power quality.
3. The rapid prototyping through dSpace real time platform can prove very useful in medium and longer term for further modelling/investigation/development of similar systems.

The chapter will also bring contributions to the development of the theoretical knowledge if the following aspects are taken into account: the complexity of the issue, its interdisciplinary, the performance of an experimental model and the necessary theoretical knowledge of the interface solutions for the renewable system, in particular for fuel cells.

Through a proper control sinusoidal input current, a nearly unity power factor (0,998), bi-directional power flow, small (up to 5%) ripple in the DC-link voltage in any operated conditions, disturbance compensation capability, fast control response and high quality balanced three-phase output voltages were obtained. By using the load feed-forward component the input reference of the current is changed with load so that a better transient response is obtained. The proposed control was successfully implemented by the author on quasi direct AC-AC power converter (Gaiceanu M., 2004b) and based on the Matlab/Simulink software the simulation test has been performed for the modified topology of the grid power inverter. The experimental results (Figs. 48, 49) have been obtained by using dSpace platform (Fig.47). The second-degree DC load current estimator for DC-AC power converter system is developed in this chapter. Since the DC-AC power converter control by means of pulse-width modulation (PWM) is based on the power balance concept, its load power should be known. In order to overcome the measuring solution with well-known disadvantages, the load power can be estimated from the DC side by using the DC load current estimator. Thus, it is mandatory to have the information regarding the DC load current. The DC voltage regulation with good dynamic response is achieved even if DC capacitance is substantially reduced. This implies also the good accuracy of the DC link load current estimation.

Author details

Marian Gaiceanu
Dunarea de Jos University of Galati, Romania

7. References

Abou El-Maaty Metwally (2005). Modelling and Simulation of a Photovoltaic Fuel Cell Hybrid System) Kassel, Germany

Candusso D. , Valero I.& Walter A. (2002). Modelling, control and simulation of a fuel cell based power supply system with energy management,IECON 2002 28th Annual Conference , pp.1294-1299

COM(2006) Action Plan for Energy Efficiency: Realising the Potential, Available fromhttp://ec.europa.eu/energy/action_plan_energy_efficiency/doc/com_2006_0545_en. pdf

EREC, Renewable Energy Technology Roadmap (2008), Available from http://www.erec.org/fileadmin/erec_docs/Documents/Publications/Renewable_Energy_ Technology_Roadmap.pdf, pp2

EREC, the European Renewable Energy Council (2011). Mapping Renewable Energy Pathways towards 2020, Available from http://www.eufores.org/fileadmin/eufores/Projects/REPAP_2020/EREC-roadmap-V4.pdf

Gaiceanu M (2004b). AC-AC Converter System for AC Drives, *IEE Conference Publication Journal*, British Library, London, Publisher: Institution of Electrical Engineers, Vol. 2, no. 498, Printed in Great Britain by WRIGHTSONS, ISSN 0537-9989, pp 724-729

Gaiceanu M. (2004a). A new load power estimator for quasi-sinusoidal ac-ac converter system," *Proceedings of the 9th International Conference on Optimization of Electrical and Electronic Equipments (OPTIM 2004)*, Vol. II: Power Electronics, Electrical Machines & Drives, ISBN 973-635-287-0, Brasov, May 20-21, pp.189-195, 2004

Gaiceanu M. (2007a) Inverter Control for Three-Phase Grid Connected Fuel Cell Power System, The *5th International IEEE Conference CPE 2007, Compatibility in Power Electronics Conference*, May 29- June 1, 2007, Gdansk, Poland, Power Electronics, 2007 Compatibility in, Conf Proceedings IEEE Product No.: EX1712, ISBN: 1-4244-1054-1

Gaiceanu, M.& Fetecau G. (2007b). Grid connected Wind turbine-Fuel Cell Power System having Power Quality Issues, EPQU'07 Barcelona, pp.7-13, 2007. ISBN 978-84-690-9441-9

Gulderin Hanifi (2005), Sliding Mode Control of DC-DC boost converter, Journal of Applied Sciences 5 (3): 588-592

Ionescu Fl. et al (1997). Electronica de putere. Modelare si simulare, Editura Tehnica

Padulles J., Ault G.W. &McDonald J.R. (2000). An integrated SOFC plant dynamic model for power systems simulation, J. Power Sources 86 495_500

Sul, S.K., & Lipo T.A. (1990). Design and performance of a high-frequency link induction motor drive operating at unity power factor," *IEEE Trans. Ind. Applicat.*, vol.26, no.3, pp. 434-440, May/June

Uhrin, R.& Profumo F. (1994). Performance comparison of output power estimators used in AC/DC/AC converters, *Industrial Electronics, Control and Instrumentation*, IECON '94., 20th International Conference on, Volume 1, 5-9 Sept. 1994 Page(s):344 - 348 vol.1, 1994

Zhu Y. &Tomsovic K. (2002). Development of models for analyzing the load-following performance of microturbines and fuel cells, Electric Power Systems Research 62 (2002) 1_/11

MATLAB for Educational Purposes

Chapter 5

Education of Future Advanced Matlab Users

Michal Blaho, Martin Foltin, Peter Fodrek and Ján Murgaš

Additional information is available at the end of the chapter

1. Introduction

Technology surrounds us in every step we take. Computers, mobile phones or cars would not exist without smart researchers and innovators. We need more and more engineers and scientists to sustain technological growth. The current state of technology and technological growth is facing two problems. The first problem is population declining in many countries. Germany is a country with least population growth in Europe, for example. The second problem is that many industrial and research centres demand high quality engineers (Blau, 2011). These two problems come hand in hand as you can imagine. Society can affect both of them in some way but providing high quality engineers is what we can affect at fastest. Learning is an important process in our lives. Educational institutions prepare students to fulfil requirements from the society. There are many modern methods and technologies for learning but most of them have one in common today – computers.

Computer aided learning has found a way in learning process from primary schools to universities (Abdullah et al., 2010, Bertrand, 1989). Computers are also significantly involved in teaching technology serving sciences like mathematics, physics and information technology. Technical computing plays an important role in these specializations. Many software applications are accessible for teaching as Matlab, Octave, Scilab and Mathematica, for example. Other specialized programs exist as well, but they are often used to solve specialized problems and tasks. Therefore we are not going to mention them. The worldwide most spread applications at educational institutions used by is Matlab, which is considered as standard in technical computing and science (The MathWorks, 2012a). Matlab is a very powerful tool for computing and simulation. Basic mathematical core provides functions for high performance computing. On top of that, Matlab provides add-ons (toolboxes) to enhance its usage via adding more functions in specialized fields of technology, economics, medicine or biology. Matlab is also applied in many publications in different fields. Matlab is not only exploited in computations but also in the process of teaching and learning. In the Matlab environment there are small GUI applications that can be created to improve learning (Andreatos & Zagorianos, 2009).

Extensive usage of Matlab demands high quality courses at educational institutions (Dogan, 2011). In fact multiple courses for different topics can be taught with the use of Matlab. To provide students with solid background for these topics, an introductory course for Matlab can be created. At our faculty we create such a course. The aim of this course is to gain basic skills that students can use in more advanced courses. Our course is divided into two parts. In the first part there are Matlab basics that every student must to know (Matlab basics, graphics and Simulink). At top of the basic specialized topics a more advanced courses are introduced to help during teaching topics that students will need later. Although we teach the Matlab course at our faculty we believe that Matlab can be used at secondary schools as supporting tool for the teachers. Matlab basics and graphics can be also taught to students at secondary school level (M. Varga & Z. Varga, 2010).

Students have different types learning capabilities. We cannot satisfy all of them, but we could motivate them to achieve the best possible performance. One of the proper motivator is their evaluation (Blaho et al. 2010a, 2010b). If students can see that the hard effort is rewarded than they want to learn more and more. The other motivator is collaboration. Many students are competitive by nature and they want to achieve better performance than others. On the other hand the collaboration can help them to solve problems that they are not able to solve for hours or days. Therefore collaborative learning is a very important for them because students learn to work in the team as well.

The Internet is popular among the students. Students search more and more for information on the Internet. Studies show that many students consider the Internet as a great source of information and using it during learning process. The Internet is full of e-learning projects, documents, presentations and multimedia content that students may find useful for their learning process (Foltin 2012b, 2012c). It is necessary that all our contents for courses are available online as well. Courses can be also supported with custom video tutorials where topics are explained and shown. Mathworks also provide online content like the documentation, webinars and events on their official web site. Conferences are also good events for students to exchange their knowledge among each other (MathWorks 2012a, 2012b, 2012c). Learning and teaching process is often high cost. Free software and open source applications are possible solution (Foltin et al. 2011).

In this chapter we will describe possibilities for an introductory Matlab course. We will show how to divide lectures and practices into several topics necessary and helpful for the students. Weekly task evaluations are proposed to motivate students to achieve better results. We will described how to find an interesting resources for the course or how to create own one. Collaboration among students is described within the Internet with the Facebook, articles or forums. Over all we focused on the educational use of Matlab, concepts for lecturers and the course improvements.

2. Matlab course

Matlab is a very powerful tool for technical computing and simulation. It is time saving tool for high performance computations. Matlab is optimized for this kind of tasks. It supports us when we lack of real world system in the education. Matlab contains many add-ons that are very useful in many fields of science. Matlab usage is a very popular in many science projects, bachelor, master and dissertation theses in the university environment. The basic Matlab course was established at the Faculty of Electrical Engineering and Information Technology in Bratislava to teach students to use Matlab and its add-ons. Matlab is a basic tool for every student at our faculty. We try to move this course into the first year of study for this reason. The knowledge, which students take from this course is a very useful in the other technical courses.

2.1. Lectures

As we mentioned before at the Faculty of Electrical Engineering and Information Technology Bratislava there is Matlab used in many mathematical and technical courses. Students use Matlab for their computations and solutions in their bachelor, diploma or dissertation theses. Matlab course is introductory course to Matlab, Simulink and Matlab toolboxes. The faculty has two terms per year. Each term lasts twelve weeks. Course can be taken in second term of the first year of undergraduate study. It consists of one lecture (100 minutes) and practice (100 minutes) per week. The lectures are not compulsory, but practices are. Count of the attendance at lectures is more than a half of all students. The lectures are combination of explanation of the current topic, solving of basic tasks and discussion. All of tasks are solved directly on the computer using Matlab. The students are allowed to see how to solve the concrete problem and can write the notes into their hand-out. The full preprint of lecture is available a week ahead on the web pages of the course. The students can print this hand-out before the lecture. The hand-out with notes are useful source of the information for the practices. For this reason there are usually students who attend the lectures more successful than students who do not have the notes from the lectures. The aim of the Matlab course is to introduce students to the Matlab, to learn basic principles, syntax and solutions of some common problems. We focus on the most common problems which students may use in their future study or on the others courses. We cover these topics:

- Matlab basics and programming
- Graphics and GUI
- Simulink
- LTI continuous and discrete systems
- Non-linear systems
- Identification
- Fuzzy logic
- Virtual reality
- Stateflow
- Neural networks
- Real-time

As you can see, there are many topics for just one course. But with the lecture time we just cover a simple introduction to these topics. That is not a big problem because they will have detailed courses for most of the mentioned topics in the future. The main idea is to show basic principles and solutions to students that Matlab could provide. They can extend knowledge gained from the Matlab course on the other courses.

2.2. Practices

The practices are related to the lectures. Students are solving some problems similar to the topic on the actual lecture. Problem is at the first solved verbally and using the board. Students then try to find out solutions in the Matlab environment. This is a time for notes from the lecture. Practices are set up in the way that students have not much time to learn the topic on the exercise and they have to always come prepared. Every student has his computer and work alone. They can use the computers with Microsoft Windows, GNU/Linux or Mac OS X operating systems. Students can also use their own notebooks. These facts improve the environment in the class. There are two lessons that take hour and forty minutes together. Teacher checks and rate every students work about ten minutes before end of the practice. The tasks are prepared for students that they should finish the given tasks before hour and half without problem. Many of students can solve given problems successfully in time.

2.3. Matlab at secondary schools

Although we teach Matlab course at university the question is if we could find usage of Matlab at lower levels of education. The answer to this question is of course yes. We think that Matlab is great supportive program for secondary schools teachers and it should be used in mathematics and physics courses. For example let us look at this two equations:

$$x = x_0 + v_0 \, t \cos(\alpha) \tag{1}$$

$$y = y_0 + v_0 \, t \sin(\alpha) - 0.5 \, g \, t^2 \tag{2}$$

Equations represents trajectory of an object thrown in 2D plane from start point (x_0, y_0) with speed (v_0) at some angle (α). With given acceleration due to gravity (g) we can compute distance (x) and height (y) of objects trajectory at certain time (t). In the next figure you can see trajectories for different angles with same start point, speed and gravity.

In the most of the secondary schools teachers and students compute results on the table or the paper. Matlab can be used to visualize different trajectories in just few lines of code for better understanding and imagination of the problem. With additional commands we could animate whole movement. This is one of the examples how to use Matlab in secondary schools physics classes. Another question is if Matlab should be considered only as a supporting program for the teachers or if students should also learned know how to create own scripts and programs. We think that we should consider both. Benefits of the first part of the question were answered with our example before. Writing Matlab scripts and programs should not be a problem for the students also because of its simplicity. We think that for students it would be also interesting. They would also learn some basic concepts of algorithm writing.

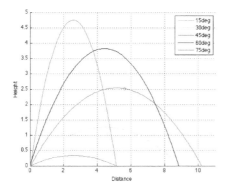

Figure 1. Trajectories of thrown object

3. Matlab course topics

In previous chapter we generally talked about the Matlab practices and lectures at the universities. We briefly showed how you could use the Matlab benefits in secondary schools also. This chapter will discus topics suitable for basic Matlab course. We divided topics into three categories. Essential topics are parts of Matlab that every student should know because they provide strong platform for advanced topics and other Matlab toolboxes. Advanced topics should cover additional parts of the Matlab necessary for later student courses. We will describe topics that we cover in our course but other interesting parts of the Matlab suitable for other study programs are described in other interesting topics.

3.1. Essential topics

With Matlab core components come several add-ons as well. It is necessary to know all about basic Matlab concepts before we start to use specializes toolboxes suitable for our needs. In our opinion the essential topic for advanced Matlab users should be Matlab basics, graphics, Graphical User Interface and Simulink. Next we will talk in the detail about each of them and on what we should focus at most.

3.1.1. Matlab basics

Understanding of the Matlab basic principles is key to be successful advanced Matlab user. Students should know how to use Matlab windows (Command Window, Workspace, History) and the benefits of each of them. Effective usage of Matlab help system is also necessary to solve Matlab warnings and errors. It is our choice if we use fast help command or Matlab Product help where user can find detailed information. Basic computations can be made in the Command Window through statements or in scripts (M-files) for example area of the circle. For additional support we can use the built-in Matlab functions for complex numbers or trigonometry functions. What makes Matlab powerful tool are vectors and matrices. There are several ways to create and manipulate them. Working with indexes of matrix is a very important and challenging parts in the Matlab for students, even harder with indexes range. Programing in the Matlab with functions, loops or conditions is one of the highlights of Matlab basics. In our course we are creating simple sorting algorithms. Students must then use almost every part of Matlab basics that we mentioned in this section. We are also teaching advanced data types – structures and cells. Data types are often used as types for output or input arguments to several Matlab functions.

3.1.2. Graphics and graphical user interface

Functions and scripts provide sets of commands necessary for computing output data. Reading plain data is hard and we need some mechanism to represent them. Matlab contains several plotting commands for 2D and 3D figures. In 3D plotting we need to create grid for 3D space through meshgrid command. Some students have a hard time to understand this concept. Changing plot properties is another important knowledge. We must create handler to plot and using get and set commands we can change line colour or type. We can also use standard Matlab handles like current axis (gca), current figure (gcf) or current object (gco). Matlab enable creating graphical user interface. With objects like buttons, labels, inputs or check box we can create interactive experience for users with no prior Matlab knowledge. Students like creating user interfaces, but concept of the handles structure and callbacks can be sometimes difficult for them. We are trying explained this concept clearly and showed them how to call callback from another to reduce necessary commands.

3.1.3. Simulink basics

We can start model dynamical systems after Matlab basics lectures and practices. Dynamics of any system can be expressed with differential equations and computed by ode solvers. With Matlab ode solvers users must write functions with differential equations. More natural way provides the Matlab extension Simulink. In Simulink we building simulation schema from graphical blocks, signals and then customizing parameters in the blocks. Simulation can be continuous or discrete. After Simulink basics we create simple DC motor model schema from differential equations of the mechanical and electrical parts. Critical part for the students is relation between variable and variables differential, how this is modelled through integrator block and how to set initial conditions. On the practice students are modelling following equations:

$$x_1' = x_2 \tag{3}$$

$$x_2' = -g/l \, \sin(x_1) - k/m \, x_2 + 1/(l^2 m) \, T \tag{4}$$

Equations represent simple pendulum differential equations where variables can be mass (m), length of the pendulum (l), acceleration due to gravity (g) and k is representative of the amount of damping present. Simulation schema for these equations is in the next figure.

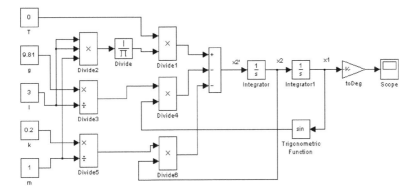

Figure 2. Simulink schema of simple pendulum

Students can change system parameters to simulate how motion of the pendulum change. Standard simulation is with no input (T) and 90 degrees as initial pendulum position.

3.2. Advanced topics

After the essential topics lectures and practices it is time to choose advanced topics. Advanced topics depend on a study program of the students. Because our students studying cybernetics and robotics we focused after basic topics to topics related to their curriculum. In this session we are describing some of them next.

3.2.1. Identification

In real world we often do not know structure of the systems (gain, constants, etc.). Systems can be identified through regression methods with input and output data. Regressions methods are part of the Matlab in System Identification Toolbox. Widely used model estimations are ARX and ARMAX models. Another possibility to achieve approximation of the system is with neural networks. In our course there we use both of them to introduce basic principles of both methods for the system identification.

3.2.2. Virtual reality

Signal values from the Simulink models can be plotted into charts. These signals can be also used for animation of models and Simulink 3D Animation provides this capability. Virtual Reality Mark-up Language represents 3D models using basic shapes and properties like geometry, appearance or translation. Virtual reality worlds can be built using several programs but the Simulink 3D Animation includes V-Realm Builder. Build 3D world is saved as *wrl file and with VR Sink Simulink block we can interact with our simulation. Building 3D animations is one of the interesting topics of our course for students and they are really enjoying it. With the differential equations from previous practices we are animating simple pendulum that oscillates from right angle to equilibrium. Visualization of this system is in the next figure.

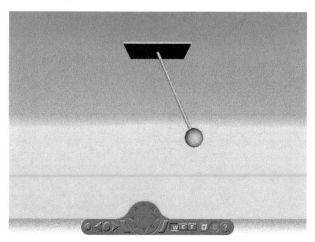

Figure 3. Trajectories of thrown object

3.2.3. Fuzzy logic

Describing behaviour of real world systems with differential equations is often very challenging. Humans can control cars without knowing its precise description. Fuzzy logic can model systems in the terms of If-Then rules natural to our thinking. Inputs and outputs to the fuzzy system are modelled through fuzzy membership functions. In our course there we introduce students into the basic concepts of fuzzy logic and then they modelling some decision problem. One of the problems is student own grading system where there are two tests, one exam and they must write rules based on the point gain for each one of them. Some interesting grade scales came often as result.

3.2.4. Stateflow

Most of the systems can be described as continuous (variables depends on time) or discrete (variables are time-sampled). Some systems react to events and we do not know exactly when system change happens. These systems are called event-driven. Event-driven systems are important to know because they can be found in the industrial applications. They can be modelled by several methods like Petri nets or Statecharts. Matlab prefers Statecharts through Stateflow, which is design environment for developing them. The states and transitions between states are represented graphically. Graphical representation is very useful within simulation where user can see which states are active and when system reacts to event through the transitions. For the Stateflow practise we are asking students to observe real word and look for examples of event-driven systems. They came out with interesting observations like the elevators, intelligent traffic light sensors or door openers in public transportations which all react to the human touch. We are choosing and modelling one system into the Stateflow together.

3.2.5. Real time

Simulation in the Simulink does not respect real time. If the Simulink schema is simple to the simulation it will be faster than in real time and if schema is complex simulation will be slower than in real time. If we interact with real systems though the Simulink we must ensure precise timing. Interaction with the real time systems is necessary for the measuring physical values (inputs) and reaction to them through outputs. Port of computers can be used to do that with sound card, USB, parallel or serial port even with specialized measuring cards. Real Time Toolbox that is not part of the Matlab can provide real time in Simulink (Humusoft s.r.o., 2012).

Real Time toolbox is only available for the 32 bit Microsoft Windows operating systems and can provide precise timing (standard usage is around 0.1s). Another real time communication can be made by OPC toolbox. With OPC toolbox we can connect, read and write data to OPC server. With large amount of OPC server distributors we can communicate with almost every Programmable logic controller widely used in praxis. For the educational purposes OPC server simulators can be used for example from the company named Matricon (MatriconOPC 2012). This server generates signal that we can read and draw in the Matlab/Simulink. We can also write our data to provided space of the server and then to the process or controller.

3.3. Other interesting topics

In the advanced topics there we described topics that are useful for students at our faculty. There are many toolboxes suitable not only for engineering study programs but also for other like economics (Financial Toolbox, Fixed-Income Toolbox, Financial Derivatives Toolbox) or natural sciences (Bioinformatics Toolbox, SimBiology). Toolboxes that we did not mention in this session can be introduced in other courses, bachelor or master theses. We think that future is in code generation for various devices (FPGA, Embedded devices), or hardware in the loop simulation but variety of the Matlab toolboxes specialised for other topics are popular as well.

4. Tasks evaluation

Results of the students are evaluated through point assigning for each course independently at the Faculty of Electrical Engineering and Information Technology Bratislava (Blaho et al. 2010a, 2010b). Students can achieve 100 points at most. Most times points are divided into two parts. The first amount of the points can student achieved for their activity at practices or tests through term. The second part they can achieve on the exam test. In the most cases it is 30/70 (practice/exam) or 40/60. Weight is on the exam as you can see. Maximum amount of the points allowed during term is 50 for the undergraduate courses.

4.1. Week task

There are two main evaluation (or result classification) systems. The first system classifies students via two or three checkpoints through term. All comes to these tests at the end. Point results depends on how successful are students to answer the test tasks. It is a little bit problematic when students doing great at the practices, but they vacillate on the tests at the end of course. They also do not have to learn until a test is in sight. This problem had been observed long time ago at the mathematics teaching. Students came from high schools and they were not used to learn so much or they had different knowledge background of the mathematics. Many of them fail some of the basics mathematics courses.

Mathematicians try another pointing system that "forces" students to learn more often than just before the tests. Students were evaluated at the every exercise. On the next exercise they had small test on previous topic. The results of the student grow significantly. We also used this schema. We had two reasons for that. One reason was that we had many topics covered in our course. It would be not useful to test student on topics they forget long time ago. Another was that we want to "force" students to do something more. We choose to give more points during the term, so we give 40 points maximum for the practices. There were 10 practices for 4 points each. The first and the last were not evaluated. You can see results from year 2011 course classification distribution in the next figure.

With weekly tasks evaluation students gained good amount of point that they carry to the exam. This type of evaluation does not fit everyone and in the next part of this session we will be talking about its advantages and disadvantages.

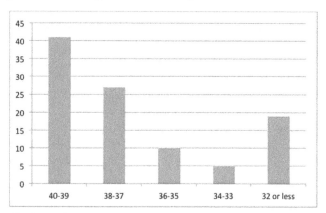

Figure 4. Point distribution for practices

4.2. Advantages and disadvantages

Every student has different capability to learn. We cannot choose unified methodology to learn them all that we know. But with proper motivation they will be willing to learn by themself more within their free time outside the university campus. Our week task evaluation is kind of motivation factor. Reachable classifications are motivators for being excellently prepared for practices. Now it is time to talk about advantages and disadvantages of our method. We think of these advantages:

- Students must come prepared for practice
- Student are evaluated for what they learned on the lectures last week
- No homework
- Students will also learn work under time limit and stress

Of course every method has some disadvantages. We think of these disadvantages:

- Limited time for educating outside of exercises
- Collision with other courses tests
- Limited time for finishing tasks
- Work under stress
- Problem with student absence on practice (small ability of repeat the same practice)

This method has also some advantages and disadvantages as you can see. The question is if this system works for students and if it is acceptable for them.

5. Study materials

Computers really changed our lives and today are almost impossible to imagine life without them. We often use them without knowing it. Computer by itself is a really powerful tool for computing, but for many years also for communication and sharing information. In fact, the basic idea for the Internet was collaboration across the continents with other researchers. We significantly use this tool today not only for sharing information but also in the teaching process. E-learning is most popular and modern activity in this process. We are also using web technologies for improving our student's results. Although possible we do not use any Learning management system (LMS).

5.1. Open source technologies

For some student education can be expensive even if it is for free (like in our country). Reduction of the costs is our priority too and we try to be supportive for them. We are trying to work with open source technologies that are comparable to commercial technologies. We support students to use free UNIX-based operating systems (Linux distributions). For creation of lectures and practices we use Open source productivity suites like OpenOffice.org or LibreOffice. They are used to exchange documents and spread sheets. All presentations are created using these office suites.

5.2. Course online study materials

Internet is great source for information exchange as we mentioned before. Modern student's first choice for material search is Internet at the moment as well. For this fact we build web page for the course to make it easy for them to find materials. On our web page students can find all about the course. They can find contacts to us in case they forgot them, some news for the course and another useful page links. Our web pages are prepared using iWeb software. This is WYSIWYG editor for doing web pages. The advantage of this software is they provide very good graphical user interface. It is not a problem to add the new lectures and important information for students by several clicks. For this reason it is possible to update the web page as often as possible. Web pages are divided into sections. The most wanted sections are about the lectures and practices. Students can find lectures and exercises materials there in electronic form. Also detailed information about both is available from there. A few topics have own video tutorials and students are able to view them at home and they can be better prepared for the practices. Video tutorials have main advantage. Students can directly see what the teacher is doing and therefore that is easier to then to understand topic. Some of the video tutorials are mentioned in references. We would like to publish these free video tutorials in Apple Store iTunes U in the future.

Computers connected to the Internet access are present at the practice room. Students can find their problems solutions on the web pages. On our webpage at which we publish student's articles we decided to write small papers about Matlab in Slovak language. Papers slowly cover the Matlab topics so the students have many tutorials. Beyond the articles discussion to the paper is available. We also publish some experiences on our publishing portal named Posterus (Systémy priemyselnej informatiky s.r.o. [SPR] 2012a).

5.3. Mathworks online study materials

The lectures are not only source of the materials. Students use many different materials at the practices. The main material for Matlab study could be the Matlab reference manual that covers all topics and functions that students can use. Matlab reference manual is also accessible online. Student can search the Matlab topics and functions help without installing Matlab tools. Mathworks support education of all parts of Matlab through various online content (The Mathworks 2012a, 2012b, 2012c). Online events called webinars are recorded regularly and they are available for later use. Webinars are categorized by date of the recording, application, product and industry. This helps users to fast find necessary contents. Many languages are supported as well and that helps overcome language barrier for the novice users. We also contributed by creating webinar for Stateflow introduction.

5.4. Seminars and conferences

Online content is very useful but human interaction is important as well. This can be done on events like seminars and conferences. Seminars take place regularly by local Matlab providers just like webinars. Participants from other institutions come to seminars to learn and discus about related topics. Another types of interactions are conferences where students or scientists can present their work. We are trying to participate at Matlab conferences to extend our knowledge and trying to incorporate student in them as well.

5.4.1. Conferences for students

Conferences for the students are great place to present their results. At our faculty students can present their work at two conferences. SVOC conference is for the students from bachelor and master level of study. On this conferences student can also gain some presentation skill that will help them at the final exams later. ELITECH conference is for the students from postgraduate level of study. This conference is more scientific oriented and can be as start conference for other local or international conferences.

5.4.2. Conferences for scientist and educators

The Humusoft Company organizes conference focus on the technical computing every autumn. Past events were hosted at the Congress Center of the Czech Technical University in Prague. Conferences were dedicated to presentations of the MATLAB / Simulink, dSPACE and COMSOL Multiphysics users. Program of the conference also included the latest information on these products and seminar for COMSOL Multiphysics. We participate at this conference and present out results in the education and science. We also motivate students to participate on the conference. Many of them have bachelor or master thesis in Matlab. We try to direct them to work on interesting topics that are worth to present on the conference. One or two papers at the conference come from our student every year.

Every year Mathworks is hosting global event. MathWorks Academic Virtual Conference is joining professors, educators and Matlab users from the praxis. The aim of the conference is to bridge the gap between theory and practice. Participants are learning how to incorporate latest MathWorks technologies into the classrooms and laboratories. Conference is divided into the three regions (Asia-Pacific, Europe, America) for people from the different time zones. Between the presentations it is the time to visit the exhibition hall. At the hall participants could visit booths to chat with staff, view products demonstrations and download literature. Two kinds of booths are available – MathWorks booths and Participating partners booths. We actively are participating on this conference. After presentations we discussed the topics and try to ask the questions online to the speakers. In the exhibition hall time we joined some booths to talk with MathWorks experts about topics that we are interested in.

6. Interaction of students

Collaborative learning is a very interesting area. Students are helping each other to better understand some topics. Main advantage of this method is that student did not stuck and some part of topic that he did not understand. This is much more times efficient and students can learn much more. This helps collaborative learning type students as well as individual learning type students to achieve better results.

6.1. Matlab forum

To support collaborative learning we founded Matlab forum. Students can ask any Matlab related questions on the forum. It is not forum just for our course. The questions can be related to various problems at which students came through on their study in every course and are about Matlab. We answer most of the questions, but there are some others responders that can easily support us when we have not enough time. They include local Matlab software distributor employers. Now students from different faculties around Slovak Republic and Czech Republic come to our forum and ask questions about Matlab. Foreign students are also welcomed as they can ask us in English as well (SPR 2012b).

6.2. Facebook

Speaking of the Internet and collaborative learning we must also mentioned social networking. Social networks are very popular today. Majority of people are present at least at one social network. Most favourite social network is the Facebook today. Like the Internet, Facebook also started on the academic field. The website's membership was initially limited by the founders to the Harvard university students at Cambridge, Massachusetts, but was expanded to other colleges in the greater Boston area. Facebook enables to create groups. Groups can be created by topics like interests or activities. We established new Facebook group for the students of the Matlab course (Foltin 2012a). This group has several active members who are mainly students of our course. We use this group for quick and short information about the course. Every member can comment tasks from the practices and lectures. It is very useful feedback from students to teachers. Lot of students use this group for publicity their works. They want to show results of their work to other students and share the algorithm. It can be a platform for new projects in the future. It can be also used as a sort of learning management and e- learning system.

7. Results and opinions of the students

To improve our course even more we study the students study results and their feedback every term. First of all we compare distributions from practices and grade results. Then we are giving some questions to the students at the end of the term. Some information and feedback we have already gained through the Facebook and Matlab forum during the term.

7.1. Results

The figure 4 shows that students did very well in tasks during term. Almost half of them gained maximum points. But the question is: How well did students at exam succeeded? Firstly we must look at the exam grades and the relevant points for that grade:

- A – excellent results with minimal errors (100 – 92 points)
- B – above-average results with less errors (83 – 91 points)
- C – fairly well, average results (74 – 82 points)
- D – satisfactory results but with significant errors (65 – 73 points)
- E – sufficient results that satisfactory minimal criteria (64 – 56 points)

- FX – insufficient results, completing of the course expect more efforts and knowledge form student (less than 56 points)
- FN -student did not come to the exams test.

Points are sum of points acquired during term and exam. Next figure shows final grade for our students.

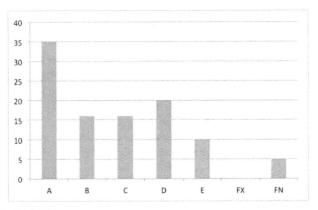

Figure 5. Grade distribution

As you can see there is a change between graphs at exercises and at exam. From the first graph we would expect more students with better grades. We have to ask our-self, what could cause such difference. The first reason could be exam itself. On exam students can acquired up to 60 points. It is a lot education classification so they have to be divided into several questions. The questions have to reflect whole course knowledge so students have to repeat and learn more at the exam. The second reason could be psychological. The good educating result from the exercises could not motivate students enough. Student with high quality result probably thought that they have enough grade of result to pass exam and did not needed to get better grade. Maybe they concentrate elsewhere to pass on the other courses more.

7.2. Opinions of the students

Most valuable information in control comes from the feedback. Such data comes from student responses to the anonymous survey. Our university information system supports such surveys for each course. Most interesting answers are for listed questions:

- How would you rate the lectures?
- How would you rate the practices?
- Were the topics explained clearly?
- How do you rate the course difficulty?
- Do you like the system of work evaluation on every exercise?

The answers depend on the individual students, but most of them agreed at some points. The lectures and practices were rated positive. Explanation was clear, but they want more practical examples. Most of the students answered that course difficulty was normal or course was easy. In the comparison with other courses was that the Matlab course difficult same or easier. The last question was about the evaluation system. Almost everyone thought that this system was suitable. This quiz was taken before exam and therefore the results were not affected by exam results.

8. Conclusion

In this chapter we described the educational side of Matlab usage. Different specializations can benefit from many Matlab products in high quality education. We described how we teach Matlab at our faculty and how are dividing lectures into several topics. We also talked about how to incorporate Matlab into secondary schools education. Topic for future engineers was divided into three categories as well. Basic topics should every engineer to be able to pass, advanced topics depend on study program specialization and other topics are suitable for the research or student thesis. Evaluation of student's performance is a difficult process. In the most cases students are evaluated few times a term. With our proposed evaluation student are forced to study before every practice. Internet is first choice for seeking information for students. It is necessary that we adapt to this fact. We are preparing much online content for students like articles or videos. Collaboration between students is beneficial and we should use social networking. Events like conferences and seminars are helping with education as well. Student's opinion showed that proposed evaluation strategy for the practices suits almost every one of them. Our novel approach to the Matlab teaching process is recommended to copy for another universities as well. We hope that this chapter will helped create high quality courses.

Author details

Michal Blaho, Martin Foltin, Peter Fodrek and Ján Murgaš
Slovak University of Technology, Slovak Republic

Acknowledgement

We would like to thank Slovak Cultural and Educational Grant Agency KEGA under contract number 032STU-4/2011 and Slovak Scientific Grant Agency VEGA under contract number 1/1256/12 for their support of this paper.

9. References

Abdullah, K.A. & Hashim, N. & Yusof, Z. (2010). The development of computer-aided learning for computer numerical control machine: A pilot study, In: *2nd International Congress on Engineering Education (ICEED)*, pp. 94-99, ISBN: 978-1-4244-7308-3

Andreatos, A. S. & Zagorianos, A. D. (2009) Matlab GUI Application for Teaching Control Systems, In: *Proceedings of the 6th WSEAS International Conference on ENGINEERING EDUCATION*, 2009, pp. 208-211

Bertrand, I. (1989). Software engineering techniques for computer-aided learning, In: *Education and Computing*, Vol. 5, Iss. 4, (1989), pp. 215–222

Blaho, M. & Foltin, M. & Fodrek, P. & Poliačik, M. (2010a). Preparing Advanced Matlab Users, *WSEAS Transactions on Advances in Engineering Education*, Vol. 7, Iss. 7, (2010), pp. 234-243, ISSN 1790-1979

Blaho, M. & Foltin, M. & Fodrek, P. & Murgaš, J. (2010b). Research on Preparing Control Engineers and Advanced Matlab Users, *Latest Trends on Engineering Education: 7th WSEAS International Conference on Engineering Education*, pp. 211-214, ISBN 978-960-474-202-8, Corfu, Greece

Blau, J. (September 2011). Germany Faces a Shortage of Engineers, In: *IEEE Spectrum*, 2012, Available from <http://spectrum.ieee.org/at-work/tech-careers/germany-faces-a-shortage-of-engineers>

Dogan, I. (2011). Engineering simulation with MATLAB: improving teaching and learning effectiveness, In: *Procedia Computer Science*, 2011, Vol. 3, pp. 853-858, ISSN: 1877-0509

Foltin, M. & Fodrek, P. & Blaho, M. & Murgaš, J. (2011). Open Source Technologies in Education, *Recent Researches in Educational Technologies: Proceedings of the 8th WSEAS International Conference on Engineering Education (EDUCATION'11) and 2nd International Conference on Education and Educational Technologies (WORLD-EDU'11)*, pp. 131-135, ISBN 978-1-61804-021-3, Corfu Island, Greece

Foltin, M. (March 2012a) Modelovanie a simulácie In: *Facebook*, 2012, Available from <http://www.facebook.com/#!/group.php?gid=313543668309>

Foltin, M. (March 2012b). Vlastnosti grafických objektov In: *Posterus.sk*, 2012, ISSN 1338-0087, Available from <http://www.posterus.sk/wpcontent/ uploads/ML018.mov>

Foltin, M. (Match 2012c). Fuzzy logic toolbox In: *Posterus.sk*, 2012, ISSN 1338-0087, Available from <http://www.posterus.sk/modsim/fuzzy_tbx.mov>

Humusoft s.r.o. (2012). Real Time Toolbox, In: *Humusoft.cz*, 2012, Available from < http://www.humusoft.cz/produkty/rtt/>

MatriconOPC (2012). Introduction to OPC – Tutorial, In: *MatriconOPC.com*, 2012, Available from <https://www.matrikonopc.com/downloads/549/software/index.aspx>

Systémy priemyselnej informatiky s.r.o. (March 2012a). Posterus.sk, In: *Posterus.sk*, 2012, ISSN 1338-0087, Available from <http://www.posterus.sk >

Systémy priemyselnej informatiky s.r.o. (March 2012b). Matlab.sk, In: *Matlab.sk*, 2012, Available from <http://www.matlab.sk >

The Matworks (March 2012a). R2012a Documentation, In: *The Matworks*, 2012, Available from <http://www.mathworks.com/help/index.html>

The Matworks (March 2012b). Mathworks Events, In: *The Matworks*, 2012, Available from <http://www.mathworks.com/company/events/index.html>

The Matworks (March 2012c). MATLAB Virtual Conference 2012, In: *The Matworks*, 2012, Available from
<http://events.unisfair.com/index.jsp?eid=1128&seid=23&code=ConfLstng>

Varga, M. & Varga, Z. (2010) Utilizing Matlab in secondary technical education, In: *Proceedings of the 33rd International Convention, MIPRO*, 2010, pp. 970-974, ISBN: 978-1-4244-7763-0

Chapter 6

An Interactive Tool for Servo Systems Learning

Nourdine Aliane, Rafael Pastor Vargas and Javier Fernández Andrés

Additional information is available at the end of the chapter

1. Introduction

Servo systems play an important role in industry. They are found in most automated manufacturing systems, machine tools, and robotic systems to cite but a few examples. Servo systems fundamentals have become an integral part of industrial electronics and other related fields in engineering, such as electrical engineering or computer disciplines. Servo systems topics should be extended to all engineering curricula [1]. It is therefore a major challenge to ensure that future engineers should be familiar with servo systems, and be able to analyze and control them.

A direct current controlled motor (DC motor) is considered to be the simplest form of servo system, and is used as a starting point for understanding all other electric machines. Control of DC motors is widely taught in control engineering and robotics courses, and is commonly used in laboratory experiments as providing an excellent case study. The importance of the material is well-evidenced in many textbooks [2]-[5]. However, in most of these texts, servo system problems are highly simplified for pedagogical purposes, and the given examples focus on the linear parts, and do not take into account practical issues such as compliance coupling, trajectory generation, the wind-up effect, feed-forward compensation, or torque limitation.

This paper presents an interactive learning module focused exclusively on servo systems. It is aimed at bridging the gap between theoretical background and experimentation, providing insight into fundamental concepts. The tool is based on exploiting interactivity as a pedagogical basis in teaching and learning activities. Although many interactive tools have been developed for general topics in control education [6]-[9], interactive tools focusing on servo systems are practically nonexistent.

There are several works in the literature which deal with the use of Matlab-Simulink for servo systems simulations for educational purposes [10]-[13], but the tools presented in these works lack interactivity. The Matlab Central File Exchange [14] is also used as a source to search for servo systems educational tools. Several excellent demonstrations can be found, but none of them meet the criteria for simulating practical aspects of servo systems. It is also worth mentioning the use of remote laboratories, where DC motors are successfully integrated in remote experimentation platforms [15]-[16]. However, remote experimentation is currently limited to performing simple experiments, and topics such as the effects of disturbances, anti-windup, or feed-forward, are not considered.

The development of the module presented in this paper is based on Simulink models used in combination with the Matlab graphical user interface (GUI). The choice of the Matlab platform is due to the fact that it is by far more productive than many other high level programming languages. Simulink, on the other hand, is used to easily model and simulate a variety of systems using intuitive block diagrams. Wrapping Simulink models within Matlab-GUI is advantageous and improves interactivity. This feature allows users to change parameters and view simulations without having to deal directly with Simulink blocks. Indeed, Matlab includes a built-in tool called GUIDE, which permits developers to design GUIs for Matlab applications.

The remainder of the paper is organized as follows: Section 2 presents the objectives and scope of the tool. Section 3 gives some theoretical background on servo systems. Section 4 describes the interactive module and shows how Simulink models can be integrated within an interactive Matalb-GUI. Section 5 describes usage experiences and gives some classroom examples. Section 6 describes the methodology used in evaluation and discusses the results obtained. Finally, Section 7 concludes the paper.

2. Objectives and scope

In the author's institution, servo systems topics are an integral part of undergraduate control engineering and robotics courses. This part of the material examines servo systems principles, providing students with modeling techniques for DC motors, the formulation of the control problem, and an introduction to the basic treatment of feedback design. The theoretical background is supplemented with hands-on laboratory work. The laboratory activities are aimed at showing the students some qualitative aspects of servo systems control and giving them a broad picture of axis control. However, there is neither enough time nor sufficient equipment to experiment with all the practical aspects of servo systems.

To remedy this situation, the methodology was recently modified to place greater emphasis on fundamental concepts, because the tuning of servo systems can be confusing due rather to unfamiliar principles than to their complexity. Thus, to help students develop their knowledge of, and intuition for, servo systems and their control, an interactive module, dedicated exclusively to this topic, was developed. The tool is aimed at speeding up learning by reducing the time needed to design simulations. It is also intended to be interactive in the sense that it allows students to see immediately the effects of changing parameters on the behavior of systems. Finally, the tool is intended to complement rather than replace laboratory work.

The developed tool simulates the behavior of a separately-excited DC motor, and covers several practical issues of servo systems. Students can, among other capabilities, configure the model, perform simulations of position and speed control, interactively tune the controller, specify trajectories, and compare different control algorithms. Lastly, the user can perform comparisons of simulations by evaluating some performance measures.

3. Servo system background

3.1. Servo system modelling

Servo systems topics, as treated in many textbooks, consider simple models and assume that the motor shaft and its load are rigidly coupled. In practice, however, most servomechanisms contain flexible modes in the actuator or the structure being controlled. This is particularly true in systems such as disk drives, antennae and radar pointing or robotics axes, where coupling might have significant compliance. For a model to be useful, it must be realistic and yet simple enough to understand and manipulate. In general, flexible coupling is modeled as a rotational spring, which is sufficient to yield models of high order.

The interactive tool presented in this paper simulates a DC motor coupled to its load through a shaft with variable compliance (see Figure. 1). The user can set the model to what s/he considers relevant (a compliantly or rigidly coupled model).

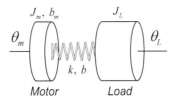

Figure 1. Model of motor and load compliantly coupled.

In the case of an armature-controlled DC motor, the control input is the armature voltage U. The torque T provided by the motor is proportional to the armature current i, and the back emf e is proportional to the motor's velocity ω, by the following equations

$$T = k_m i$$
$$e = k_m \omega$$

(1)

The electrical equation is

$$U - e = L\frac{di}{dt} + Ri$$

(2)

where R is the armature resistance and L is the armature winding inductance.

The torque provided by the motor is transmitted to the load through the compliant shaft, which is modeled as a rotary spring with constant k and damping constant b. The mechanical equations of the motion are:

$$J_m\ddot{\theta}_m + b_m\dot{\theta}_m + b\left(\dot{\theta}_m - \dot{\theta}_L\right) + k\left(\theta_m - \theta_L\right) = k_m i$$
$$J_L\ddot{\theta}_L - b\left(\dot{\theta}_m - \dot{\theta}_L\right) - k\left(\theta_m - \theta_L\right) = 0 \tag{3}$$

where subscript m refers to the motor, subscript L refers to the load, J is an inertia, and b is a damping constant.

Defining the sate vector as $x = \left[i, \theta_m, \dot{\theta}_m, \theta_L, \dot{\theta}_L \right]^T$, the state space representation of the DC motor with compliant coupling

$$\dot{x} = \begin{bmatrix} -R/L & 0 & -k'_m/L & 0 & 0 \\ 0 & 0 & 1 & 0 & 0 \\ k_m/J_m & -k/J_m & -(b+b_m)/J_m & k_m/J_m & b/J_m \\ 0 & 0 & 0 & 0 & 1 \\ 0 & k/J_L & b/J_L & -k/J_L & -b/J_L \end{bmatrix} x + \begin{bmatrix} 1/L \\ 0 \\ 0 \\ 0 \\ 0 \end{bmatrix} u \tag{4}$$

If the coupling shaft is rigid, then $k \rightarrow \infty$, and $\dot{\theta}_m = \dot{\theta}_L$. Adding the two mechanical subsystem equations (3) yields

$$J_m\ddot{\theta}_m + J_L\ddot{\theta}_L + b_m\dot{\theta}_m = k_m i \tag{5}$$

Thus, the mechanical subsystem becomes

$$\left(J_m + J_L\right)\ddot{\theta}_m + b_m\dot{\theta}_m = k_m i \tag{6}$$

Defining the total moment of inertia as $J = J_m + J_L$, and the state as $x = \left[i, \theta_m, \dot{\theta}_m \right]^T$, the state space equation is now simplified as

$$\dot{x} = \begin{bmatrix} -R/L & 0 & -k'_m/L \\ 0 & 0 & 1 \\ k_m/J & 0 & -b_m/J \end{bmatrix} x + \begin{bmatrix} 1/L \\ 0 \\ 0 \end{bmatrix} u \tag{7}$$

3.2. Servo system control

Despite the development of more advanced control techniques, the PID controller is still the most common algorithm used in servo systems applications [17]. The attractiveness of PID resides in the fact that an accurate model is not required and its control capabilities have been proven to be adequate for controlling servo systems. Indeed, PID controllers are used in many dedicated motion-control, such as LM628/629 [18], Magellan [19], Galil boards [20], or the Quanser DC motor model for training and education [21].

The mathematical expression in the time domain is given by the equation (8).

$$u(t) = K_p\left(r(t) - y(t)\right) + K_i \int \left(r(t) - y(t)\right) dt + K_d \frac{d\left(r(t) - y(t)\right)}{dt} \tag{8}$$

where u(t) is the controller output, r(t) is the reference, y(t) is the measured system output, and K_p, K_i and K_p are the PID adjustable parameters. In real servo systems, PID controllers can perform poorly when used alone. To enhance the system performance, a number of additional mechanisms such as handling the wind-up effect properly, combining the feedback with feed-forward control, or using a trajectory generator, are adopted as technical solutions.

3.2.1. Anti-windup correction

The elimination of the steady state error in servo systems has long been performed using the integrator action. However, this action has the disadvantage of causing the wind-up effect, which occurs when the calculated control signal exceeds its saturation limits and the controller is unable to respond immediately to changes in the error signal. To prevent the windup effect, the operating range of the control signal should be limited to the range of the voltage input of the servo [22]. This ad-hoc solution provides instant recovery when the error signal changes signs. There are many way to ovoid the integrator wind-up and one of these possibilities is illustrated in the following Simulink diagram.

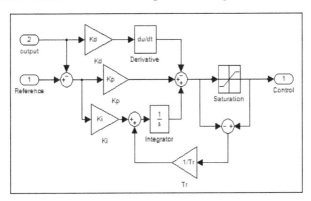

Figure 2. PID controller with Anti-Windup correction.

3.2.2. Feed-forward control

Feed-forward is another technique used to improve servo systems performance and is essentially used to reduce the tracking error in high performance motion control problems. Theoretical developments show that the feed-forward transfer function is the inverse dynamic of the servo. In general, feed-forward compensation is performed through the required acceleration and velocity.

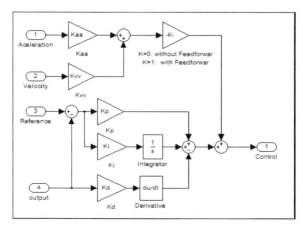

Figure 3. PID controller with feed-forward control.

3.2.3. Motion control

In real servo systems control, the position step references can cause controller saturation and lead to significant overshoot, and indeed, this kind of references are hardly used. The step response is actually used as a measure of system performance. To overcome these problems, references known as S-curves, such as parabolic or trapezoidal profiles, are used instead. These S-curves are provided by a trajectory generator, which is an algorithm at the top of control hierarchy.

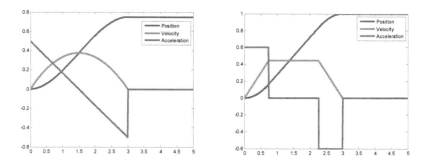

Figure 4. Parabolic and trapezoidal profiles for motion control.

4. Interactive tool description

As mentioned above, the interactive tool is composed of two parts: a Matlab-GUI application and a Simulink model. The Simulink model is completely transparent for end users, and is automatically opened and runs in the background. The tool is freely available on the World Wide Web [23]. The layout of the GUI of the interactive module is shown in Figure 5.

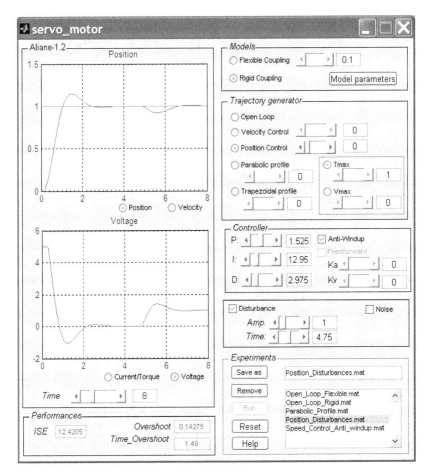

Figure 5. The servo systems learning module main user interface.

Its interface visually displays all the actions that users may execute. In the first group of controls, users can select between a rigid or flexible coupling model. The difference between these models can be visualized by their open-loop step response. Furthermore, the compliance of the flexible coupling can be changed interactively which allows students visualize the significance of coupling stiffness better. Users can also customize the model by setting the model parameters in the "model parameters" button, which displays a window for capturing model parameters.

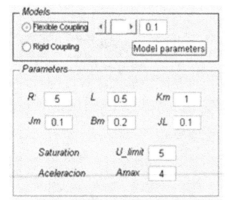

R: Electric resistance
L: Electric inductance
Km: Electromotive force constant.
Jm: Moment of inertia of the rotor
Bm: Damping ratio factor
JL: Moment of inertia of the load
U_limit: Maximal input source voltage
Amax: Maximal motor acceleration

Figure 6. DC-Motor model parameters.

This is suitable for motor modeling, and it is particularly useful for investigating the effects of some DC-motor's parameters on the speed and how the induced current is modified.

In the second group, users can select between simulating a velocity or position control. In the position besides the step input reference, users can choose parabolic or trapezoidal profiles as a trajectory reference. The third group deals with control, where users can interactively modify the PID tuning parameters and immediately see their effect on the system behavior. In addition, the feedback control can be augmented with a feed-forward and an anti-windup correction. The fourth group allows the simulation of the effect of exogenous factors such as external disturbances and noise measurements. The fifth group lets users save and retrieve simulations, which is particularly useful for drawing straightforward comparisons between different scenarios. Finally, as well as visualizing velocity, position, induced current, and voltage input, some performance measures, such as the integral of squared error (ISE) and the overshoot, are also displayed.

The design of the Matlab-GUI is easy using the Matlab GUIDE. This toolkit is opened by entering the command ">>guide" in the command line. Then, images of all the elements (sliders, axes plotting, etc) are dragged out, and then the user writes their respective callback functions. The reader can go further with the help of the Matlab GUI manuals.

The Simulink block diagram implementing the whole servo systems simulation is shown in Figure 7. Interfacing Simulink models with Matlab GUI applications is easy, but not trivial operation. The control of Simulink models can be performed through suitable Matlab commands. Simulink blocks can be accessed and their parameters changed by using the "set_param()" function. Alternatively, the communication between Simulink models and Matlab-GUI can be performed by using variables defined in the main workspace. These two mechanisms are also valid for specifying other Simulink parameters such as sample time or time simulation through the GUI. Lastly, a Simulink simulation can be run by using the "sim()" function.

As far as the trajectory generator is concerned, this is implemented as an "embedded Matlab function block," which is a Simulink block that contains a compiled Matlab code. Unlike "Matlab function blocks," which accept multiple inputs and support only a single scalar output, the functions in "embedded Matlab function blocks" allow multiple inputs and return multiple outputs.

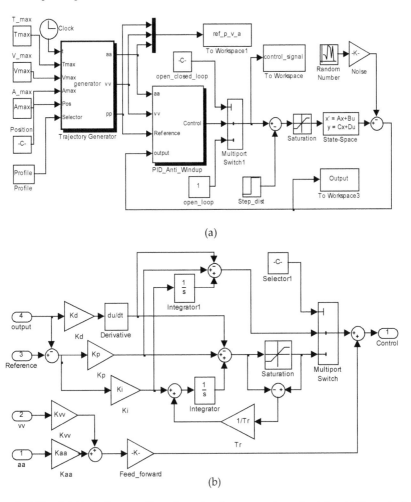

Figure 7. a) Simulink block diagrams: General structure for servo systems simulation; b) The controller subsystem: the PID, anti-windup, and feed-forward control.

5. Classroom experience

The tool was used during the 2006-07 and 2007-08 academic years at Universidad Europea de Madrid (Spain), in control engineering and robotics subjects, providing the instructor with a valuable supplement to lectures by projecting the module screenshots. The first advantage of the tool presented here is that it allows the instructor to set up simulations with minimum effort, which obviously helps him to maintain the flow of the lecture, and allows him to pose different cases quickly in response to the students' questions. The module proved to be an effective instrument to facilitate teaching, since the interactive nature of the module helps to draw comparisons between simulations, explore the effect of varying parameters, and give explanations through "what-if" scenarios.

The learning module was also used by approximately 35 students in the classroom, following guided exercises. These exercises were focused on students getting a feel for the qualitative aspects of servo systems, having them explore what would happen if a given parameter were increased or decreased. The quantitative aspects were not emphasized as much. For example, students are asked to undertake the problem of position control and tracking trajectories. After a review of the PID controller, students are asked to tune the controller through a trial and error process, taking advantage of the interactivity of the tool. As a first step, students use proportional action (P) and examine steady-state error. Next, they introduce the integral action (I) to see how the steady-state error is eliminated. Finally, the derivative action (D) is activated to increase the dumping of the system. Robustness is also an important aspect in servo systems. In another exercise, simulations are performed to assess control strategy with respect to external disturbances, considering cases where a motor is holding a final position and a disturbance is applied to its shaft. Thanks to the module's interactivity, many other concepts such as flexible coupling, anti-windup and feed-forward corrections, or the use of S-curve references are presented with animated graphs examining the effects of some parameters. These exercises are solved in group, and the use of the interactive tool provides an excellent context for provoking discussions and reflections.

To foster interest in the use of the tool, a comprehensive tutorial, providing a number of handouts on classroom activities, was also developed [23]. This tutorial starts with an introductory level on modeling techniques, and goes into more detail on using the PID controller, anti-windup, feed-forward and trajectory generation. It provides a total of ten guided examples; some are projected as demonstrations during lectures while others are developed as exercises and as a basis for group discussion on more in-depth theoretical topics.

5.1. Classroom examples

Many are the classroom activities that can be performed by the tool presented. This subsection shows three classroom examples that illustrate the module's capabilities. Although these examples do not fully exploit all of the tool's features, they illustrate some important aspects of servo systems.

Example-1: Modeling and open-loop simulation

Models are an essential element of servo system analysis and design, and serve to understand how systems behave with and without control. This aspect is covered through demonstrations shown during a lecture, carrying out comparisons of a motor's open-loop responses with rigid and flexible coupling, as well as observing dynamically how changes in the compliance parameter affects the shapes of the responses. Furthermore, different parameters of the model are taken into account and are changed dynamically in order to assess their effect in light of the modeling concept. Step responses of a DC motor with rigid and flexible coupling are shown in Figure. 8.

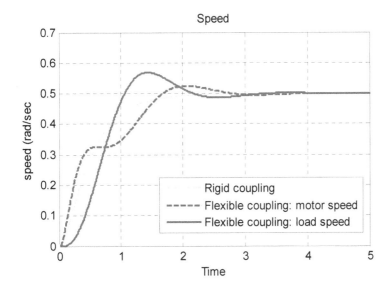

Figure 8. Step responses of a DC motor with rigid and flexible coupling (k = 0.7).

Example-2: Speed control and anti-windup correction

The tool is used to study velocity control and its characteristics. For example, one exercise is devoted to simulating PI control, applying poles placement strategy. The tuning parameters are adjusted analytically assuming a simplified model. Afterwards, students are required to compare simulation outputs applying the same controller tuning to the model with flexible coupling. In the context of speed control, another exercise is dedicated to demonstrating the benefits of anti-windup correction. In this section, students are required to compare the system's output under different conditions: namely, a simulation with no saturation limits, a simulation with saturation limits, and a simulation with anti-windup compensation. This comparison is illustrated in Figure. 9.

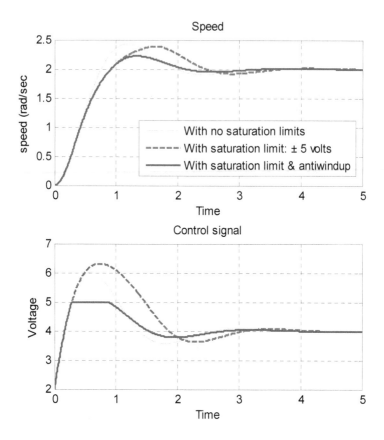

Figure 9. Speed control using a PI controller with and without anti-windup effect (P=1 I=7).

Example-3: Parabolic velocity profiling and feed-forward

Servo systems behavior is often characterized by their step responses. However, it is also useful to see how servo systems behave under S-curves, such as parabolic or trapezoidal profiles. Students are asked to investigate the effect of these trajectories and how input voltage and current are influenced. Lastly, activities concerning feed-forward compensation are also possible, demonstrating how near-zero tracking error can be achieved. Figure. 10 shows a comparison of position control through a parabolic profile, and illustrates the effect of feed-forward.

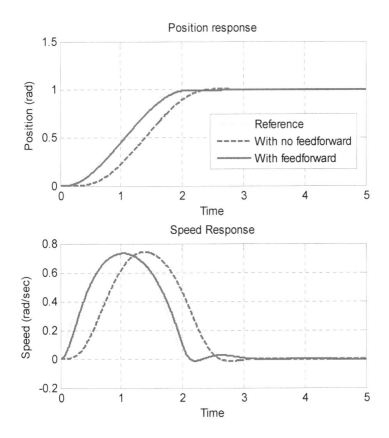

Figure 10. Illustration of a parabolic velocity move profile with and without feed-forward. (P = 12.6, I = 0.5, D = 4.25, Kv = 4.95, Ka = 0.85, T = 2).

6. Assessment and evaluation

The use of the interactive module, from the students' point of view, and how this contributes effectively to enhancing the learning of servo systems are important issues for the instructor. To this end, a qualitative assessment based on a focus group interview [24] and a traditional course survey were conducted by the instructor. Interviewing students constitutes an excellent way of assessing the use of the new learning module as well as learning outcomes. The interview consisted of discussing a set of open-ended questions with the students, raising two primary issues: the usability of the module and its effectiveness in learning. After the discussion, students were asked to give an evaluation (from 1 to 5) for each of the discussed questions. The assessment was conducted with two groups (a control engineering and robotics courses) during the second 2007 semester. In all, 34 students took part in the interview. The students' questionnaire and corresponding evaluations are summarized in Table 1.

N⁰.	Questions	score
1	The module is easy to use.	3.91 (0.79)
2	The module is productive and allows setting up simulations quickly.	3.56 (0.93)
3	The module is useful for complementing lectures.	3.88 (1.01)
4	The module gave me more motivation to learn.	3.79 (0.77)
5	Overall, the module helped me to learn servo systems.	3.88 (0.88)

Table 1. Student questionnaire. The table gives the mean and the standard deviation of students' responses. The grading scale is from 1 (low) to 5 (high).

Concerning the usability of the module, students were receptive to using the new tool. The majority agreed that it is easy to use and does not add cognitive load. They also agreed that the use of a simulation module with a GUI is much better than directly using Simulink blocks, since it helps them to proceed quickly. Students agreed that its most valuable feature is the sliders provided as a means to explore the effects of varying parameters on system behavior. The companion tutorial, with its guided exercises, is also considered important for the correct use of the module. In this aspect, students presumably limit their instructional material to the tutorials designed by the teacher.

The results from the question on whether the module is useful for complementing lectures showed that students consider that interactive tools represent a convenient way of enhancing in-class sessions and bringing new dimensions to traditional teaching methods. The majority considered that the tool presented constitutes a good complement for lectures, and many of them advocated extending the use of such modules to more topics and subjects.

Concerning learning outcomes, students uniformly agreed that the module allowed them to pay more attention to simulation results, rather than to designing Simulink diagrams. Some students declared that the interactive feature of the module activated their curiosity to discover its contents. As the interaction with the module is driven mainly by sliders, students can explore the effects of a full range of parameters by adjusting the values from low to high, or vice versa. In this aspect, the majority believed that this routine enables them to perceive clearly the qualitative aspects of servo systems. Finally, many students agreed that the tool helped them to understand servo systems problems, and many of them felt that the interactive module was an effective learning medium.

7. Conclusion

In this paper, the development of a Matlab/Simulink-GUI application for servo systems learning is described, and its use in the classroom is also addressed. The tool exposes students to servo systems concepts and allows them to experience a variety of practical scenarios. Its principal feature is that it dramatically reduces the effort needed to specify simulations. It also allows students to explore the effects of varying parameters and instantly observe their influence on the system's behavior. Interaction with the module is straightforward and is done essentially using sliders. This sort of interaction proved to be helpful since it stimulates the students, and it is found that the interactive tool provides a stronger motivation to learn than does the traditional use of Simulink blocks. Finally, extensive use of the module can give students an enhanced intuition and help to them to gain better understanding of the qualitative aspects of servo systems.

Author details

Nourdine Aliane* and Javier Fernández Andrés
Dpto: Sistemas Informáticos Automática y Comunicaciones, Universidad Europea de Madrid (UEM), Villaviciosa de Odón, Madrid, Spain

Rafael Pastor Vargas
Dpto. Sistemas de Comunicación y Control, Escuela Técnica Superior Ingeniería Informática, UNED, Spain

Acknowledgement

The authors wish to thank the Spanish Ministry of Science and Innovation and the National Plan R&D TIN2008-06083-C03/TSI "s-Labs: Integration of open services for remote and distributed virtual laboratories, reusable and safe".

8. References

[1] D. S. Bernstein, The Quanser DC motor Control Trainer (2005), *IEEE Cont. Syst. Mag.*, vol. 25, no. 3, pp. 90-94.

[2] G. F Franklin, J. D. Powell, and A. Emami-Naeini, (2006), *A. Feedback Control of Dynamic Systems*. 5th ed, New Jersey: Prentice-Hall.

[3] F. L. Lewis, (1992), *Applied Optimal Control & Estimation: Digital Design & Implementation*. 1st ed, New Jersey: Prentice Hall.

[4] G. F. Franklin, J. D. Powell and M. L. Workman, (1997) *Digital Control of Dynamic Systems*. 3rd ed, Boston: Addison Wesley.

[5] R. N. Clark, (1997) *Control System Dynamics*. Cambridge: Cambridge University.

[6] B. Wittenmark, H. Hägglund, and M. Johansson, (1998), Dynamic pictures and interactive learning, *IEEE Cont. Syst. Mag.*, vol. 18, no. 3, pp. 26-32.

[7] M. Johansson, M. Gäfvert, and K. J. Åström, (1998), Interactive tools for education in automatic control, *IEEE Cont. Syst. Mag.*, vol. 18, no. 3, pp. 33-40.

[8] S. Dormido, S. Dormido-Canto, R. Dormido-Canto, J. Sanchez, and N. Duro, (2005) The role of interactivity in control learning," *Int. J. Eng. Educ.*, vol. 21, no. 6, pp. 1122-1133.

* Corresponding Author

[9] J. L. Guzmán, K. J. Åström, S. Dormido, T. Hägglund, and Y. Piguet, (2008), Interactive learning modules for PID control, *IEEE Cont. Syst. Mag.*, vol. 28, no. 5, pp. 118-134.

[10] T. Kikuchi, T. Kenjo and S. Fukuda, (2002), "Developing an educational simulation program for the PM stepping motor," *IEEE Trans. Educ.*, vol 45, no 1, pp-70-78.

[11] S. Ayasun and C. O. Nwankpa, (2005), Induction motor tests using Matlab/Simulink and their integration into undergraduate electric machinery courses, *IEEE Trans. Educ.*, vol 48, no 1, pp. 37–46.

[12] N. Patrascoiu, (2005), Modeling and Simulation of the DC Motor Using Matlab and LabVIEW," *Int. J. Eng. Educ.*, vol 21, no 1, pp. 49-54.

[13] D. Hercog and K. Jezernik, (2005), Rapid Control Prototyping using Matlab/Simulink and DSP-based Motor Control," *Int. J. Eng. Educ.*, vol. 21 no. 4, pp.596-605.

[14] MATLAB-Central-File-Exchange [on-line], Retrieved March 2012 from: http://www.mathworks.com/matlabcentral/fileexchange

[15] Casini, M. y D. Prattichizzo, (2003), The automatic control Telelab: A user-friendly interface for distance learning," *IEEE Trans. Educ.*, vol.46, no. 2, pp. 252-257.

[16] R. Pastor, C. Martín, J. Sánchez, and S. Dormido, (2005), Development of a XML-based lab for remote control experiments on a servo motor, *Int. J. Elect. Eng. Educ.*, vol. 42, nº 2, pp. 173-184.

[17] R. Kelly and J. Moreno, (2001), Learning PID structures in an introductory course of automatic control," *IEEE Trans. Educ.*, vol. 44, no. 4, pp. 373-376.

[18] LM628/LM629 Precision Motion Controller, [on-line] Retrieved March 2012 from: http://cache.national.com/ds/LM/LM628.pdf

[19] MAGELLAN Motion Control ICs, [on-line] Retrieved March 2012 from: http://www.pmdcorp.com/downloads/Magellan_PUG_v23_Feb_2008.pdf

[20] GALIL Controllers, [on-line] Retrieved March 2012 from: http://www.galilmc.com/about/index.html

[21] J. Apkarian and K. J. Astrom, (2004), A laptop servo for control education, *IEEE Cont. Syst. Mag.*, vol. 24, no. 5, pp-70-73.

[22] K. J. Åström and T. Hägglund, (2005), Advanced PID Control, ISA-Society.

[23] The Matlab interactive module for servo systems learning: [on-line]: http://www.esp.uem.es/aliane/servosystems/ss.zip

[24] B. M. Olds, B. M. Moskal and R. L. Miller, (2005), Assessment in Engineering Education: Evolution, Approaches, and Future Collaborations," *J. Eng. Educ.*, vol. 94, no. 1, pp. 13-25.

Chapter 7

Using MATLAB in the Teaching and Learning of Semiconductor Device Fundamentals

Ian Grout and Abu Khari Bin A'ain

Additional information is available at the end of the chapter

1. Introduction

Mathematical analysis tools provide an invaluable (and sometime essential!) tool for use within the engineering disciplines and are readily found in education, research and industrial applications. For example, within the industrial applications, mathematical analysis tools provide an essential aid at all stages of a product development from design through manufacture to test. Although there are a number of useful tools available, since its inception, MATLAB [1] has found a unique role within the engineering disciplines. Given the need to utilise this tool ultimately in both a research context and an industrial application context, there is a need to introduce students at the university level to the effective use of MATLAB, with a focus on the particular discipline area of the student.

In this chapter, the use of MATLAB is presented and discussed within a university education context and in particular the integration of MATLAB into the teaching and learning of semiconductor device fundamentals for electronic and computer engineering students. The aim is to support the student learning of semiconductor device operation, primarily diodes (silicon, germanium, Schottky barrier and Zener) and transistors (bipolar junction transistors (BJTs), junction field effect transistors (JFETs) and metal-oxide semiconductor field effect transistors (MOSFETs)).

MATLAB is primarily used as a data analysis, presentation and reporting tool in this context, but the natural integration of MATLAB into the teaching and learning environment has two real purposes:

1. Firstly, it is an introduction to the tool for generic engineering and scientific design and data analysis.
2. Secondly, it is used to support the learning of semiconductor device operation.

The basic idea is that experiments are undertaken on practical devices, the results obtained are then analysed in MATLAB and finally compared to the ideal device (mathematical) models. Hence, within MATLAB, actual data is used and mathematical models of ideal devices are developed. This is aimed as an introduction (targeting first year undergraduate students) to both semiconductor devices and to mathematical analysis tools (here MATLAB which would then be used by the students later on in more advanced subjects).

Three different teaching and learning scenarios are presented and the integration of MATLAB into a computer aided learning (CAL) environment that has been custom developed are provided:

Firstly, students undertake experiments in a *traditional learning scenario*. In the laboratory, electronic circuits using semiconductor devices are built and tested. Experimental results are then taken and analysed using MATLAB; specifically, results are entered into arrays (the term *array* used here to mean a *1 x m* matrix) within MATLAB which then allows these results to be analysed and graphically plotted. These results are also compared to the ideal mathematical equations for the devices considered (specifically diodes and transistors). Hence, the learning experience naturally includes an introduction to concepts such as scalar types and arrays (in a generic context, matrices and matrix manipulation), building and manipulating equations, manipulating experiment results, results comparison, graphical plotting and m-files. The student therefore gains experience in both electronic hardware build and test, and results analysis using MATLAB. This is suitable for electronic and computer engineering students at an introductory level. This idea is depicted in figure 1.

Secondly, students undertake experiments using *computer aided learning (CAL) environment*. The experiment electronic hardware is pre-built and connected to a PC via an *experiment interface electronics* unit (essentially a computer port connection such as RS-232 (readily extended to USB) interface that allows for analogue voltages to be created and sampled in the same manner as would manually be done, but now through a software graphical user interface (GUI)). The student therefore gains experience in computer control of experiments and results analysis using MATLAB. This is suitable for electronic and computer engineering students at an introductory level who would not necessarily need to physically build electronic hardware. This idea is depicted in figure 2.

Thirdly, students undertake experiments via a *distance mode of learning* in that they access the experiment electronic hardware and MATLAB via an Internet browser. This arrangement forms a *remote laboratory* whereby the experiment is controlled and results accessed remotely and via an Internet browser. Essentially, the CAL arrangement identified in figure 2 is "web enabled" – that is made accessible via the Internet. The student gains therefore experience in computer control and results analysis using MATLAB, but in a distance mode of learning. This idea is depicted in figure 3.

The above three teaching and learning scenarios provide ways in which MATLAB can be integrated into a flexible teaching and learning environment. However, given that the idea here is that both the use of MATLAB and the electrical characteristics of basic semiconductor devices are to be introduced, the structure of the laboratory experiments must be carefully considered. For example, it would be necessary to introduce the basic concepts of MATLAB as well as the key commands to be used before attempting to analyse experiment data. One possible laboratory experiment flow is shown in figure 4.

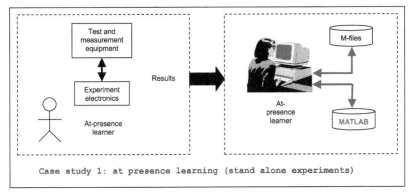

Figure 1. The traditional learning scenario

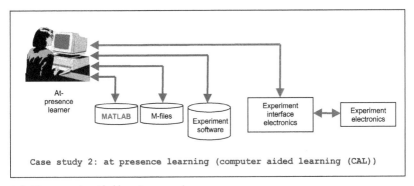

Figure 2. The computer aided learning scenario

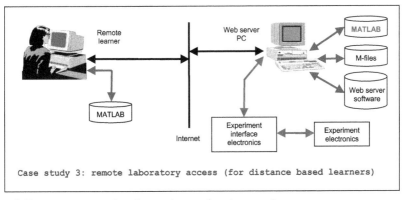

Figure 3. Remote user access via an Internet browser learning scenario

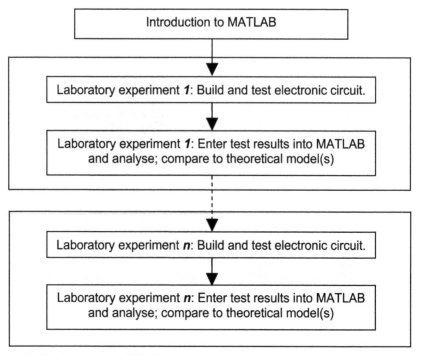

Figure 4. Laboratory experiment "flow"

The development of the hardware-software infrastructure and use of the three above teaching and learning scenarios are introduced here with reference to an experiment consisting of a BAT86 Schottky barrier diode [2] and are presented in this chapter. The remainder of the chapter is structured as follows:

Section 2: The use of MATLAB within an education environment

The use of MATLAB as an aid to teaching and learning for a wide range of engineering and scientific applications is presented. A rationale for using MATLAB is provided and how it may be used is identified. Reference is made to the teaching and learning in the computer and electronic engineering disciplines.

Section 3: Teaching and learning semiconductor device fundamentals

The teaching of semiconductor device fundamentals at an introductory level within the university sector is presented with reference to current teaching undertaken by the authors. The need for teaching semiconductor devices and their application in the electronics and microelectronic industries is provided, along with the need to relate the theory to real (practical) devices through the use of suitable laboratory experiments undertaken by the students. The use of MATLAB as an integrated mathematical analysis tool is presented where theory and practice are compared.

Section 4: Case study 1: at presence learning (stand alone experiments)

The use of MATLAB is presented whereby physical circuits with the semiconductor devices of interest are developed and tested by the student. Results are then entered into MATLAB and analysis undertaken, comparing the real devices with their mathematical ideal models. Current and voltage relationships are then identified. The student gains hands-on experience with both electronic hardware and computer based software.

Section 5: Case study 2: at presence learning (computer aided learning (CAL))

The use of MATLAB is presented as in case study 1, but now pre-built experiments are accessed through a custom software application and the experiments are accessed via a PC interfaced electronic hardware arrangement. The student concentrates on the MATLAB and software side of the experiment activity.

Section 6: Case study 3: remote laboratory access (for distance based learners)

The use of MATLAB is presented as in case study 2, but now the interface is via a remote laboratory arrangement, accessed via an Internet browser and web server arrangement. With this arrangement, remote learners are supported.

Section 7: Conclusions

Conclusions to the work that has been undertaken are presented.

Section 8: References

References used in the development of the chapter are provided.

2. The use of MATLAB within an education environment

2.1. Introduction

MATLAB is an invaluable tool for use within the engineering disciplines for education, research and industrial purposes. In this chapter, the use of MATLAB is presented and discussed within a university education context. MATLAB is an almost universal tool for engineering education. It provides a cost-effective *what if* platform where users can manipulate and explore functions to discover and explore the response of a system. Here, the system is an electronic circuit where the focus of the circuit operation is discovering and exploring the behaviour of semiconductor devices.

2.2. Why use MATLAB?

MATLAB is a high-level language and interactive environment that enables a user to perform computationally intensive engineering and scientific calculations tasks faster than with traditional programming languages such as C. It includes a set of integrated graphics and plotting capabilities allowing users to visualise their data and analysis results and which can also be extended by the user to suit his or her own needs. As such, it provides the student and practising engineer with a suite of useful tools for analysing and solving engineering related problems. For semiconductor devices made from semiconductor materials such as silicon, which the work discussed in this chapter are aim at exploring, MATLAB is the perfect tool to use as it allows the student to undertake directed and self study activities, even outside laboratory. As the calls for innovation and creativity become stronger, students cannot afford to limit their experiments and exploration within physical laboratory. By integrating MATLAB within experiments and the course syllabus, it supports self-directed learning and also does not cost anything to make mistakes!

2.3. Important concepts to introduce

With the integration of MATLAB into a course syllabus, there is a need to identify the key concepts to introduce and for the students to practice. It is therefore important for the course developer to ensure that there is a seamless integration of MATLAB into the course syllabus and for there to be a clear focus on why and how this mathematical analysis tool is used. Therefore the course developer needs to consider a wide range of aspects including:

1. The role of MATLAB
   Why is MATLAB utilised in the course with a focus on the engineering discipline concerned? How would there be a suitable and seamless integration of the analysis tool with the core engineering topics in the course? How much time should be allocated to the teaching and learning of MATLAB core concepts Vs the use of MATLAB to solve engineering problems?

2. What is important for electronic and computer engineering students
   Why utilise mathematical analysis tools in electronic and computer engineering and how can they be used to support the practicing engineer? With MATLAB being introduced to the students for the first time, how can this support more advanced engineering topics? For example, MATLAB with its toolbox Simulink is widely used in control engineering and where students are introduced to control engineering concepts, their knowledge of MATLAB from this introductory course could be used to allow the teaching of the control engineering to concentrate on using MATLAB rather than reintroducing the core MATLAB concepts.

3. Consider a stand-alone module (i.e., just MATLAB) or integrate MATLAB into subject (as considered here)
   The introduction to students of MATLAB can be either the main focus of a course whereby the introduction to MATLAB is the purpose of the course, or MATLAB can be introduced as a tool to use in supporting engineering disciplines. Whilst allocating a complete course to MATLAB would allow students to consider both the introductory concepts and the more advanced concepts (such as the use of the toolboxes), it might not necessarily provide a link to the use of this tool in solving engineering discipline specific problems. It also means that valuable and restricted time within the overall programme of study (the available time needs to be allocated to many different aspects of engineering) which should be focused on the specific engineering discipline is not necessarily allocated to the focus area of the overall programme of study. The alternative approach, as considered here, is to provide a more generic introduction to

the tool before using it to solve problems relating to a specific electronic and computer engineering discipline, namely semiconductor devices.

4. Navigating the MATLAB desktop
    The MATLAB desktop provides the method in which a user interfaces to MATLAB and hence a working knowledge of the desktop must be obtained. However, learning the structure of the desktop should not become the focus of the learning and so detract from learning how to use the tool to solve real engineering problems.

5. Dealing with errors
    When learning how to use any software application and a new language, errors in the use of the software application, along with syntax and semantic errors with the language will inevitably be experienced by the student. How to deal with these errors can be a daunting task for a student and so the prompt correcting of these errors would be important. It would be expected that there would be a common set of errors encountered by many students and so many errors should be readily identifiable and corrected.

6. Matrix manipulation
    Within MATLAB, everything is treated as a matrix. Hence, the students would need to revise their previous learning of matrices and apply the concepts within the MATLAB environment, learning how to create and manipulate matrices using the native syntax. For example, a common problem encountered when learning how to use MATLAB is in the multiplication of matrices (for example, such as determining the square of an $n \times m$ matrix named y if attempting to use the command y^2 directly and y is not a square matrix).

7. Command line entry Vs m-files
    The starting point of learning the tool is how to effectively use the MATLAB command line for data and command entry. Once the basic concepts are learnt, the use of m-files (both script m-files and function m-files [3]) can then be introduced and from there onwards, m-files may become a more convenient manner in which to enter data and commands.

8. Arithmetic operators
    The use of arithmetic operators (addition, subtraction, multiplication, division, left division, power) when considering scalar values (1×1 matrices) and matrices ($n \times m$ matrices). How the arithmetic operations are undertaken – operations undertaken on the complete matrix or matrix element-by-element in turn. This requires a working knowledge of matrix algebra.

9. Logical operators
    The use of logical operators (less than, less than or equal to, greater than, greater than or equal to, equal to, not equal to, logical AND, logical OR) for determining conditions of the variables within the MATLAB workspace.

10. Functions
    A number of mathematical functions are available to create equations (including absolute value, square root, sine (value in radians), cosine (value in radians), tangent

(value in radians), the exponential operator, the logarithmic operator, the value of pi (Π), the imaginary unit (i or j = √(-1))).

11. Program (flow) control

Program (flow) control allows for the development of scripts that control how the script (program) operates depending on specific conditions. There are three types of control statement in MATLAB, along with a program termination statement: **conditional control**, **loop control**, **error control** and the program termination statement **return**. **Conditional control** statements are *if* (together with *else* and *elseif*) and *switch* (together with *case* and *otherwise*) to execute MATLAB statements based on some logical condition. Loop control statements are *for* to execute MATLAB statements a fixed number of times, *while* to execute MATLAB statements an indefinite time based on some logical condition and *continue* to pass control to the next iteration of the *for loop* or *while loop* in which it appears and skips any remaining statements in the body of the loop. **Error control** (*try … catch*) changes the flow control if an error is detected during execution. The program termination statement **return** causes execution to return to the invoking function.

12. 2D and 3D plotting

MATLAB includes a large number of plotting functions which allow the user to view their data as both two-dimensional (2D) plots and three-dimensional (3D) plots.

13. MATLAB toolboxes

Whilst probably not appropriate to include in an introductory course, the MATLAB toolboxes such as Simulink and DSP toolbox provide for powerful extensions to the basic MATLAB commands and would typically be used in more advanced courses. For example, Simulink is widely used in the control engineering discipline and, with its block diagram graphical model generation approach, provides for a useful and important tool for the engineer.

14. Integration of other languages

Whilst probably not appropriate to include in an introductory course, the ability to create MATLAB scripts which interact with code developed in other languages (such as FORTAN, C/C++ and Java) provide for a useful extension and enhanced flexibility in the use of MATLAB for system modelling and analysis.

15. Graphical user interface (GUI) development

MATLAB provides for the ability to create graphical user interfaces which allow the user to interact with MATLAB through a suitable user interface rather than the command prompt or directly writing m-files.

16. Dealing with terminology

Finally, as with anything that the engineer is involved in, there is a need to learn and correctly use the terminology specific to the domain that is being worked in.

3. Teaching and learning of semiconductor device fundamentals

For electronic and computer engineers, the use of semiconductor devices is integral to everything that they do, whether they design electronic circuits using semiconductor devices or program processors to control specific electronic circuits. Whilst practising engineers may not necessarily investigate the physics of the devices on a day-to-day basis, it is essential that they understand the behaviour of the devices at the material level (how they behave and why) in order to use these devices effectively within the electronic circuits they design or use. There are therefore two key aspects to the teaching and learning of semiconductor device fundamentals:

1. The **theory underpinning the device operation** – what is happening at the physical material level and how the behaviour can be related to device terminal behaviour in terms of voltages and currents (the development of theoretical mathematical models for idealised and more realistic device models).
2. How the **device terminal behaviour in terms of voltages and currents** (using the developed idealised and more realistic device models) can be used in practical and useful electronic circuits.

For example, consider an introduction to diodes. Both semiconductor (p-n junction) and Schottky barrier (metal-semiconductor contact) diodes are encountered and so must be introduced. The concepts identified in theses devices (such as a.c. signal rectification) would then be extended to more complex devices such as transistors, thyristors, triacs and integrated circuits (ICs).

Consider the Schottky barrier diode. The initial starting point is the structure and underlying mathematical equations (current-voltage (I-V) relationship) for this device. These are summarised in figure 5.

The starting point for understanding the device operation would need to introduce semiconductor materials, what their properties are and how they can be considered to behave (electrons and holes as charge carriers, intrinsic and extrinsic semiconductors, and the effects material doping [4, 5]). Based on these principles then the behaviour of the metal-semiconductor contact can be introduced and developed:

1. The behaviour of the materials around the contact junction and away from the contact junction at thermal equilibrium and non-equilibrium conditions (forward bias and reverse bias conditions).
2. The differences between ohmic and rectifying contacts. It is the rectifying contact (allowing current to flow through the metal-semiconductor contact under forward bias conditions but blocking current flow under reverse bias conditions) that would be of interest in the Schottkty barrier diode discussions.
3. The current-voltage (I-V) relationship at forward and reverse bias conditions at the anode and cathode device terminals would be developed and the use of the diode in

electronic circuits would be introduced and discussed. Reference would initially be made to a rectifier circuit using the diode and a resistor connected in series as shown in figure 6(a) [note that the standard diode symbol is shown here rather than the Schottky barrier diode symbol].

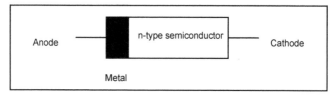

Schematic symbol with diode current and voltage in forward bias identified

Diode equations (forward and reverse bias)

$$I_D = I_S [e^{(qV_D/nkT)} - 1]$$

$$I_D = -I_S$$

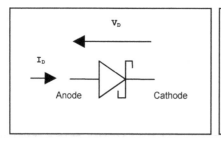

Simplified structure for n-type semiconductor diode

Figure 5. Schottky barrier diode summary (n-type semiconductor type)

With reference to the diode rectifier circuit (figure 6(a)), this can be modelled mathematically for both forward bias and reverse bias in MATLAB to show the principle of operation. A sample m-file for modelling and simulating the Schottky barrier diode is shown in listing 1 and the output plot is shown in figure 7. Note that this code works for versions of MATLAB after v6.5. Here:

1. An idealised diode model is created which has a forward voltage drop of 0.3 V (Vd) when conducting (line 14).
2. The resistor (R) is set to 2 Ω for illustration purposes (line 15).
3. A sine wave voltage source (Vin) is created with an amplitude of 1 V and ten complete cycles of the sine wave are generated (lines 17 to 22).
4. The resistor voltage drop in forward bias and reverse bias is calculated (lines 24 to 30).
5. The resistor current and hence the diode current (Id) is calculated (line 32).
6. Four sub-plots are created with time along the x-axis (lines 38 to 73). There is then a delay of five seconds before the script code continues (line 74).
7. The plotted values are scrolled across the sub-plots (lines 80 to 90).

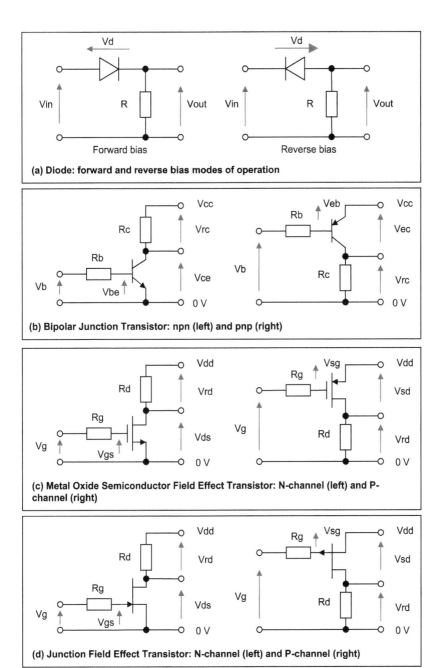

Figure 6. Basic test circuits for diodes and transistors

```
1   %%----------------------------------------------------
2   %% Function to create the waveforms and subplots
3   %% for a Schottky diode model.
4   %%----------------------------------------------------
5
6   function Schottky_animation()
7
8   %%----------------------------------------------------
9   %% Create the variables and equations
10  %%----------------------------------------------------
11
12  clear Degrees Time R Vin Vr Vd Id;
13
14  Vd = 0.3;
15  R = 2;
16
17  for (j=0:1:9)
18      for (k=1:1:360)
19          Vin(k + (j* 360)) = 1.0 * sind(k - 1);
20          Time(k + (j* 360)) = (k + (j * 360)) / 360;
21      end
22  end
23
24  for (i=1:1:length(Vin))
25      if (Vin(i) > 0.3)
26          Vr(i) = (Vin(i) - Vd);
27      else
28          Vr(i) = 0;
29      end
30  end
31
32  Id = (Vr / R);
33
34  %%----------------------------------------------------
35  %% Create the subplots and wait for 5 seconds
36  %%----------------------------------------------------
37
38  scrsz = get(0,'ScreenSize');
39  figure('Name', 'Ideal Schottky Diode Half-Wave Rectifier Circuit', ...
40      'OuterPosition',[scrsz(3)/8 scrsz(4)/16 (3 * (scrsz(3)/4)) (15 * (scrsz(4)/16))])
41
42  ha(1) = subplot(4,1,1);
43  plot(Time, Vin,'YDataSource', 'Vin');
44  hold on;
45  grid;
46  plot(Time, Vr, 'r', 'YDataSource', 'Vr');
47  title ('\it{Time Vs Vin & Vr}', 'Color','k', 'FontWeight', 'bold');
48  xlabel('Time (seconds)');
49  ylabel('Vin & Vr (V)');
50
51  ha(2) = subplot(4,1,2);
52  plot(Time, Vin,'YDataSource','Vin');
53  grid;
```

```
54 title ('\it{Time Vs Vin}', 'Color','b', 'FontWeight', 'bold');
55 xlabel('Time (seconds)');
56 ylabel('Vin (V)');
57
58 ha(3) = subplot(4,1,3);
59 plot(Time, Vr, 'r', 'YDataSource', 'Vr');
60 grid;
61 title ('\it{Time Vs Vr}', 'Color','r', 'FontWeight', 'bold');
62 xlabel('Time (seconds)');
63 ylabel('Vr (V)');
64
65 ha(4) = subplot(4,1,4);
66 plot(Time, Id, 'm', 'YDataSource', 'Id');
67 grid;
68 title ('\it{Time Vs Id}', 'Color','m', 'FontWeight', 'bold');
69 xlabel('Time (seconds)');
70 ylabel('Id (A)');
71
72 linkaxes(ha, 'xy');
73 axis([0 3 -1.1 1.1]);
74 pause(5);
75
76 %%-------------------------------------------------
77 %% Create the scrolling plot
78 %%-------------------------------------------------
79
80 for k = 0:0.1:7
81
82     refreshdata(ha(1),'caller');
83     refreshdata(ha(2),'caller');
84     refreshdata(ha(3),'caller');
85     refreshdata(ha(4),'caller');
86     axis([k (k + 3) -1.1 1.1]);
87     drawnow;
88     pause(0.5);
89
90 end
91
92 end
93
94 %%-------------------------------------------------
95 %% End of code
96 %%-------------------------------------------------
```

Listing 1. Schottky barrier diode model – MATLAB m-file code to show signal rectification

In figure 7 then:

1. Time is plotted on the horizontal axis.
2. The top plot shows the input sine wave voltage (*Vin*) and the half-wave rectified voltage across the resistor (*Vr*) are plotted on the vertical axis.
3. The second plot shows the input voltage (*Vin*).
4. The third plot shows the resistor voltage (*Vr*).
5. The bottom plot shows the diode current (*Id*).

When the plot scrolls, after an initial delay of five seconds, it shows a similar waveform to that which would be seen on an oscilloscope display; it would be seen here that as time increments, the viewed waveforms scrolls across the screen. This shows how theoretical models can be created and analysed in MATLAB. Simulation however is only part of the overall story. Relating theory to the "real world" requires suitable the *design, build* and *test* of real circuits. Then, MATLAB could be used to analyse the results from a physical circuit prototype, and the theoretical model and practical circuits could be compared.

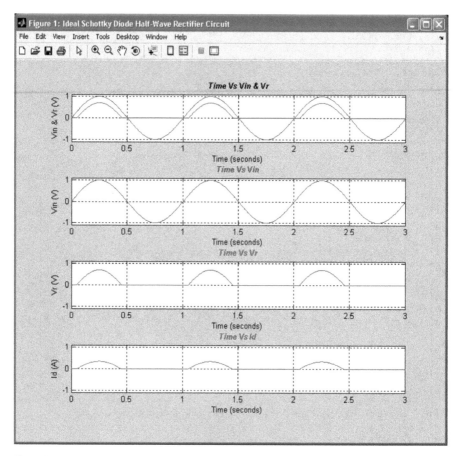

Figure 7. Schottky barrier diode model – MATLAB plot from listing 1

In more general terms, the above discussion flow would be extended to any semiconductor device, given the ability to create and measure the required range of voltage levels. For example, figure 6(b) shows a test circuit for a bipolar junction transistor (both npn and pnp types), figure 6(c) shows a test circuit for a metal oxide semiconductor field effect transistor (both N-channel an P-channel types) and finally, figure 6(d) shows a test circuit for a junction field effect transistor (both N-channel an P-channel types). These test circuits are suitable for the experimentation arrangements considered here. However, it is possible to create different test set-ups given the availability of suitable test and measurement equipment. Care however has to be taken in order to ensure that:

1. Suitable device types are used.
2. The applied voltages operate the devices in the intended modes of operation.
3. Damage to the devices would not occur in the physical test set-up if specified and used correctly (maximum device ratings are never encountered or exceeded).

Device damage would not occur in a simulated mathematical model, but could occur in a real device. For example, in N-channel JFET circuits, the gate-source voltage is to be zero or negative for correct device operation with the drain-source voltage zero or positive. The gate resistor (Rg) is included here to ensure that if a positive gate-source voltage were to be applied then the current through the JFET gate node would be limited to a safe value by suitable choice of the resistor value. When gate-source voltage is to be zero or negative, no current flows through the transistor gate (the p-n junction created is reverse biased) and for d.c. gate-source voltages, the resistor has no effect (although for a.c. signals the value of the resistor would affect the circuit operation).

4. Case study 1: The traditional learning scenario

This section will describe the use of the experiment via a traditional laboratory scenario. In this arrangement, the student builds a test circuit (either using a suitable solderless prototyping board or physically soldering the components to a suitable printed circuit board (PCB)) and runs a number of electrical tests on the electronic circuit. The tests are chosen to operate the particular device under the modes of operation that are of interest for the student to investigate. Once the tests have been completed, the student would plot the results (by-hand) on graph paper and then import the results into MATLAB for analysis and computer based graphing of the results. Here, it would then be possible to consider the physical process of setting-up an experiment, running the experiment and taking results before utilising a suitable mathematics tool for analysis purposes. However, the traditional *manual* way of plotting the graph from experiment data is slow and sometimes not convenient. Both the idealised (theoretical mathematical equation model) and the operation of an actual semiconductor device could then be analysed and compared, with differences between the practical device test results and idealised models analysed using MATLAB. Using the analysis tool to analyse the behaviour of and to plot the experiment data means that various analyses can be performed on the data and the results quickly plotted.

Within the teaching and learning of semiconductor device fundamentals, the basic devices to initially introduce to the student are the diode and transistor. To illustrate this, figure 8 shows the device to discuss here, the Schottky barrier diode. The circuit here shows the BAT86 Schottky barrier diode in a forward bias mode of operation. In this mode of operation, when the input voltage applied is positive, the diode will allow the flow of current through the load resistor and the diode will have a voltage drop of approximately 0.3 V when conducting (the actual device voltage drop being dependent on the level of current flowing through the diode). If the diode is connected in the reverse direction, the reverse bias mode of operation will be encountered and the diode will block the flow of current until a reverse bias junction breakdown voltage is encountered at which point the diode will conduct current. In reverse bias junction breakdown, if the current flow is not limited then damage to the diode will occur.

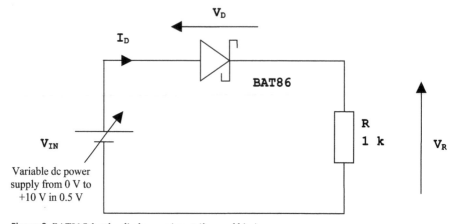

Figure 8. BAT86 Schottky diode experiment (forward bias)

The I-V mathematical model characteristic of the diode in figure 9 shows both the expected forward and reverse bias modes of operation and the ideal device equation are also noted:

Forward bias:

$$I_D = I_S \left[e^{(qV_D / nkT)} - 1 \right]$$

Reverse bias (prior to breakdown):

$$I_D = -I_S$$

Here:

- I_D is the diode current.
- I_S is the diode saturation current.
- q is the charge on an electron.
- V_D is the forward bias diode voltage drop.
- n is the ideality factor and is set to 1.
- k is Botzmann's constant.
- T is the temperature in degrees Kelvin.

The current-voltage (I-V) relationship that should be encountered during an experiment is that as shown in figure 9. The regions of operation of interest are the forward bias (to the right of the I_D-axis) and the reverse bias (to the left of the I_D-axis) prior to reverse bias junction breakdown.

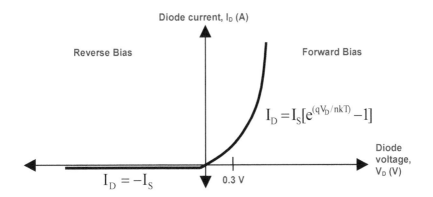

Figure 9. Schottky diode I-V characteristic (before reverse bias junction breakdown is encountered)

In forward bias, the diode current increases in an exponential manner with a linear increase in diode voltage. The diode voltage is around 0.3 V when current flows through the device, the exact value of diode voltage dependent on the value of the diode current. In reverse bias and prior to reverse bias breakdown occurring, the diode current is essentially independent of the diode voltage and is approximately the value of the saturation current (I_S). This effect can readily be modelled in MATLAB as shown in listing 2, here using the *for loop* in the calculation of the diode current for set values of diode voltage.

For comparison purposes, from the BAT86 Schottky barrier diode datasheet, the diode parameters can be identified. These are summarised in table 1.

Parameter	Conditions	Maximum value
Forward bias		
Forward bias voltage drop	Forward current = 0.1 mA	300 mV
	Forward current = 1 mA	380 mV
	Forward current = 10 mA	450 mV
	Forward current = 30 mA	600 mV
	Forward current = 100 mA	900 mV
Reverse bias		
Reverse bias current	Reverse bias voltage = 40 V	5 μA

Table 1. BAT86 Schottky barrier diode [2] datasheet forward and reverse bias parameters

In listing 2, both the forward bias mode of operation and the reverse bias mode of operation are modelled and plotted, where:

- The forward bias voltage is *Vd_forward*.
- The forward bias current is *Id_forward*.
- The reverse bias voltage is *Vd_reverse*.
- The reverse bias current is *Id_ reverse*.

One way in which the ideal device equations can be modelled in MATLAB is shown in listing 2:

```
1   %%---------------------------------------------------------------------
2   %%-- Schottky barrier diode forward bias equation
3   %%-- x-axis scaling (voltage) from 0 V to +0.8 V
4   %%---------------------------------------------------------------------
5
6           Vd_forward = (0:0.01:0.8)
7
8           T = 300
9           k = 1.38066e-23
10          q = 1.60218e-19
11
12          Is_sch = 1e-9
13          n = 1.0
14
15          for i=(1:1:length(Vd_forward))
16
17              Id_forward = Is_sch * (exp((q * Vd_forward)/(n * k * T)) - 1)
18
19          end
20
21  %%---------------------------------------------------------------------
22  %%-- Schottky barrier diode reverse bias equation
23  %%-- x-axis scaling (voltage) from 0 V to -10.0 V
24  %%---------------------------------------------------------------------
25
26          Vd_reverse = (0:-0.01:-10.0)
27
28          Is_sch = 1e-9
29
30          for i = (1:1:length(Vd_reverse))
31
32              Id_reverse = -Is_sch
33
34          end
35
36  %%---------------------------------------------------------------------
37  %% End of code
38  %%---------------------------------------------------------------------
```

Listing 2. Calculating the forward and reverse bias operation of the Schottky diode

These values and equations can be entered into MATLAB and plots of the I-V characteristic can be produced (by adding code for plotting the results to the code shown in listing 2).

Figure 10 shows a figure where the forward and reverse bias diode characteristics are plotted. The top subplot shows the forward and reverse bias characteristic (V_D shown from -10 V to +0.6 V) and the bottom two subplots show the forward bias characteristic zooming in on different ranges of V_D. Hence, specific areas of device operation can easily be identified from the overall set of data and individual plots created for understanding and analysis purposes.

The experiment can then be prototyped on a solderless prototyping board as shown in figure 11. Connecting this circuit to a dual d.c. power supply and digital voltmeter will provide all the necessary circuitry and equipment to undertake the experiment shown in figure 8. Table 2 shows the forward bias results (measuring Vin and Vr, and calculating Vd and Id). Table 3 shows the reverse bias results. Both sets of diode currents are calculated using the calculated resistor current and the actual measured resistor value ($Rm = 997\ \Omega$)

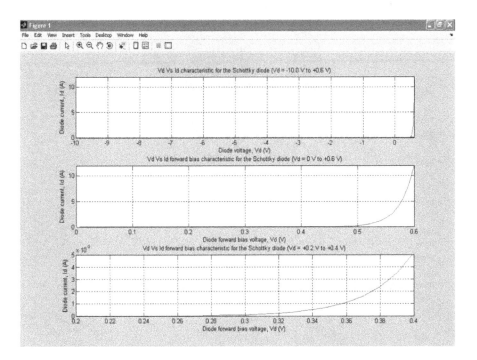

Figure 10. Ideal Schottky barrier diode equation plots

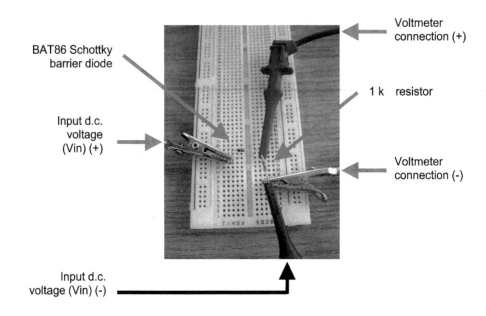

Figure 11. Prototyping the experiment

The measured values of voltage (*Vin* and *Vr*) can be entered into MATLAB and the diode voltage and current (*Vd* and *Id*) can then be calculated. The results can be entered into MATLAB and plotted with the MATLAB m-file code as shown in listing 3. Note also that the actual resistance value (*Rm*) of the 1 kΩ resistor was used in the current calculation in order to account for the tolerance of the resistor used. Figure 12 shows the resulting MATLAB plot with the forward bias shown on the top sub-plot and the both forward and reverse bias shown on the bottom sub-plot.

Vin (V)	Vr (V)	Vd = (Vin – Vr) (V)	Id = Ir = (Vr / Rm) (A)
Measured	Measured (to nearest 1 mV)	Calculated (to nearest 1 mV)	Calculated (to nearest 1 μA)
0	0	0	0
0.5	0.268	0.232	269 μA
1.0	0.739	0.261	741 μA
1.5	1.223	0.277	1.227 mA
2.0	1.712	0.288	1.717 mA
2.5	2.204	0.296	2.211 mA
3.0	2.697	0.303	2.705 mA
3.5	3.190	0.310	3.200 mA
4.0	3.685	0.315	3.696 mA
4.5	4.180	0.320	4.193 mA
5.0	4.675	0.325	4.689 mA
5.5	5.170	0.330	5.186 mA
6.0	5.666	0.334	5.683 mA
6.5	6.162	0.338	6.181 mA
7.0	6.659	0.341	6.679 mA
7.5	7.155	0.345	7.177 mA
8.0	7.651	0.349	7.674 mA
8.5	8.148	0.352	8.173 mA
9.0	8.645	0.355	8.671 mA
9.5	9.141	0.349	9.169 mA
10.0	9.637	0.363	9.666 mA

Table 2. Diode forward bias test results

Vin (V)	Vr (V)	Vd = -(Vin – Vr) (V)	Id = -Ir = -(Vr / Rm) (A)
Measured	Measured (to nearest 1 mV)	Calculated (to nearest 1 mV)	Calculated (to nearest 1 µA)
0	0	-0	0
0.5	0	-0.5	0
1.0	0	-1.0	0
1.5	0	-1.5	0
2.0	0	-2.0	0
2.5	0	-2.5	0
3.0	0	-3.0	0
3.5	0	-3.5	0
4.0	0	-4.0	0
4.5	0	-4.5	0
5.0	0	-5.0	0
5.5	0	-5.5	0
6.0	0	-6.0	0
6.5	0	-6.5	0
7.0	0	-7.0	0
7.5	0	-7.5	0
8.0	0	-8.0	0
8.5	0	-8.5	0
9.0	0	-9.0	0
9.5	0	-9.5	0
10.0	0	-10.0	0

Table 3. Diode reverse bias test results

```
1   %%-------------------------------------------------------------
2   %%-- BAT86 Schottky barrier diode test
3   %%-------------------------------------------------------------
4
5   %%----------------------------------------
6   %% Test conditions
7   %%----------------------------------------
8
9   Rm = 997
```

```
10
11 Vin = [0 0.5 1 1.5 2 2.5 3 3.5 4 4.5 5 5.5 6 6.5 7 7.5 8 8.5 9 9.5 10]
12
13 %%-------------------------------------
14 %% Diode in forward bias
15 %%-------------------------------------
16
17 Vr_forward = [0 0.268 0.739 1.223 1.712 2.204 2.697 3.190 3.685 4.180 ...
18     4.675 5.170 5.666 6.162 6.659 7.155 7.651 8.148 8.645 9.141 9.637]
19
20 Vd_forward = (Vin - Vr_forward)
21 Id_forward = (Vr_forward / Rm)
22
23 %%-------------------------------------
24 %% Diode in reverse bias
25 %%-------------------------------------
26
27 Vr_reverse = [0 0 0 0 0 0 0 0 0 0 0 0 ...
28     0 0 0 0 0 0 0 0]
29
30 Vd_reverse = -(Vin - Vr_reverse)
31 Id_reverse = -(Vr_reverse / Rm)
32
33 %%-------------------------------------
34 %% Plot results
35 %%-------------------------------------
36
37 subplot(2, 1, 1)
38 plot(Vd_forward, Id_forward, 'k')
39 hold on
40 grid
41 plot(Vd_forward, Id_forward, 'o')
42
43 title('Vd Vs Id for measured BAT86 Schottky Barrier Diode (forward bias)')
44 xlabel('Vd (V)')
45 ylabel('Id (A)')
46
47 subplot(2, 1, 2)
48 plot(Vd_forward, Id_forward, 'k')
49 hold on
50 grid
51 plot(Vd_forward, Id_forward, 'o')
52
53 plot(Vd_reverse, Id_reverse, 'r')
54 plot(Vd_reverse, Id_reverse, 'o')
55
56 title('Vd Vs Id for measured BAT86 Schottky Barrier Diode')
57 xlabel('Vd (V)')
58 ylabel('Id (A)')
59
60 %%-----------------------------------------------------------------------
61 %%-- End of BAT86 Schottky barrier diode test
62 %%-----------------------------------------------------------------------
```

Listing 3. M-file code for entering and plotting the test results for the BAT86 Schottky barrier diode

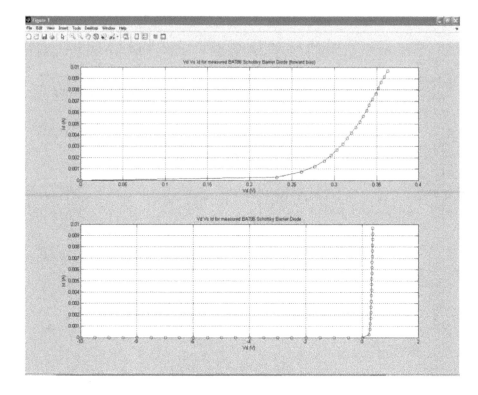

Figure 12. BAT86 Schottky barrier diode test results (forward and reverse bias)

In order to create the plots then there are three main parts to the m-file:

1. Entering the device test data (measured values) as scalar values and arrays:
   a. The measured resistor value (*Rm*) (line 9).
   b. The input voltage values (*Vin*) (line 11).
   c. The measured resistor voltage with the diode in forward bias (*Vr_forward*) (lines 17 and 18).
   d. The measured resistor voltage with the diode in reverse bias (*Vr_reverse*) (lines 27 and 28).
2. Creating the equations to determine the diode voltage and current values:
   a. The diode voltage in forward bias (*Vd_forward*) (line 20).
   b. The diode current in forward bias (*Id_forward*) (line 21).
   c. The diode voltage in reverse bias (*Vd_reverse*) (line 30).
   d. The diode current in reverse bias (*Id_reverse*) (line 31).
3. Plotting the currents and voltages on a single figure using subplots (lines 37 to 58).

5. Case study 2: Computer aided learning scenario

This section will describe the use of the experiment via a computer interface. In this arrangement, the student does not build the circuit – the circuit experiment is pre-built and connected to a computer via a suitable computer serial port. In this discussion, the RS-232 serial port is used and this interfaces to the diode experiment via an interface circuit consisting of a suitably configured Spartan-3 field programmable gate array (FPGA) [6, 7] and digital-to-analogue converter (DAC) and analogue-to-digital converter (ADC) arrangement.

This structure of the hardware and software interface is shown in figure 13.

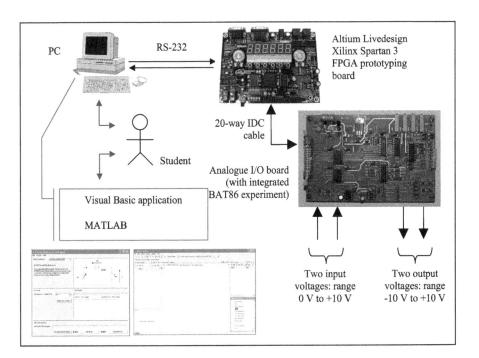

Figure 13. Tester hardware interface set-up

Here, the PC connects to an FPGA prototyping board via an RS-232 interface. The FPGA prototyping board also houses a voltage level shifter circuit (the MAX3232 IC) to interface the RS-232 voltage levels to the FPGA +3.3 V power supply voltage levels. Digital inputs and outputs (I/O) of the FPGA then connect to an analogue I/O board. This houses a power supply, two DACs (providing two independent voltage outputs in the range -10 V to +10 V) and two ADCs (receiving two input voltages in the range 0 V to +10 V). The analogue I/O board consists of a custom made printed circuit board (PCB) with an on-board BAT86 Schottky barrier diode experiment and a connector to interface to additional experiments.

Figure 14 shows the manufactured PCB in more detail. It is of course possible to utilise an existing hardware arrangement rather than designing a custom made solution.

In addition, the computer runs a suitably designed software application which gives the user access to the tester hardware. It is possible to use any suitable programming language (including the MATLAB GUI (Graphical User Interface) builder) to provide for a user interface and suitable software applications to access to the computer RS-232 port. However, here, a Visual Basic [8] application was used with Visual Basic here being the language of preference. Figure 15 shows the GUI as designed. The user selects the experiment (diode in forward bias or reverse bias mode of operation) and then runs a test by setting the input voltage (*Vin*) to apply to the circuit and then sending this to the experiment. The results from the experiment then are displayed on the GUI.

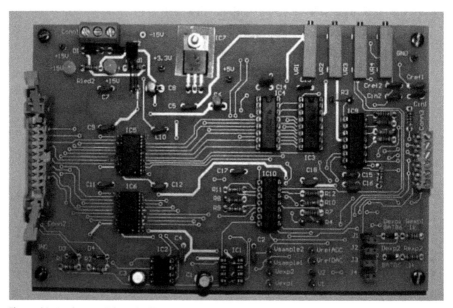

Figure 14. Analogue I/O board PCB

On completion of the experiment, the experiment results are saved into an automatically generated MATLAB m-file template (essentially the input and output voltages are saved in arrays in the m-file). The user then edits the m-file (adding his or her own results analysis and plotting commands), and runs MATLAB to analyse the test results. Listing 4 shows an example m-file template automatically generated by the software application.

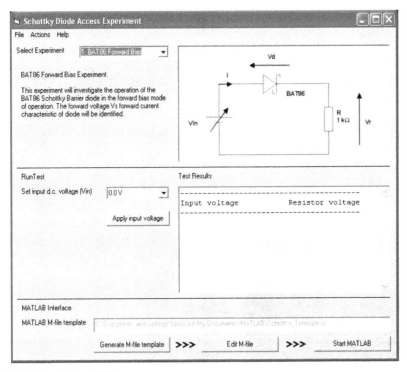

Figure 15. User interface GUI

```
1    %---------------------------------------------------------------------%
2    % MATLAB template file for BAT86 Schottky barrier diode experiment.
3    % BAT86 Forward Bias mode of operation.
4    %---------------------------------------------------------------------%
5    % Experiment undertaken on 13/01/2012 14:25:43
6    %---------------------------------------------------------------------%
7
8    %%-------------------
9    %% Test Results
10   %%-------------------
11
12   R = 1e+3
13
14   Vin = [0, 0, 0]
15   Vr  = [0.00, 0.00, 0.00]
16
17   %%-------------------
18   %% Analysis section
19   %%-------------------
20
21
22
23   %---------------------------------------------------------------------%
```

Listing 4. Automatically generated m-file template

The equipment set-up is shown in figure 16. Here, a laptop PC runs the software application and interfaces to the FPGA prototyping board via an RS-232 serial data link. The analogue I/O board operates on a +/-15 V d.c. power supply and test points are provided on the board to allow for the measurement of specific circuit voltages. The BAT86 Schottky barrier diode experiment is also incorporated on the analogue I/O (experiment) board.

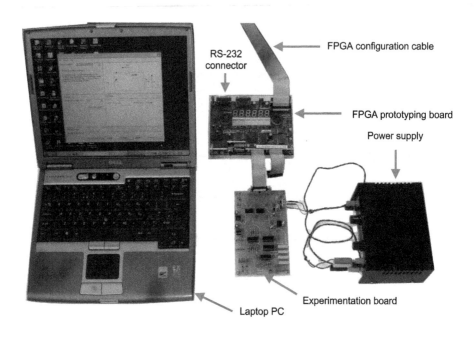

Figure 16. Computer set-up

6. Case study 3: Distance education learning scenario

Increasingly, universities are providing access to courses in a distance mode of operation – that is students are not physically located within the institution, but learn from an alternative (remote) location. In the simplest terms, students are registered to study for a qualification within the institution but access course material (lecture notes and assignments) via a suitable Internet connection and learning management system (LMS) such as Moodle [9] or a custom LMS solution. However, such a simplistic statement does not tell the whole story.

In engineering and science, there is a need to undertake experiments and analyse experiment results. This is traditionally undertaken *at-presence* where the learner undertakes the experiment within the laboratory facilities hosted by the institution. This approach might not be possible for distance learners and so alternative approaches to providing access to experimentation have been developed – distance learning utilising remote experimentation accessed through a remote laboratory [10]. The role that distance learning now undertakes within the teaching and learning environments on a global scale has gained widespread acceptance over the last number of years. Textural based teaching material, enhanced with graphics and animation, is now supported through the use of remote experimentation. Remote experimentation is essentially physical laboratory experiments that are set-up to be accessible via the Internet. Many institutions and organisations now provide for their laboratory experimentation to be Internet-enabled, so providing access via a web browser for remote users who may be in a location in the world that provides the user with an Internet access capability. This has been shown to be of high value from university education through to E-Science applications [11].

Industry can also benefit from the concept of distance access and learning scenario. Imagine for example, a parent company which has invested heavily in expensive equipment, for example integrated circuit (IC) testers. When the company extends its operations into other locations, it does not then need not to invest in the same equipment again. This is where the remote logging into the tester for device testing and data collection purposes can be done, and the analysis can carried out using MATLAB. In another scenario, the after sales service of a product can be made more friendly, easier and cost effective. In traditional approach, when a machine is down (i.e., not operational due to a fault), the customer has to wait for the service engineer to arrive from another part of the world to repair the machine. Using the concept of distance access, the service engineer needs only to be remotely connected to the down machine and MATLAB can once again be useful to analysis the symptoms and suggest possible causes, along with solutions. Of course the symptom has to be first modelled accurately just like the diode and other devices are modelled.

Here and in this distance based learning scenario, the basic experimentation set-up and discussed in section 5 (Case study 2: computer aided learning scenario) can be modified to be accessible via the Internet. Essentially, a web-server arrangement (a WAMP (Windows, Apache [12], MySQL [13] and PHP [14])) system is set-up here and the experiment user interface is via a series of Internet browser pages (web pages). Figure 17 shows the home page set-up for the experiment.

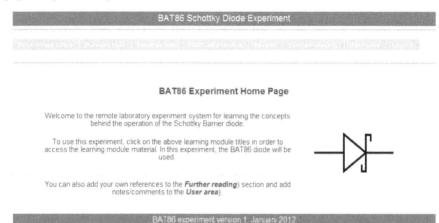

Figure 17. User interface (home page)

In the user interface, the user is considered to already have successfully logged in to the remote laboratory via a username/password arrangement and is then given access to a diode experiment menu system (top of the page) for accessing different parts of the experiment. These options are identified in table 4. The user is prompted to access the different web pages in order to access different aspects of the experiment, including access to MATLAB via the web server arrangement.

Option	Option description
Experiment home	Return to this (home) page.
Forward bias	Run the diode forward bias experiment.
Reverse bias	Run the diode reverse bias experiment.
MATLAB analysis	Create a MATLAB function to enter and analyse the experiment results.
Results	View the results from previously run experiments and MATLAB analyses.
Further reading	List of references (which can be added to by users).
User area	Area to allow users to add notes for all users to access.
Logout	Log out from the overall remote laboratory arrangement.

Table 4. User interface options

In order to run an experiment, the user chooses the diode in forward bias or reverse bias mode of operation via the top menu system. Figure 18 shows the forward bias experiment web page. This provides for an introduction to the experiment and an area to enter the values of the input voltage (*Vin*) to apply to the test circuit. This is via an HTML form seen to the right of the page. All values are entered into the form and then submitted to the web server (and hence the experiment) using the *Submit* button.

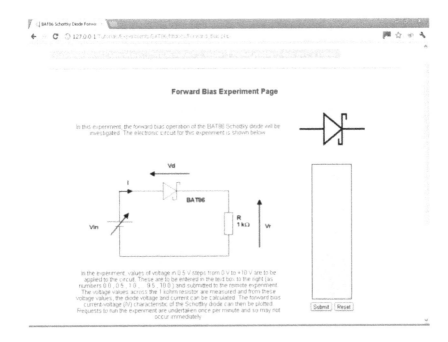

Figure 18. Remote submission of diode forward bias experiment input voltage values

Figure 19 shows the reverse bias experiment web page. This page has the same form as the forward bias experiment, except now on submission of the input voltage values, the reverse bias experiment is selected rather than the forward bias experiment.

As the experiments are performed remotely with the experiment electronic hardware connected to the web server PC, the user has a much more restricted and controlled access to the experiment. In this arrangement, the experiment is run on the remote web server and the results are accessible via a web page. Here, the user does not have interactive control of the experiment, rather they submit their values and the web server treats this as a job to complete, allowing the same experiment to be used by multiple users without the need for the user to pre-book the experiment.

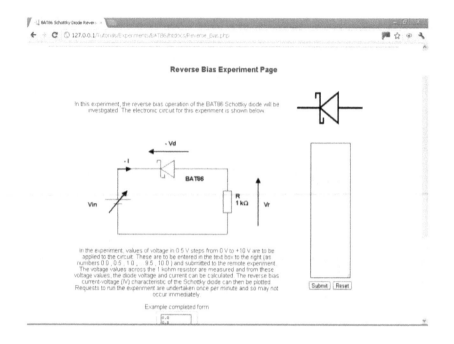

Figure 19. Remote submission of diode reverse bias experiment input voltage values

Figure 20 shows the experiment results page that the user sees. Their submitted test values and the experiment results are available as hypertext links via this web page. Hence, the user can see the text based experiment results which would then be used in MATLAB to analyse the results.

The MATLAB analysis is undertaken by entering the code for a MATLAB *function* into a form on the web page and then submitting the *function* to the web server for remote processing. On completion of the processing, the results are available for the user to access.

In figure 21, a template form for the MATLAB code as a function is automatically presented to the student and they complete the function with their own comments. This is shown in more detail in figure 22 and listing 5. The user does not modify this code structure, but inserts their own code between the "% Start of user commands" and "% End of user commands" comments.

On submission of the completed form, the code is automatically saved in a function m-file, MATLAB automatically executes the m-file commands and the results are saved to suitable results files.

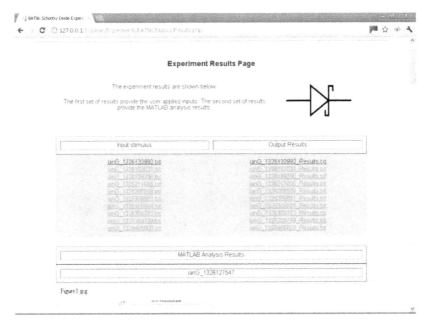

Figure 20. Viewing experiment results

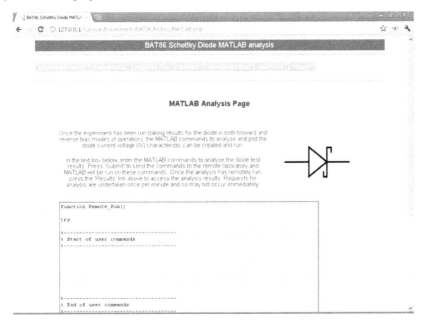

Figure 21. Remote submission of MATLAB commands to web server for remote processing

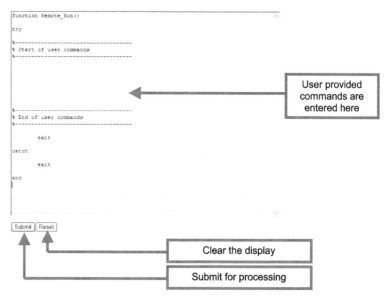

Figure 22. Remote submission of MATLAB commands to web server for remote processing

The function template code is shown in listing 5. On submission, this function is saved into the m-file and MATLAB is executed on the web server PC. In order to handle possible errors in the submitted code, then the *try – catch* error control is used.

```
1    function Remote_Run()
2
3    try
4
5    %-----------------------------------
6    % Start of user commands
7    %-----------------------------------
8
9
10
11
12
13
14
15   %-----------------------------------
16   % End of user commands
17   %-----------------------------------
18
19            exit
20
21   catch
22
23            exit
24
25   end
```

Listing 5. MATLAB function template

Two important aspects of using MATLAB in this manner are:

1. MATLAB is run remotely on a different computer and so any instant visual feedback that a user would see when running MATLAB on his or her own computer is not immediately available.
2. If any errors are encountered in the user provided code, MATLAB must exit "gracefully" and not simply crash. It must also be able to provide suitable error feedback to the user.

To this extent, the above function template captures and reports errors, and the text feedback that would normally be seen in the MATLAB Command Window is automatically outputted to a text log file (and this file is available via the Results Page).

A third aspect of using MATLAB in this manner is that any figures to plot the results would not be seen if simply the plot(x, y) command was used.

To this extent, whenever a figure plot is to be produced, this will need to be saved as an image file (using the commands of the form shown in listing 6) and if the image file is in JPEG format, it will be displayed in the Results page along with the MATLAB log file and the uploaded analysis code.

```
1    figH = figure('visible', 'off')          Create figure
2
3
4        plot(Vd_forward, Id_forward)          Plot to figure
5        grid                                  Add grid
6        title('Vin Vs I (Forward biased diode)')  Add title
7        xlabel('Vin (volts)')                 Add x-axis label
8        ylabel('I (amps)')                    Add y-axis label
9
10
11       print(figH, '-djpeg', 'Figure1.jpg')  Print figure to JPG file
12
13
14   close(figH)                               Close figure
```

Listing 6. MATLAB: plotting the figure to a JPEG image file

Here in listing 6, a figure is created and plotted to (along with the annotation required by the user). Here, a figure called *figH* is created and plots the variables **Vd_forward** and **Id_forward** along with a figure title and axis labels. This is then saved to an image file in JPEG format with the file name Figure1.jpg.

Once an analysis has been undertaken, the results are available for viewing on the results page in the format as shown in figure 23. Here, the analysis run name (a unique run name), the image files produced, the generated MATLAB m-file and the MATLAB log file are available for viewing.

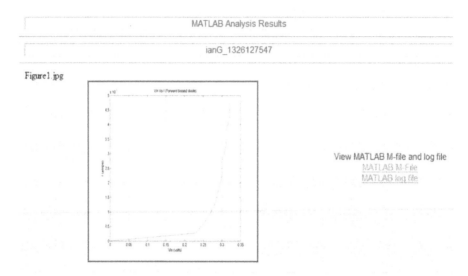

Figure 23. MATLAB analysis results access

The user can click on the computer mouse on the image and this shows the full-size figure in a new browser window. Where the user runs an m-file to create multiple figures and save these as image files, each generated image file is shown in the results window and is therefore accessible. The image file can then be saved to the student's own computer for later inclusion in experiment reports.

In this work, the infrastructure to support the use of MATLAB to be accessed via an Internet browser page is developed and discussed.

A final comment to make however relates to the use of the MATLAB software license where MATLAB runs on a particular computer, but is accessed remotely from a separate computer. It is not the intention to discuss specifics about the use of the software license and if there is any doubt about the use of the license in this mode then the provider of the license should be consulted.

7. Conclusions

This chapter has presented and discussed the use of MATLAB within an education environment with reference to the teaching and learning of semiconductor device fundamentals. Specifically, MATLAB can be integrated into the education curriculum as a tool to provide specific analysis and results presentation operations, these being (i) physical electronic circuit test results data entry, analysis and graphical plotting; (ii) idealised device characteristic equation modelling and graphical plotting; (iii) comparisons between idealised and actual device performance; and (iv) documentation preparation purposes. In this work, consideration was given to the use of MATLAB in three teaching and learning scenarios; (i) at-presence "traditional" laboratory experiments; (ii) at-presence computer aided learning laboratories; and (iii), distance based remote access to laboratory experiments. Each scenario was introduced and the development of the laboratory experiments discussed. The physical infrastructure (electronic hardware and software) was identified and the role in which technology is utilised in the education environment was presented. In particular, the way in which MATLAB was considered to be used and how it was integrated into custom developed education technology tools were highlighted. The discussions were based on the evaluation of the Schottky barrier diode, specifically the BAT86 Schottky barrier diode. However, the discussions, arguments and experimentation hardware and software can be readily adapted to other forms of semiconductor devices.

Author details

Ian Grout
Department of Electronic and Computer Engineering, University of Limerick, Limerick, Ireland

Abu Khari Bin A'ain
Faculty of Electrical Engineering, Universiti Teknologi Malaysia (UTM), Skudai, Johor, Malaysia

8. References

[1]   The Mathworks Inc., MATLAB®, 2012, www.themathworks.com

[2]   NXP, BAT86 Schottky barrier diode product datasheet, 2004, www.nxp.com/documents/data_sheet/BAT86.pdf

[3]   Duane Hanselman and Bruce R. Littlefield, Mastering MATLAB 6, 6th Ed., Prentice Hall; 1 edition (14 Dec 2000), ISBN 0130194689

[4]   Pierret R.F., Semiconductor Device Fundamentals, 1996, Addison-Wesley Publishing Company, ISBN 0-13-178459-5x

[5]   Sze S.M., Semiconductor Devices Physics and Technology, 1985, John Wiley & Sons. Inc., ISBN 0-471-83704-0

[6]   Xilinx Inc., Spartan-3 FPGA Family Data Sheet, 2009, www.xilinx.com/support/documentation/data_sheets/ds099.pdf

[7]   Altium, TR0104 LiveDesign Evaluation Board Technical Reference Manual, 2004

[8]   Microsoft Corporation, 2012, Visual Basic 6.0, msdn.microsoft.com/en-us/vstudio/ms788229

[9]   Moodle, 2012, moodle.org/

[10] Ian Andrew Grout and Alexandre César Rodrigues da Silva, "Analysis Tool for Remote Laboratory Structures", Proceedings of the Remote Experimentation and Virtual Instrumentation conference (REV 2010), Stockholm, June 29 - July 2, 2010, www.rev-conference.org/REV2010/

[11] R. Ratering et al., "GridBeans: Supporting e-Science and Grid Applications", Proceedings of the 2nd IEEE International Conference on e-Science and Grid Computing", 4-6 Dec. 2006, Amsterdam, The Netherlands

[12] The Apache Software Foundation, Apache HTTP Server Project, 2012, httpd.apache.org/
[13] MySQL, 2012, dev.mysql.com/
[14] PHP, PHP Hypertext Preprocessor, 2012, www.php.net/

Illustrating Amazing Effects of Modern Physics with Numerical Simulations Conducted in the Classroom

Eric Anterrieu

Additional information is available at the end of the chapter

1. Introduction

Real experiments are sometimes missing or highly expensive to implement when teaching modern physics. This is an important issue, especially when the theories are not intuitive. However, with the incorporation of computers into the classroom it has become much easier to illustrate some amazing effects of modern physics that cannot be brought to the attention of students without the aid of numerical simulations. Thanks to the performance of MATLAB langage, as well as to the easiness to code a theoretical problem, the students can really conduct numerical expriments and play with them almost in real time. This computer-based teaching approach is illustrate here with the capabilities to use MATLAB for solving initial values problems of ordinary differential equations encountered in relativistic electrodynamics [2] as well as in non-linear optics [3].

2. Ordinary differential equations in Matlab

In mathematics, an ordinary differential equation (or ODE) is a relation f that contains one or more derivatives of a dependent variable y with respect to a single independent variable t, usually referred to as time. Many studies have been devoted to the solution of ODEs. In the case where the equation is linear, it can be solved by analytical methods. Unfortunately, most of the interesting ODEs are non-linear and, with a few exceptions, cannot be solved analytically. However, in science and in engineering, a numeric approximation to the solution is often good enough to solve a problem. Numerical integration is that part of numerical analysis which studies the numerical solutions of ODEs with the aid of iterative solvers.

MATLAB offers several numerical algorithms to solve a wide variety of ODEs. These solvers are designed to handle only explicit ODEs of the form $y' = f(t,y)$, linearly implicit ODEs of the form $M(t,y) \cdot y' = f(t,y)$ as well as fully implicit ones of the form $f(t,y,y') = 0$. Generally there are many functions that satisfy a given ODE, and additional information is necessary to specify the solution of interest. In an initial value problem, the solution of interest satisfies a specific initial condition $y(t_o) = y_o$ at a given initial time t_o. Finally, the ODE solvers available in MATLAB accept only first-order ODEs. However, ODEs often involve derivatives of order higher than one. As a consequence, to use the ODE solvers for solving an ODE of order n, the equation has to be rewritten as an equivalent system of n first-order ODEs.

All the ODE solvers proposed in MATLAB share a common syntax that makes them easy to try if it is not apparent which one is the most appropriate. To apply a different method to the same problem, simply change the name of the ODE solver function. The simplest syntax, common to all the solver functions, is:

```
>> [t,y] = solver(odefun,tspan,y0,options);
```

where `solver` is one of the ODE solver functions available in MATLAB.

The input arguments are:

- `odefun`, a handle to a function that evaluates the ODE.
- `tspan`, a vector specifying the interval of integration.
- `y0`, a vector of initial conditions for the problem.
- `options`, a structure of optional parameters to change the default integration properties of the solver.

The output arguments contain the solution approximated at discrete points:

- `t`, a vector of time points.
- `y`, a solution array with the values of the solution y at the time t returned in `t`.

Beginning with initial condition, the solver steps through the time interval, computing a solution at each time step. If the solution for a time step satisfies the solver's error tolerance criteria, it is a successful step. Otherwise, it is a failed attempt; the solver shrinks the step size and tries again. The solver `ode45` is based on a RUNGE-KUTTA formula [6] and is according to MATLAB documentation "the best function to apply as a first try for most problems."

3. Non-linear optics

Ray optics is the branch of optics [4] in which all the subtle wave effects are neglected: the light is considered as travelling along rays which can only change their direction by refraction or reflection. The usefullness of the computer for studying, or designing, optical systems within an educational frame, is well known and it has been already suggested [10], but only in the paraxial approximation of geometrical optics. Indeed, when light propagates in media with constant refractive index, the SNELL-DESCARTES laws can be applied for implementing a fast numerical ray-tracing procedure based on a geometrical approach of the problem. However, when propagation takes place in media with non-homogeneous refractive index, the differential equation governing the propagation of light has to be solved with the aid of the computer. This section describes a fast, accurate and easy to use code for illustrating the propagation of light in such media, sometimes with amazing effects that cannot be brought to the attention of students without the aid of numerical simulations, or except at an expensive cost.

3.1. Solving the iconal equation

The iconal equation [4], which describes the path of the light propagating in a medium with refractive index n, is an ODE of the second order:

$$\frac{d}{ds}\left(n\frac{d\mathbf{r}}{ds}\right) = \nabla n, \tag{1}$$

where $\mathbf{r}$ denotes the position vector of a point on the ray and ds is an element of length along the path. From the point of view of the numerical implementation of a ray tracing procedure, it is more convenient to set $d\ell = ds/n$ so that (1) now reads:

$$\frac{d^2\mathbf{r}}{d\ell^2} = \frac{1}{2}\nabla n^2. \tag{2}$$

When light is propagating in a plane, the vector equation (2) reduces to a system of two scalar equations of the second order. We therefore have in Cartesian coordinates:

$$\begin{cases} \dfrac{d^2x}{d\ell^2} = \dfrac{1}{2}\dfrac{\partial n^2}{\partial x}, \\[2mm] \dfrac{d^2y}{d\ell^2} = \dfrac{1}{2}\dfrac{\partial n^2}{\partial y}. \end{cases} \tag{3}$$

As soon as the refractive index does not vary with x and y, (3) is straiforward to integrate and leads to a straight line path. When n is not uniform and according to the dependency of n with respect to x and y, it may not be possible to integrate (3) without the aid of the computer. This is why the capabilities of MATLAB to quickly solve an ODE is used here for studying the propagation of light in non-homogeneous media. However, since MATLAB can only solve ODEs of the first order, (3) has to be rewritten:

$$\begin{cases} \dfrac{dp_x}{d\ell} = \dfrac{1}{2}\dfrac{\partial n^2}{\partial x}, \\[2mm] \dfrac{dp_y}{d\ell} = \dfrac{1}{2}\dfrac{\partial n^2}{\partial y}, \end{cases} \quad \text{with} \quad \begin{aligned} \dfrac{dx}{d\ell} &= p_x, \\[2mm] \dfrac{dy}{d\ell} &= p_y. \end{aligned} \tag{4}$$

The MATLAB function `iconalODE` contains the final definition of the problem: in vector f are stored the values of x, y, p_x and p_y for a given value of ℓ, whereas the vector df returns the values of p_x, p_y, $dp_x/d\ell$ and $dp_y/d\ell$ for the same value of ℓ.

```
function df=iconalODE(l,f)
x = f(1);   px = f(3);
y = f(2);   py = f(4);
% gradient of n^2
[dn2dx, dn2dy] = dn2(x,y,param);
% ode
dpxdl = 0.5*dn2dx;
dpydl = 0.5*dn2dy;
df = [px; py; dpxdl; dpydl];
```

The students have to supply a function dn2 which should return the Cartesian components of the gradient of n^2 at any point (x, y), the expression of which may depend on parameters stored in the param vector. The equation described in iconalODE is solved with the aid of the built-in function ode45 provided by MATLAB:

```
>> [l,f] = ode45('iconalODE',l,fi);
>> X = f(:,1);
>> Y = f(:,2);
>> dYdX = f(:,4)./f(:,3);
```

The solver is fed with a vector fi which contains the initial settings of the problem, namely x_i, y_i, $(dx/d\ell)_i$ and $(dy/d\ell)_i$ at a given starting point M_i. The values of the solution, namely x, y, $dx/d\ell$ et $dy/d\ell$ along the ray path, are returned in the array f: here, for convenience reasons, vectors X, Y and dYdX are used for storing the values of x, y and dy/dx.

3.2. Application in non-homogeneous media

In this study, the refractive index of the non-homogeneous media satisfies the law:

$$n^2(\rho) = 1 + \frac{\rho_o^2}{\rho^2} \quad \text{with} \quad \rho = \sqrt{x^2 + y^2}. \tag{5}$$

Another choice would have been to study the propagation of light in LUNEBURG lens [9], however contrary to expression (5) the refractive index would have not present a singularity and consequently the example would have been less constraining from the computational point of view and less illustrative from the point of view of the propagation of light in non-homogeneous media. However, according to the approach adopted here, moving from one study to another just requires to change the lines of code written in the function dn2 supplied by the students: this is exactly what is done in a classroom.

Coming back to (5), the region where the media is non-homogeneous is restricted to a disk $\mathcal{D}$ with radius R. Outside $\mathcal{D}$, n is supposed to be uniform and equal to

$$n_i = \sqrt{1 + \rho_o^2/R^2}, \tag{6}$$

so that no discontinuity occurs at the boundary. According to (5), within $\mathcal{D}$ the components of the gradient of n^2 in Cartesian coordinates are:

$$\frac{\partial n^2}{\partial x} = -\frac{2x\rho_0^2}{(x^2+y^2)^2},$$

$$\frac{\partial n^2}{\partial y} = -\frac{2y\rho_0^2}{(x^2+y^2)^2},$$

(7)

whereas they are null outside $\mathcal{D}$ since n is there uniform and equal to n_i given by (6). The function dn2 is therefore reduced to:

```
function [dn2dx,dn2dy]=dn2(x,y,param)
Ro = param(1);
R  = param(2);
if (sqrt(x^2+y^2) > R)
     dn2dx = 0;
     dn2dy = 0;
else
     dn2dx = -2*x*Ro^2/(x^2+y^2)^2;
     dn2dy = -2*y*Ro^2/(x^2+y^2)^2;
end
```

where Ro is used for storing the value of parameter ρ_0 and R that of the radius R of $\mathcal{D}$.

Before solving the ODE described in functions iconalODE and dn2 it is necessary to set the initial conditions of the problem. Let us consider an incident ray starting at a point $M_i(x_i, y_i)$ and making an angle α with the Ox axis. In the neighbourhood of M_i, we have $dx = ds\cos\alpha$ and $dy = ds\sin\alpha$. Since at any point on the ray path $d\ell = ds/n$, we therefore have:

$$(dx/d\ell)_i = n_i\cos\alpha \quad \text{and} \quad (dy/d\ell)_i = n_i\sin\alpha.$$

Finally, the radius of $\mathcal{D}$ is set, for example, to $R = 4\rho_0$ with $\rho_0 = 1$. Since the system exhibits a central symmetry, the study is restricted here to incidents rays parallel to the Ox axis, so that $\alpha = \pi$, and starting from M_i located at a distance $y_i = h = 2\rho_0$ from the Ox axis and with $x_i = 6\rho_0$. The following lines are the MATLAB code corresponding to all these initial settings.

```
>> Ro = 1;
>> R = 4*Ro;
>> h = 2*Ro;
>> Xi = 6*Ro;
>> Yi = h;
>> alpha = pi;
>> Ni = sqrt(1 + (Ro/R)^2);
>> dXidl = Ni*cos(alpha);
>> dYidl = Ni*sin(alpha);
>> fi = [Xi Yi dXidl dYidl];
```

After point M_i, the light travels according to the ODE described in the functions `iconal0DE` and `dn2`. The complete path of the ray returned by the `ode45` solver is represented on Figure 1. It corresponds to the following lines:

```
>> figure(1);
>> plot(X/Ro,Y/Ro,'r-');
```

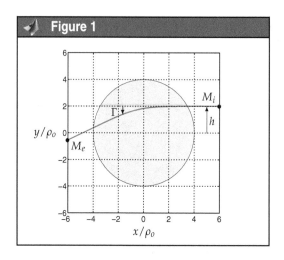

Figure 1. An example of a ray path (in red) between points M_i and M_e. Outside the disk $\mathcal{D}$ (in grey) the media is homogeneous with a constant refractive index: the light is travelling in straight line. On the contrary, the media in $\mathcal{D}$ is non-homogeneous with spatially varying refractive index: the path of the light is curved.

As expected, outside the disk $\mathcal{D}$, the light is travelling in straight line since the media is homogeneous with uniform refractive index given by (6). On the contrary, within $\mathcal{D}$ the path is curved since the light is here travelling in a non-homogeneous media with spatially varying refractive index according to (5). The curvature of the path is oriented towards the center of the disk $\mathcal{D}$, that is to say towards the direction of the gradient of n. The ray continuously tends towards the center without reaching it. According to the inverse return of light, the path of the light obtained when solving the iconal equation (1) from M_i to M_e and that obtained when solving it from M_e to M_i in the reverse direction of propagation are nothing but the same. In addition, owing to the central symmetry of the system, the path of the light is symmetrical with respect to the location where the distance from the center of $\mathcal{D}$ is minimal.

Coming back to the situation of Figure 1, the deviation angle Γ after travelling from M_i through the non-homogeneous media can be computed at any point M_e in the homogeneous media according to:

$$\Gamma = \arctan(dy/dx)_e + \pi$$

that is to say in MATLAB language:

```
>> gamma = atan(dYdX(end))+pi
```

As observed by the students, h is playing the role of an impact parameter with respect to the singularity of the refractive index at the center of the disk $\mathcal{D}$ and the angle Γ that of a scattering angle with regards to the direction of the incoming ray. Shown in Figure 1, for $h = 2\rho_0$, the deviation is about 25° with respect to the incident direction.

An interesting and convenient aspect of conducting numerical simulations with the aid of the computer in a classroom with MATLAB is the capability to re-run the code with different initial settings and to obtain the new path of the light almost immediately. This is exactly what is done by the students for investigating the influence of the parameter h on the deviation angle Γ. As shown in Figure 2, Γ varies with h in a non-linear manner. Values of Γ greater than $\pi/2$ correspond to rays which make a half turn, or even more than a complete turn, before leaving the non-homogeneous media.

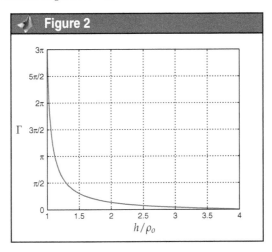

Figure 2. Variations of the deviation (or scattering) angle Γ with the (impact) parameter h.

Some particular situations are shown in Figure 3 for different values of the ratio h/ρ_0. Although trajectories for large values of Γ are not without surprise for the students, they usually accept that the light can make a large number of turns before leaving the disk $\mathcal{D}$. However, their reaction is simply incredible when they discover, even with numerical experiences, that below a limit for the ratio h/ρ_0 the path of the light identifies to that of a spiral: the ray seems to be attracted by the singularity of the refractive index of the non-homgeneous media for $\rho = 0$ and does not emerge from the disk $\mathcal{D}$. Such an amazing situation is represented in Figure 4 for $h = 0.965\,\rho_0$.

Coming back to the analogy between h and an impact parameter and between Γ and a scattering angle, these trajectories remind those of a particule captured by a KEPLER or COULOMB potential [5].

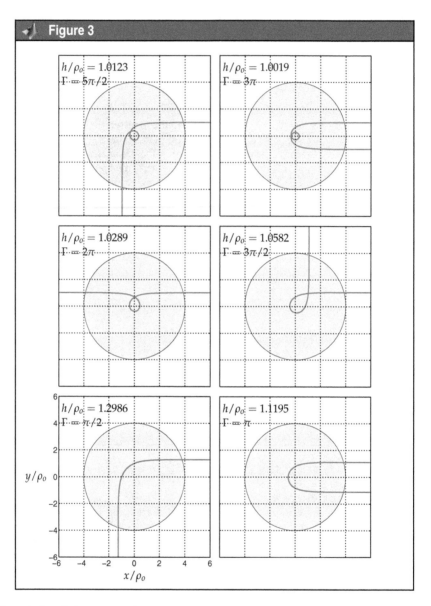

Figure 3. Some light trajectories for various values of h. According to the inverse return of light, all the trajectories are valid solutions for propagation in both directions.

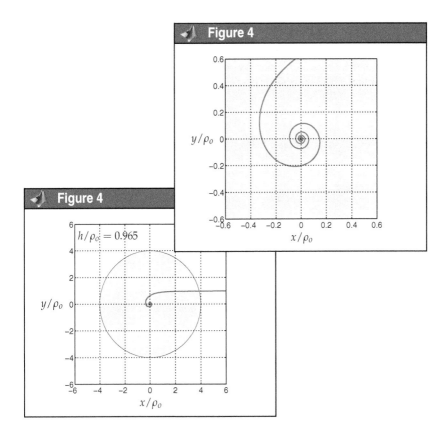

Figure 4. Ray path for $h = 0.965\,\rho_0$ (central part is enlarged on the top-left).

4. Relativistic electrodynamics

Classical electrodynamics is an important branch of the theoretical physics [7], which has numerous applications in physical engineering. On one hand, the usefulness of the computer for studying the movement of particles in electromagnetic fields is now well known and it has been already suggested [11], but only in the Newtonian approximation. However, the trajectory becomes complicated to establish when the electric and magnetic fields are acting together, whatever the initial velocity. On the other hand, the teaching of relativity to undergraduate electrical engineers appears also to be a necessity [8]. A stimulated way to gain the attention and the interest of students for relativity, which is not an intuitive theory, is precisely to begin by studying the movement of fast particles in electromagnetic fields because the applications are numerous and surprising. This section describes a fast, accurate and easy to use code for computing the trajectories of charged relativistic particles under the action of the LORENTZ force and illustrating some effects of relativity that cannot be brought to the attention of students without the aid of numerical simulations, or except at an expensive cost.

4.1. Solving the movement equation

The equation which describes the trajectory of a relativistic particle of mass m and charge q under the simultaneous actions of an electric field $\mathbf{E}$ and a magnetic one $\mathbf{B}$ is an ordinary differential equation (ODE) of the first order [7]:

$$\frac{d\mathbf{p}}{dt} = q(\mathbf{E} + \mathbf{v} \times \mathbf{B}), \tag{8}$$

where $\mathbf{v}$ is the velocity of the particle, $\mathbf{p} = \gamma m\mathbf{v}$ is the relativistic expression of the momentum with $\gamma = 1/\sqrt{1 - \mathbf{v}^2/c^2}$ the relativistic factor and c is the speed of light. In Cartesian coordinates, the previous vector equation can be put in the form of a system of three scalar ODEs of the first order:

$$\begin{cases} \dfrac{dp_x}{dt} = q(E_x + v_y B_z - v_z B_y) \\[2mm] \dfrac{dp_y}{dt} = q(E_y + v_z B_x - v_x B_z) \\[2mm] \dfrac{dp_z}{dt} = q(E_z + v_x B_y - v_y B_x) \end{cases} \tag{9}$$

Owing to the factor γ, solving this system of ODEs is harder in the relativistic case than in the Newtonian one. Indeed, expression of the first derivatives of the components p_x, p_y et p_z of the momentum $\mathbf{p}$ is not simple because of the expression of the first derivative of γ itself. It is necessary to express the speed $\mathbf{v}$ as a function of the momentum $\mathbf{p}$ without involving the LORENTZ factor γ. This is done by introducing the energy $\mathcal{E}$ of the free particle:

$$\mathbf{v} = \frac{\mathbf{p}}{\gamma m} = \frac{\mathbf{p}c^2}{\mathcal{E}} = \mathbf{p}\frac{c^2}{\sqrt{\mathbf{p}^2 c^2 + m^2 c^4}}. \tag{10}$$

This vector equation reduces again to three scalar equations in Cartesian coordinates:

$$\begin{cases} v_x = p_x c^2 / \sqrt{(p_x^2 + p_y^2 + p_z^2)c^2 + m^2 c^4} \\[2mm] v_y = p_y c^2 / \sqrt{(p_x^2 + p_y^2 + p_z^2)c^2 + m^2 c^4} \\[2mm] v_z = p_z c^2 / \sqrt{(p_x^2 + p_y^2 + p_z^2)c^2 + m^2 c^4} \end{cases} \tag{11}$$

Finally, solving (8) in Cartesian coordinates in the relativistic case is equivalent to solve the system of ODEs (9) together with (11). However, owing to the coupling between these equations, it may not be possible to integrate them without the aid of the computer. This is why the capabilities of MATLAB to quickly solve ODEs is used here for tackling this problem.

The MATLAB function odeEB contains the definition of the system to solve: in vector f are stored the coordinates (x, y, z) of the particle as well as the components (p_x, p_y, p_z) of the momentum $\mathbf{p}$ at a given time t, whereas the vector df returns the components dx/dt, dy/dt and dz/dt of the speed vector $\mathbf{v}$ as well as the components of the first derivative of the momentum dp_x/dt, dp_y/dt and dp_z/dt at the same time.

```
function df=odeEB(t,f,q,m)
% particle coordinates
x   = f(1);
y   = f(2);
z   = f(3);
% particle momentum
Px = f(4);
Py = f(5);
Pz = f(6);
% particle energy
P = sqrt(Px.^2+Py.^2+Pz.^2);
E = sqrt(P^2*c^2+m^2*c^4);
% particle velocity
Vx = Px*c^2/E;
Vy = Py*c^2/E;
Vz = Pz*c^2/E;
% electric and magnetic fields
[Ex,Ey,Ez]=fieldE(x,y,z,t);
[Bx,By,Bz]=fieldB(x,y,z,t);
% ode
dPxdt = q*(Ex + Vy*Bz - Vz*By);
dPydt = q*(Ey + Vz*Bx - Vx*Bz);
dPzdt = q*(Ez + Vx*By - Vy*Bx);
df = [Vx; Vy; Vz; dPxdt; dPydt; dPzdt];
```

This function is general enough for solving various problems without re-writing any code since the mass m and the electric charge q of the particle are given to the function. The students have only to supply the two functions fieldE and fieldB which should return the Cartesian components of **E** and **B** at any point (x, y, z) and at any time t. The equation described in odeEB is solved again with the aid of the built-in function ode45:

```
>> [t,f] = ode45('odeEB',t,fi);
```

The solver is fed with a vector fi which contains the initial settings of the problem, namely the initial position of the particle $(x, y, z)_i$ as well as the initial components of the momentum $(p_x, p_y, p_z)_i$ at a given starting point M_i. The values of the solution, namely the successive positions of the particle (x, y, z) along the trajectory as well as the components (p_x, p_y, p_z) of the momentum **p** at the corresponding time, are returned in the array f.

```
>> x = f(:,1);   Px = f(:,4);
>> y = f(:,2);   Py = f(:,5);
>> z = f(:,3);   Pz = f(:,6);
```

Here, for convenience reasons, vectors x, y and z are used for storing the values of x, y and z. Likewise, vectors Px, Py and Pz are used for storing the values of p_x, p_y and p_z.

```
>> P = sqrt(Px.^2+Py.^2+Pz.^2);
>> E = sqrt(P.^2*c^2+m^2*c^4);
>> Vx = Px*c^2./E;
>> Vy = Py*c^2./E;
>> Vz = Pz*c^2./E;
```

The final step performed outside the solver is the computation of the components (v_x, v_y, v_z) of the speed vector **v**, according to (10). The corresponding values are written in vectors Vx, Vy and Vz.

4.2. Applications in uniform fields

The applications presented in this section are concerned with the movement of a relativistic electron under the simultaneous action of an electric field **E** and a magnetic one **B**.

```
>> c =   2.99792458E+08; % m/s
>> q = -1.60217649E-19; % C
>> m =   9.10938215E-31; % kg
```

Depending on the orientation of **E** with respect to that of **B**, the trajectory of the electron may be very different.

4.2.1. **E** and **B** collinear

In this first case, **E** and **B** are collinear, oriented along the Oz axis, $\mathbf{E} = E\,\mathbf{e}_z$ and $\mathbf{B} = B\,\mathbf{e}_z$, and uniform with intensities E and B set to $3 \cdot 10^6$ V/m and 0.05 T, respectively. The functions fieldE and fieldB supplied by the students are therefore reduced to:

```
function [Ex,Ey,Ez]=fieldE(x,y,z,t)
% cartesian components of electric field
Ex = 0;
Ey = 0;
Ez = 3.00E+06;
```

and

```
function [Bx,By,Bz]=fieldB(x,y,z,t)
% cartesian components of magnetic field
Bx = 0;
By = 0;
Bz = 0.05;
```

The electron is injected in the region where the electromagnetic field is applied from a point M_i with an initial speed vector $\mathbf{v}_i = v_i\mathbf{e}_x$ perpendicular to **E** and **B** and a velocity $v_i = 2c/3$. The coordinates of M_i are chosen in such a way that the trajectory rolls up along the Oz axis: $x_i = 0, y_i = \rho_i$ and $z_i = 0$, for example, where $\rho_i = \gamma_i mv_i/qB$ is the initial radius of curvature. We therefore have the following initial conditions:

```
>> Vi = 2*c/3;
>> Pxi = gamma(Vi)*m*Vi;
>> Pyi = 0;
>> Pzi = 0;
>> Xi = 0;
>> Yi = Pxi/(q*0.05);
>> Zi = 0;
```

After point M_i, the electron is under the influence of **E** and **B**: its trajectory is the solution of the ODE described in function odeEB with the previous initial conditions. The complete path returned by the ode45 solver is represented on Figure 5:

```
>> figure(5);
>> plot3(x,y,z,'r-');
```

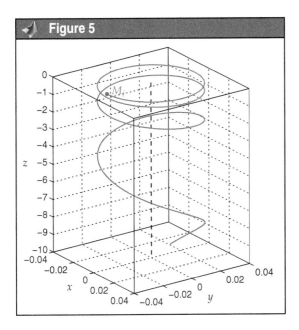

Figure 5. Trajectory of a relativistic electron in an electromagnetic field when **E** and **B** are collinear: $E = E\,e_z$, $B = B\,e_z$ and $v_i = v_i e_x$ with $v_i = 2c/3$.

The trajectory is that of a circular helix with a variable step which rolls anticlockwise (from Ox to Oy) along the Oz axis (in the opposite direction of the **E** because here $q < 0$).

According to the LORENTZ force law (8), a charged particle can gain (or lose) energy from an electric field **E**, but not from a magnetic field **B**. Indeed, by definition the magnetic force $q\,\mathbf{v} \times \mathbf{B}$ is always perpendicular to the particle's direction of motion and therefore does not work on the particle. Consequently, as expected from the theory of relativity, the students can easily observed on Figure 6 that the velocity of the particle $v = (v_x^2 + v_y^2 + v_z^2)^{1/2}$ along the trajectory increases rapidly (under the only action of the electric field **E**) from $v_i = 2c/3$ up to the very limit c:

```
>> figure(6);
>> plot(t/1E-09,sqrt(Vx.^2+Vy.^2+Vz.^2)/c,'r-');
```

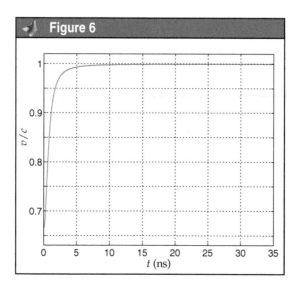

Figure 6. Relative velocity v/c of a relativistic electron along the trajectory shown in Figure 5.

4.2.2. **E** and **B** perpendicular

Now **E** and **B** are perpendicular to each other, $\mathbf{E} = E\,\mathbf{e}_x$ and $\mathbf{B} = B\,\mathbf{e}_y$, and uniform with intensities E and B set to $3 \cdot 10^6$ V/m and 0.02 T, respectively. The functions `fieldE` and `fieldB` are modified accordingly by the students:

```
function [Ex,Ey,Ez]=fieldE(x,y,z,t)
% cartesian components of electric field
Ex = 3.00E+06;
Ey = 0;
Ez = 0;
```

and

```
function [Bx,By,Bz]=fieldB(x,y,z,t)
% cartesian components of magnetic field
```

```
Bx = 0;
By = 0.02;
Bz = 0;
```

The electron is injected in the region where the electromagnetic field is applied from a point M_i with a initial speed vector $\mathbf{v}_i = v_i\mathbf{e}_z$ perpendicular to both $\mathbf{E}$ and $\mathbf{B}$ and a velocity $v_i = 2c/3$. The complete path returned by the ode45 solver is represented on Figure 7. The trajectory is now confined to a plan perpendicular to $\mathbf{B}$ and containing both $\mathbf{E}$ and the speed vector $\mathbf{v}$. More exactly it is a sinusoidal curve with amplitude and period depending on $\mathbf{v}_i$, $\mathbf{E}$ and $\mathbf{B}$. Indeed, only the magnetic force can periodically return the particle since $q\,\mathbf{v} \times \mathbf{B}$ operates in the $0xz$ plan sometimes in a direction, sometimes in the other one, depending on the direction of $\mathbf{v}$. On the other hand, the electric force $q\,\mathbf{E}$ also operates in this plan but always in the same direction, namely $-\mathbf{e}_x$ because here $q < 0$.

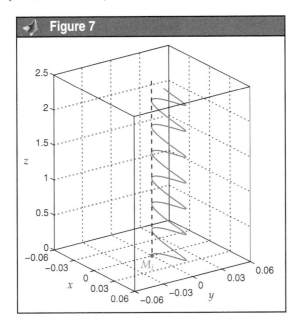

Figure 7. Trajectory of a relativistic electron in an electromagnetic field when $\mathbf{E}$ and $\mathbf{B}$ are perpendicular: $\mathbf{E} = E\,\mathbf{e}_x$, $\mathbf{B} = B\,\mathbf{e}_y$ and $\mathbf{v}_i = v_i\mathbf{e}_z$ with here $v_i = 2c/3$.

An interesting and convenient aspect of conducting numerical simulations with the aid of the computer in a classroom with MATLAB is the capability to re-run the code with different initial settings and to obtain the new trajectory almost immediately. As observed by the students in such a situation, as soon as the value of v_i becomes closer to the ratio E/B, the amplitude of the oscillations decreases as illustrated in Figure 8. When $v_i = E/B$, the actions of the electric and magnetic forces offset each other so that the trajectory reduces to a straight line. Such

Figure 8

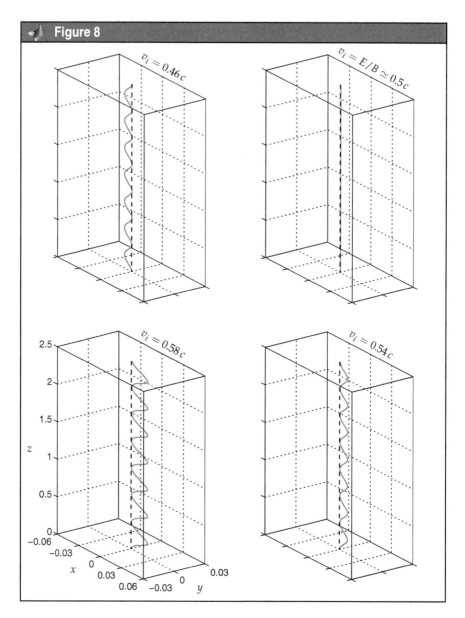

Figure 8. Same as Figure 7 for various initial velocities v_i: when $v_i = E/B$, the trajectory of the electron identifies to that of a straight line.

an amazing situation is encountered in a WIEN filter [12] which is a device used for filtering charged particles with a given velocity (or energy), for example in electron microscopes or in spectrometers.

4.3. Applications in time/space varying fields

In the previous applications, the students dealt with uniform electromagnetic fields. Since the time and space coordinates are given to the functions `fieldE` and `fieldB`, some time and/or space variations in the intensity E and B of the electric and magnetic fields can be easily introduced. This is exactly what is done by the students in the classroom.

Here, the particle is under the lonely action of a static but non-uniform magnetic field **B**, the components of which are:

$$
\begin{cases}
B_x = -B_0 \dfrac{xz}{z_0^2} \\[2mm]
B_y = -B_0 \dfrac{yz}{z_0^2} \\[2mm]
B_z = B_0\left(1 + \dfrac{z^2}{z_0^2}\right)
\end{cases}
\tag{12}
$$

where B_0 and z_0 are taken equal to 0.05 T and 1 m, respectively. The functions `fieldE` and `fieldB` are modified accordingly by the students to reflect this new experimental setup.

The initial conditions of the problem are now the following ones. The electron is injected in the region where the magnetic field is applied from a point M_i with an initial speed vector $\mathbf{v}_i = v_i(\sin\alpha_i \mathbf{e}_x + \cos\alpha_i \mathbf{e}_z)$ with a velocity $v_i = 2c/3$ and $\alpha_i = 20°$, for example. The coordinates of M_i are chosen in such a way that the trajectory rolls along the Oz axis. The complete path returned by the `ode45` solver is shown in Figure 9. The trajectory reminds that of a circular helix with a fixed step but with a variable radius of curvature ρ which raises its maximum for $z = 0$ where B_z raises its minimum and where $B_x = B_y = 0$.

Shown in Figure 10 are the variations of the velocity of the particle $v = (v_x^2 + v_y^2 + v_z^2)^{1/2}$ along the trajectory as well as those of the axial and radial components $|v_z|$ and $v_\rho = (v_x^2 + v_y^2)^{1/2}$ of the speed vector **v**:

```
>> figure(10);  hold('on');
>> plot(t/1E-09,abs(Vz)/c,'b-');
>> plot(t/1E-09,sqrt(Vx.^2+Vy.^2)/c,'g-');
>> plot(t/1E-09,sqrt(Vx.^2+Vy.^2+Vz.^2)/c,'r-');
```

Contrary to what is observed in Figure 6 where the particule is moving under the simultaneous action of an electric field **E** and a magnetic one **B**, here the velocity v of the particle is constant and equal to v_i since it is under the lonely action of a (non-uniform) magnetic field **B** which cannot give (or take) energy to (or from) the particle because it does not work.

Coming back to the trajectory observed in Figure 9 in the light of Figure 10, as soon as B_z grows from $z = 0$, the particle draws circles around the Oz axis which become continually

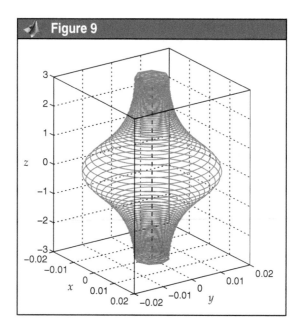

Figure 9. Trajectory of a relativistic electron in the non-uniform magnetic field described in (12).

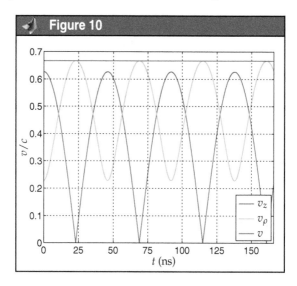

Figure 10. Relative velocity v/c of a relativistic electron along the trajectory shown in Figure 9.

smaller and closer. At the same time, the axial contribution to the kinetic energy is converted into a rotational one up to v_z is cancelled out and v_ρ reach its maximum (v remaining constant and equal to v_i). Then, the particle turns and goes back, drawing again circles in the opposite direction which become larger and more distant up to $z = 0$. The particle has been reflected by the magnetic field **B**. Such an experimental setup is called a magnetic mirror [1]. It is encountered, for example, in a magnetic bottle which is the superposition of two magnetic mirrors used together for confinement purpose.

5. Conclusion

This contribution has described MATLAB codes for solving ordinary differential equations that cannot be solved without the aid of the computer in the field of non-linear optics as well as in relativistic electrodynamics. Since these two domains of modern physics are associated to non intuitive theories, concrete illustrations are welcomed to gain the attention and the interest of the students. The code is fast, accurate and easy to use. It has to be fed with few functions supplied by the students for switching from one study to another, the initial conditions of the problem being changed accordingly. Since the results are obtained almost in real time, these initial settings can be changed at will so that an interactive study is often conceivable with the computers in a classroom. Numerical examples have demonstrated the capabilities of these codes for illustrating in teaching conditions some amazing effects of modern physics that cannot be brought to the attention of students without the aid of the computer, or at an expensive cost. In a classroom setting, the time to be allocated between the underground physics, the modeling issues and the freewheel experimentation is of course left to the teacher and it may vary from one student to another.

Author details

Eric Anterrieu
National de la Recherche Scientifique & Université de Toulouse, France

6. References

[1] Allen R.J. (1962). A demonstration of the magnetic mirror effect, *American Journal of Physics*, Vol. 30, No. 12, pages 867-869, 1962.

[2] Anterrieu E. & Pérez J.-P. (2011). How to make attractive the teaching of relativistic electrodynamics?, *Proceedings of IEEE International Conference on Computer as a Tool*, pages 1-4, Lisbon (Portugal), 27-29 April 2011.

[3] Anterrieu E. & Pérez J.-P. (2010). Illustrating amazing effects of optics with the computer, *Proceedings of IEEE Engineering Education Conference*, pages 180-185, Madrid (Spain), 14-16 April 2010.

[4] Born M. & Wolf E. (1999). *Principles of optics*, 7th edition, Cambridge University Press, Cambridge.

[5] Boyer T.H. (2004). Unfamiliar trajectories for a relativistic particle in a Kepler or Coulomb potential, *American Journal of Physics*, Vol. 72, No. 8, pages 992-997, 2004.

[6] Dormand J.R. & Prince P.J. (1980). A family of embedded Runge-Kutta formulae, *Journal of Computational and Applied Mathematics*, Vol. 6, No. 1, pages 19-26, 1980.

[7] Feynman R.P. (2005). *The Feynman lectures on physics: the definitive and extended edition*, 2nd edition, Addison Wesley, Boston.

[8] Hoefer W.J.R. (1973). On teaching relativity to undergraduate electrical engineers, *IEEE Transactions on Education*, Vol. 16, No. 3, pages 152-156, 1973.

[9] Luneburg R.K. (1964). *Mathematical theory of optics*, 1st edition, University of California Press, Berkeley.

[10] Petouris A., Humphries J., Russell P., Vourdas A. & Jones G.R (1994). Computer aided design for teaching modern optics to electronic engineering undergraduates, *IEE Proceedings Science, Measurement & Technology*, Vol. 141, No. 3, pages 171-176, 1994.

[11] Sader U. & Jodl H.J. (1987). Computer-aided physics-particles in electromagnetic fields, *European Journal of Physics*, Vol. 8, No. 2, pages 88-92, 1987.

[12] Wien W. (1898). Untersuchungen über die electrische entladung in verdünnten gasen, *Annalen der Physik*, Vol. 301, No. 6, pages 440-452, 1898.

Chapter 9

Using a Low Complexity Numeric Routine for Solving Electromagnetic Transient Simulations

Rafael Cuerda Monzani, Afonso José do Prado, Sérgio Kurokawa,
Luiz Fernando Bovolato and José Pissolato Filho

Additional information is available at the end of the chapter

1. Introduction

Different methods can be applied to accomplish the analysis of transmission lines. Many mathematical tools can be used, the main tools used are: circuits analysis with the use of Laplace or Fourier Transform, State Variables and Differential Equations. These tools can be included in a numeric routine in order to obtain voltage and current values in simulation of electromagnetic transients, at any point of the circuit.

The EMTP (ElectroMagnetic Transient Program) [1] is the main kind of this software. The prototype was developed in 60's by professionals of power system area led by Dr. Hermann Dommel (University of British Columbia, in Vancouver, B.C., Canada), and Dr. Scott Meyer (Bonneville Power Administration in Portland, Oregon, U.S.A.). Currently, EMTP is the basis of electromagnetic transients simulations in power systems.

With EMTP type programs, the following analysis can be done: simulation of switching and lightning surges, transient and temporary overvoltage, electrical machines, resonance phenomena, harmonics, power quality and power electronics applications. The most known programs of EMTP type are:

- MicroTran Power Systems Analysis of the University of British Columbia, Vancouver, Canada, founded in 1987 by: Hermann W. Dommel, Jose R. Marti (University of British Columbia), and Luis Marti (University of Western Ontario, Hydro One Networks Inc.).
- PSCAD®, also known as PSCAD®/EMTDC™ of Manitoba HVDC Research Centre. Commercially available since 1993, PSCAD® is the result of continuous research and development since 1988.
- ATP has been continuously developed through international contributions by Drs. W. Scott Meyer and Tsu-huei Liu, the co-Chairmen of the Canadian/American EMTP User

Group. The birth of ATP dates to early in 1984. For the free software, however there are some rules for using it.

This kind of program, in general, doesn't present an easy interface where data can be included [5]. Thus, many times, undergraduate students may not be interested in initiateing works in this area because the transmission lines studies involve complex models and numeric routines which are truly complex if earth effect and line parameters are considered to be frequently dependent ones.

The objective of this chapter is to introduce concepts about power systems, more especifically, in transmission lines, considering a simplified model of monophasic line in order to analyze electromagnetic transients. [2]-[6].

Considering this purpose, a transmission line can be represented as a monophasic circuit and modeled by circuits (Fig. 1). State variables are used to represent this model. The obtained linear system can be solved by using trapezoidal integration techniques.

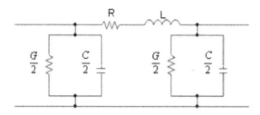

Figure 1. π circuit

Based on these conditions, a simplified numeric routine for a first contact of undergraduate students with the study of travelling waves was obtained. This numeric routine can led to a satisfactory precision and accuracy for the simulation of electromagnetic transients for a monophasic line transmission representation. The numeric routine was developed with the use of MatLab™.

2. Mathematical model

In order to equate the linear system Kirchhoff's Laws should be used. Nodal analysis is used to calculate the algebraic sum of the currents. Given that the current in the capacitor is defined as the time derivative of the voltage multiplied by the capacitance factor, the first state equation is obtained. Mesh analysis is used to calculate the algebraic sum of the voltages, the voltage across the inductor is defined as the time derivative of the current multiplied by the inductance factor, the second state equation is obtained.

A linear system can be described algebraically by using state equations variables as it follows:

$$\dot{x} = Ax + Bu \tag{1}$$

where: x – vector of state variables;
u – vector of linear system entries;
A and B – matrices which feed the system.

The solution of this system can be obtained numerically by trapezoidal rule.

$$x[k+1] - x[k] = \frac{T}{2}(Ax[k+1] + Bu[k+1] + Ax[k] + Bu[k]) \tag{2}$$

On the other hand, to solve the linear system of equations of state variables above, an interactive method can be used, where T is the integration step applied for the system solution. For time domain simulations, the integration step is a time step.

Rearranging equation (2), one can obtain:

$$x[k+1] = x[k] + \frac{T}{2}(Ax[k+1] + Bu[k+1] + Ax[k] + Bu[k]) \tag{3}$$

Solving this equation by using numeric methods, the equation can be rewritten as:

$$\left[I - \frac{T}{2}A\right]x[k+1] = \left[I + \frac{T}{2}A\right]x[k] + \frac{T}{2}B[u[k] + u[k+1]] \tag{4}$$

Verifying the equation (4), there are some constant terms, thus the equation can be simplified to:

$$A'x[k+1] = A''x[k] + B'[u[k] + u[k+1]] \tag{5}$$

A', A'' e B' are constant matrices and can be described by the following equations:

$$A' = \left[I - \frac{T}{2}A\right]$$

$$A'' = A' \cdot \left[I + \frac{T}{2}A\right] \tag{6}$$

$$B' = A' \cdot \frac{T}{2}B$$

In these equations, I is eye matrix of order($2nx2n$), n is the number of π circuits. A a matrix is based on a cascade of π circuits. B is a matrix that inserts the entry values of the system. If the entrance signal is a voltage source, the inductor will be the component introduced in B matrix for the correspondent π circuit. If the entrance signal is a current source, the element will be a capacitor.

The line transmission model for analysis without frequency influence over longitudinal parameters is based on a cascade of π circuits, which is constituted of a branch of resistor and inductor in series with a branch of capacitor and conductor in parallel. The precision of system is higher as the amount of π circuits increase.

For the transmission line represented in Fig. 2, the A matrix is described in Eq. 7. In this case, the A matrix has a special format; it's a sparse matrix, with elements non null in the three diagonals as seen below.

$$A = \begin{bmatrix} -\dfrac{G}{C} & -\dfrac{2}{C} & 0 & \cdots & \cdots & 0 \\ \dfrac{1}{L} & -\dfrac{R}{L} & -\dfrac{1}{C} & 0 & \ddots & \vdots \\ 0 & \dfrac{1}{C} & -\dfrac{G}{C} & -\dfrac{1}{L} & 0 & \vdots \\ \vdots & 0 & \ddots & \ddots & \ddots & 0 \\ \vdots & \ddots & 0 & \dfrac{1}{L} & -\dfrac{R}{L} & -\dfrac{1}{C} \\ 0 & \cdots & \cdots & 0 & \dfrac{2}{C} & -\dfrac{G}{C} \end{bmatrix} \qquad (7)$$

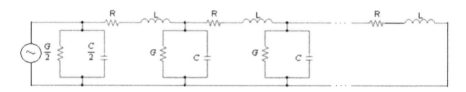

Figure 2. Transmission Line Model

In the main diagonal of the A matrix, there are the negative values of the parameters alternating between $-G/C$ and $-R/L$. In the upper diagonal, the element values alternate between $-1/C$ and $-1/L$. Considering the lower diagonal the element values are positive and similar to the upper diagonal.

The A matrix is a matrix of order $(2n \times 2n)$, if the transmission line is considered opened for sending and receiving in the terminal of the line.

On the other hand, the modeling of frequency influence over longitudinal parameters can be done when introduced branches in parallel of resistor and inductor associated in series with the main branch in series of an inductor and a resistor, in each π circuit [5]. The Fig. 3 shows this description.

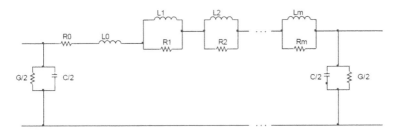

Figure 3. π circuit considering frequency dependency

The parameters R_0, L_0 refers to resistance and inductance values in series, respectively. The parameters R_m, L_m, with m being the number of branches in series, refers to value of resistance inductance of each one of the m branches in series of each π circuit, respectively. The parameters C and G, refer to the value of capacitance and conductance, respectively.

From analysis of Kirchhoff's Laws of the current in the inductor and the voltage in the capacitor, the linear system of state variables is obtained.

$$\frac{d\,i_{10}}{dt} = \frac{i_{10}}{L_0}\left(-\sum_{j=1}^{m} R_j\right) + \frac{1}{L_0}\left(\sum_{j=1}^{m} R_j i_{1j}\right) + \frac{1}{L_0}u(t) - \frac{1}{L_0}v_1(t)$$

$$\frac{di_{11}}{dt} = \frac{R_1}{L_1}i_{10} - \frac{R_1}{L_1}i_{11}$$

$$\frac{di_{12}}{dt} = \frac{R_2}{L_2}i_{10} - \frac{R_2}{L_2}i_{12} \qquad (8)$$

$$\frac{di_{1m}}{dt} = \frac{R_m}{L_m}i_{10} - \frac{R_m}{L_m}i_{1m}$$

$$\frac{dv_1(t)}{dt} = \frac{2}{C}i_{10} - \frac{G}{C}v_1(t)$$

n is the number of π circuit and m is the number of series branch. In order to represent these equations, the A matrix is square of order $(m + 2)$ and it's described by:

$$A = \begin{bmatrix} [A_{11}] & [A_{12}] & \cdots & [A_{1n}] \\ [A_{21}] & [A_{22}] & \cdots & [A_{2n}] \\ \vdots & \vdots & \ddots & \vdots \\ [A_{n1}] & [A_{n2}] & \cdots & [A_{nn}] \end{bmatrix} \qquad (9)$$

where, each A_{kk} matrix is represented by:

$$
A' = \begin{bmatrix}
-\dfrac{\sum_{j=0}^{j=m} R_j}{L_0} & \dfrac{R_1}{L_0} & \dfrac{R_2}{L_0} & \cdots & \dfrac{R_m}{L_0} & -\dfrac{1}{L_0} \\[2ex]
\dfrac{R_1}{L_1} & -\dfrac{R_1}{L_1} & 0 & \cdots & 0 & 0 \\[2ex]
\dfrac{R_2}{L_2} & 0 & -\dfrac{R_2}{L_2} & \cdots & 0 & 0 \\[2ex]
\vdots & \vdots & \vdots & \ddots & 0 & 0 \\[2ex]
\dfrac{R_m}{L_m} & 0 & 0 & \cdots & -\dfrac{R_m}{L_m} & 0 \\[2ex]
\dfrac{2}{C} & 0 & 0 & \cdots & 0 & -\dfrac{G}{C}
\end{bmatrix} \tag{10}
$$

For n π circuits, the A matrix is formed in the diagonal line by A' matrices, in the upper diagonal these matrices have just one element not null which is in the first column and in the last row and it's described by $-1/C$.

The lower matrices contain just one non null element which is in the last column in first line and it's described by $1/L_0$. Both matrices, upper and lower are $(m+2)$ order one. The B vector is an $n(m+2)$ order with the first element non null described by $1/L_0$. A generic vector x is shown below:

$$
x^T = [x_1 \cdots x_n] \tag{11}
$$

Each element of x has the following structure:

$$
x_k^T = [i_{k0} \, i_{k1} \cdots i_{km} \, v_{kn}] \tag{12}
$$

This state equation describes the transmission line represented by n π circuits, by using numeric methods.

3. Routine development

The routine used for introducing the proposed model shown in previous items is implemented in MatLab™ software. For this, only basic notions of programming are necessary to make the development of this routine easy for undergraduate students. Initially, the source values, the number of π circuits, the line length and the line parameters per unit length in the numeric routine are introduced. By using the line parameters per unit length, the parameter values for each π circuit it is determined by using the following definitions:

$$
R = \frac{R' \cdot d}{n} \tag{13}
$$

$$L = \frac{L' \cdot d}{n}$$

$$C = \frac{C' \cdot d}{n}$$

$$G = \frac{G' \cdot d}{n}$$

Where R′, L′, C′, G′ are the line parameters per unit length, d is the length of the line and n is the number of π circuits. Fig. 4 shows a window program that applies the proposed numeric routine.

In the case of frequency influence the user may choose the number of branches and also specify the value for each resistor and inductor. These values can be calculated by using any routine that considers the frequency influence in transmission line parameters. After this step, the simulation time (t), the time step (T) and the sources that are connected at the line are defined. Then, the equation that describes each source should be introduced in the numeric routine by using a specific MatLab™ tool. Simulations of electromagnetic transient of many different input signals can be obtained just by inserting their functions in MatLab™ program routine as seen in Fig. 4. After specifying all the input values, the routine generates the A and B matrices and also the input vector U in discrete time. Then, the equation (6) terms are calculated numerically by using the chosen time step and the simulation time. The chosen current and voltage output results are uploaded in a vector file. Finally, a graph is plotted with the results of the simulation.

Figure 4. MatLab window.

In order of results, both routines, with and without frequency influence, will be shown and discussed step by step. The objective of these routines is to show how to use MatLab™ by using simple functions or commands to present the wave propagation of current or voltage to undergraduate students. The functions and commands used into routine will be explained; also the loops and conditions used into it will also be explained below the routine.

The first routine doesn't consider the frequency influence.

MatLab code

```
%Clear variables and command window
clear;
clc;
%Close windows
Close all;
%Definitions of Entrance Elements
disp('Transmission Line Analyze')
P = input ('Enter the Number of Pi Circuits = ');
D = input ('Enter the line length (km) = ');
R = input ('Enter the value of distributed resistance (ohm/km) = ');
L = input ('Enter the value of distributed inductance (H/km) = ');
C = input ('Enter the value of distributed capacitance (F/km) = ');
G = input ('Enter the value of distributed conductance (S/km) = ');
T = input ('Set time step [s]: ');
t = input ('Enter the simulation total time [s]: ');
%Distributed Elements
R=R*D/P;
L=L*D/P;
G=G*D/P;
C=C*D/P;
%e = Pi circuits which will receive entries
cont=1;
while (i ~= 0)
    clc;
    disp('Indicate the input kind:');
    disp('1 - Voltage');
    disp('2 - Current');
    disp('0 - Exit');
    i = input('');
    if (i==1)
        e(cont)= input ('\n Indicate the pi circuit = ');
        fun = input('\n Enter the function:');
        fun = inline(fun);
```

```
      u(2*e(cont)-1,1) = fun;
   end
  if (i==2)
     e(cont)= input ('\n Indicate the pi circuit= ');
     fun = input('\n Enter the function:');
     fun = inline(fun);
     u(2*e(cont),1) = fun;
   end
   cont=cont+1;
end
%A matrix
for j=1:(2*P-1)
  h = rem(j,2);
  if h==1
     A(j,j)= -(R/L);
     A(j,j+1)= -(1/L);
     A(j+1,j)= 1/C;
   else
     A(j,j)= -(G/C);
     A(j,j+1)= -(1/C);
     A(j+1,j)= 1/L;
   end
end
%A (2*P,2*P)
A(2*P,2*P)=-(G/C);
%B matrix
B(2*P,1)=0;
for j=1:numel(u)
  h = rem(j,2);
  if h==1
     B(j,j)=1/L;
   else
     B(j,j)=1/C;
   end
end
%Constant terms
A1=inv(eye(2*P)-(T/2)*A);
A2=(eye(2*P)+(T/2)*A);
A2=A1*A2;
B1=(T/2)*B;
B2=A1*B1;
x(2*P,1)=0;
%Iterations to solve the linear system
```

```
j=1;
for q= 0: T: t
  u1=feval(u,q);
  u2=feval(u,q+T);
  x=A2*x+B2*(u1+u2);
  y(j,1)=q;
  y(j,2)=x(2*P,1);
  y(j,3)=x(2*P-1,1);
  j=j+1;
end
plot(y(:,1),y(:,2),'b')
title('Voltage in the end of transmission line');
ylabel('Voltage [kV]');
xlabel('Time [s]');
pause
plot(y(:,1),y(:,3),'r')
title('Current in the end of transmission line');
ylabel('Current [A]');
xlabel('Time [s]');
```

In the beginning of the routine some commands are used like:

- **clear all:** cleans all the variables existents in MatLab™.
- **clc:** cleans the command window.
- **close all:** closes all the graphics opened.

The command **disp** shows a message in the command window for users to know what happens in the routine, that way no one thinks the routine is not working, because sometimes, it does take a lot of time to finish all the procedures, thus, a message is important to enlighten that.

The command **input** asks the user to insert a value for a variable, instead of defining a constant value inside the routine, this command makes it more interactive, so the user can put any value wanted and analyze the answer for different values inserted.

The loop **while** is used with the purpose to insert voltage or current sources as many as the user wants. The user will specify if the source is of voltage (1) or current (2), after specifying the kind of source, it shall specify the π circuit that will receive the source, and finally specify the function that represents the source. A loop while is used, to mount a vector of entries. The user will get out of the loop inserting the value (0). The function of entry (voltage or current) must be inserted as a string, as explained above. At least one source for the routine works correctly is necessary, as an example, the user can insert a step function in the first circuit. Entering the following:

Indicate the input kind:

      1 – Voltage
      2 - Current
      0 - Exit
      1
      Indicate the pi circuit = **1**
            Enter the function: **'1'**

For mounting the A matrix a loop **for** is used because the number of interactions is known, inside the loop the command **if** is used to construct the mainly, upper and lower diagonals as shown in Eq. 7. The same is done in the B matrix.

Finally, a loop for is used to solve the trapezoidal rule considering the time step and the total time elapsed. The variable y retains in the first column the value of steps of time, the second column retains the value of voltage, and the third column retains the value of current in the terminal of the line transmission.

Fig. 4 shows the previous version of the routine, in that routine the command **syms** was used. This command creates a symbol as a variable to solve this. The command **subs** must be used, in order to substitute the variable in the function with the value requested. In this case, the function entry of current or voltage source didn't need to be inserted as a string, but the user always had to insert the function by using the variable specified, what was not always done. The second purpose used the command **inline** which gets a string and converts it into a function; with this command the user can use any variable, to solve this in the trapezoidal rule. It's used the command **feval**, which gets the function and substitutes the values with the time step.

The second routine considers the frequency influence. Almost all the steps used in this routine were the same as shown in the first one. Only the different steps done here will be described.

MatLab code

```
%Clear variables and command window
clear all;
clc;
%Close all graphic windows
close all;
disp('Transmission Line Analysis');
sprintf('\n');
P = input ('Enter the Number of Pi Circuits = ');
D = input ('Enter the line length (km) = ');
%It's defined R(1) and L(1) which represents R0 and L0 respectively,
%values of R1, L1, ... Rm, Lm, will be with a plus number.
R(1) = input ('Enter the value of distributed resistance (ohm/km) = ');
```

```
L(1) = input ('Enter the value of distributed inductance (H/km) = ');
C = input ('Enter the value of distributed capacitance (F/km) = ');
G = input ('Enter the value of distributed conductance (S/km) = ');
m = input ('Enter the number of coupling circuits = ');
for i=2:m+1
    R(i) = input (['Enter the value of resistance of the branch ' int2str(i-1) ' [ohm/km] = ']);
    %Distributed Resistance
    R(i) = R(i)*D/P;
    L(i) = input (['Enter the value of inductance of the branch ' int2str(i-1) ' [H/km] = ']);
    %Distributed Inductance
    L(i) = L(i)*D/P;
end
%Time step and total time
T = input ('Set time step [s]: ');
t = input ('Enter the simulation total time [s]: ');
%Distributed Elements
R(1)=R(1)*D/P;
L(1)=L(1)*D/P;
G=G*D/P;
C=C*D/P;
%A matrix
A=zeros(size(P*(m+2)));
c=0;
for i=1:m+1
    A(i,i)=-R(i)/L(i);
    A(1,i)=R(i)/L(1);
    A(i,1)=-A(i,i);
end
%First term as positive
A(1,1) = -A(1,1);
for i=1:m+1
    %c variable will get the values to put in A(1,1), uses recall
    c=A(1,i)+c;
end
A(1,1)=-c;
%Terminal elements of matrix
A(1,m+2)=-1/L(1);
A(m+2,1)=1/C;
A(m+2,m+2)=-G/C;
```

```
%Mainly matrix
AP=A;
%Putting the matrix in all the positions
for j=1:(P-1)
    AP(j*(m+2)+1:(j+1)*(m+2),j*(m+2)+1:(j+1)*(m+2))=A;
end
%Lower matrix
AI(1,m+2)=1/L(1);
AI(m+2,m+2)=0;
%Upper matrix
AS(m+2,1)=-1/C;
AS(m+2,m+2)=0;
%Putting the lower and upper matrices in their places
for j=1:(P-1)
    AP(j*(m+2),j*(m+2)+1)=-1/C;
    AP(j*(m+2)+1,j*(m+2))=1/L(1);
end
%Element of the first matrix
A(m+2,1)=2/C;
%Element of last matrix
A(P*(m+2),1)=2/C;
%e = Pi circuits which will receive entries
%cont sets which pi circuit will receive the entry
cont=1;
while (i ~= 0)
    clc;
    disp('Indicate the input kind:');
    disp('1 - Voltage');
    disp('2 - Current');
    disp('0 - Exit');
    i = input('');
    if (i==1)
        e(cont)= input ('\n Indicate the pi circuit = ');
        fun = input('\n Enter the function:');
        fun = inline(fun);
        u(e(cont)*(m+2)-(m+1),1) = fun;
    end
    if (i==2)
        e(cont)= input ('\n Indicate the pi circuit = ');
```

```
    fun = input('\n Enter the function:');
    fun = inline(fun);
    u(e(cont)*(m+2),1) = fun;
  end
  cont=cont+1;
end
%Clear the command window
clc;
disp('PROCESSING...');
%B matrix
B(P*(m+2),1)=0;
for j=1:m+2:numel(u)
  h = rem(j,2);
  if h==1
    B(j,j)=1/L(1);
  else
    B(j,j)=1/C;
  end
end
A1=inv(eye(P*(m+2))-(T/2)*AP);
A2=(eye(P*(m+2))+(T/2)*AP);
A2=A1*A2;
B1=(T/2)*B;
B2=A1*B1;
%x matrix
x(P*(m+2),1)=0;
j=1;
for q = 0: T: t
  u1=feval(u,q);
  u2=feval(u,q+T);
  x=A2*x+B2*(u1+u2);
  y(j,1)=q;
  y(j,2)=x(P*(m+2),1);
  y(j,4)=x(P*(m+2)/2,1); %middle of line
  y(j,3)=x(P*(m+2)-(m+1),1);
  y(j,5)=x((P*(m+2)/2)-(m+1),1); %middle of line
  if (q==30*T)
    for kk = 1:P
      z(kk,1)=kk*D/P;
```

```
      z(kk,2)=x(kk*(m+2),1);
   end
end
if (q==60*T)
   for kk = 1:P
      z(kk,3)=x(kk*(m+2),1);
   end
end
if (q==90*T)
   for kk = 1:P
      z(kk,4)=x(kk*(m+2),1);
   end
end
if (q==120*T)
   for kk = 1:P
      z(kk,5)=x(kk*(m+2),1);
   end
end
if (q==150*T)
   for kk = 1:P
      z(kk,6)=x(kk*(m+2),1);
   end
end
if (q==180*T)
   for kk = 1:P
      z(kk,7)=x(kk*(m+2),1);
   end
end
if (q==210*T)
   for kk = 1:P
      z(kk,8)=x(kk*(m+2),1);
   end
end
if (q==240*T)
   for kk = 1:P
      z(kk,9)=x(kk*(m+2),1);
   end
end
if (q==260*T)
```

```
   for kk = 1:P
      z(kk,10)=x(kk*(m+2),1);
   end
end
if (q==290*T)
   for kk = 1:P
      z(kk,11)=x(kk*(m+2),1);
   end
end
if (q==310*T)
   for kk = 1:P
      z(kk,12)=x(kk*(m+2),1);
   end
end
if (q==330*T)
   for kk = 1:P
      z(kk,13)=x(kk*(m+2),1);
   end
end
if (q==360*T)
   for kk = 1:P
      z(kk,14)=x(kk*(m+2),1);
   end
end
if (q==390*T)
   for kk = 1:P
      z(kk,15)=x(kk*(m+2),1);
   end
end
j=j+1;
end
plot(y(:,1),y(:,2),'b')
title('Voltage in the end of transmission line');
ylabel('Voltage [kV]');
xlabel('Time [s]');
pause
plot(y(:,1),y(:,3),'r')
title('Current in the end of transmission line');
ylabel('Current [A]');
```

```
xlabel('Time [s]');
pause
plot(z(:,1),z(:,2),'b',z(:,1),z(:,5),'r',z(:,1),z(:,11),'g',z(:,1),z(:,15),'k')
title('Voltage in line path');
ylabel('Voltage [kV]');
xlabel('Length (km)');
```

This routine uses the loop **for** in the beginning to obtain all the values series branches. The user specifies the amount of series branches and enters the resistance and inductance values for each branch. In the last loop **for**, a sequence of **if** is used to obtain the wave propagation in different time instants. This is a very important part of the routine, because it shows how the voltage or current waves propagates into the line. This representation shows to undergraduate students that a signal put in the beginning of line will not appear instantaneously in the end of line. It takes a little time, like milliseconds to arrive at the end, because the length of the line is considered, differently from a bipole, the signal put in a terminal is at the other terminal at the same time. Another observation is that, with the EMTP type programs, the user can only analyze a specific point of the circuit and in this case in a time range. The routine shows how the wave propagates into the line for different line points in the time instant.

4. Obtained results

For all simulations the following values were used: the number of π circuits was 100 and the transmission line has 10 kilometers. The resistance value was $0.05\ \Omega/Km$. The inductance value was $1\ mH/Km$. The capacitance values was $11.11\ nF/Km$. The conductance value was $0.556\ \mu S/Km$. The time step was $50\ ns$ and the period of simulation was $600\ \mu s$.

Resistors (Ω)		Inductors (mH)	
R_0	0,026	L_0	2,209
R_1	1,470	L_1	0,74
R_2	2,354	L_2	0,12
R_3	20,149	L_3	0,10
R_4	111,111	L_4	0,05

Table 1. Longitudinal parameters values using the routine considering the frequency influence

A simulation was made for voltage input unitary step signal. It was a step function with a unitary step after $t = 0s$. The result of this simulation can be seen in Fig. 5. the voltage output at the receipting line end is shown. By using the routine without frequency influence, from the results of Fig. 5, it is observed that there is a period time related to the propagation time of the signal through the line. So, it represents a time delay between the input signal and the output signal. After the time delay, there are oscillations associated to wave reflections on the sending and receipting line ends that compose the shown voltage output.

By using the routine with frequency influence at longitudinal parameters, it is obtained Fig. 6. In this figure, it is noticed that are not so many transients as in Fig. 5, because in this case the series branches dampen the signal.

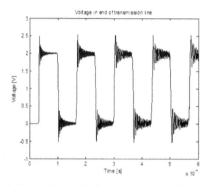

Figure 5. Voltage in the end of transmission line by using routine without frequency influence.

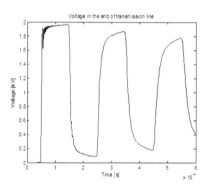

Figure 6. Voltage in the end of transmission line by using routine with frequency influence

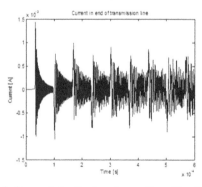

Figure 7. Current in the end of transmission line by using routine without frequency influence.

In Figs. 7 and 8, it's possible to observe the influence of frequency in the current. Without frequency influence the signal is very disturbed. On the other hand, when it is used the routine that considers frequency influence, it is noticed that in the end of the line it should not have any current, supposing an end line opened, but, there are some transients because of the last branch. As in voltage signal, the current signal is damped because of the series branches in circuit. By using the routine of frequency influence, it can also be obtained how the voltage signal goes to the path of line for the time in Fig. 9.

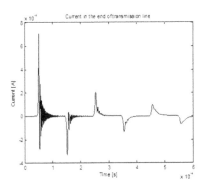

Figure 8. Current in the end of transmission line by using routine with frequency influence.

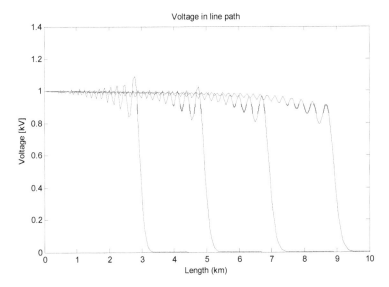

Figure 9. Voltage in line path.

5. Conclusions

By using a mono-phase circuit representation of transmission lines associated to the state variables and the trapezoidal rule, π circuits are applied for electromagnetic transient simulations. The π circuits represent the mono-phase circuit of transmission lines and considering no frequency influence, they are included in a numeric routine through a sparse matrix where only three diagonal lines have non-null elements. Considering the frequency dependent longitudinal line parameters, the parameters are included in a matrix, by using the first line, the first column and the main diagonal of this matrix. This matrix is introduced in another large matrix, rounded by other matrices with one non-null element each. In the upper matrix, the parameter is introduced $-1/C$. In the lower matrix, the parameter is introduced $1/L_0$. The obtained linear system, which is based on state variables, it is solved by using trapezoidal rule integration method. The numeric solution uses the trapezoidal rule method, which solves the numeric integration by the addition of infinitesimal trapeziums areas. This method increases the accuracy of the calculation, comparing with the Euler method for the same time step. The numeric routine is applied to a mathematical matricial program and, because of this, it is possible to simulate the propagation of electromagnetic transients on transmission lines. Using MatLab™ software, it is possible to describe the input signal through mathematical functions that are included as an initial datum of the numeric routine. It is not included in the structure of the routine, but during the routine running. By using the mentioned routine, examples of a unitary step were applied as voltage input signal and some electromagnetic transients generated from these signals are shown in this chapter. The numeric routine permits the inclusion of any function describing the voltage or current source that represents the simulated transient. The included function can be located on any point of the represented transmission line.

The shown numeric routine is simple and because of this, it can be used by undergraduate students for their first contact with electromagnetic transient phenomena, by traveling wave propagation, transmission line analyses. For the first contact with wave propagation simulations for undergraduate students, the proposed routine is an excellent tool. It is simple and its use is easy. So, by using basic concepts of traveling wave, linear systems and computing, it is possible to manipulate the numeric routine, observing the wave propagation characteristics, such as time delays, wave reflection and refraction, numeric oscillations (Gibbs' oscillations), transient oscillations. For undergraduate students, it is possible to compare the results and the modeling of the electromagnetic transients in transmission lines considering or not frequency dependent line parameters. This is possible by accessing the proposed routine numeric code. In courses related to the transmission line area, the manipulation of this code can make the course more interesting for the undergraduate students. These advantages are added to the other ones that are shown in this chapter and related to the application of the MatLab™ software. The use of this software makes the implementation of the mentioned routine extremely easy.

Author details

Rafael Cuerda Monzani, Afonso José do Prado,
Sérgio Kurokawa and Luiz Fernando Bovolato
Department of Electrical Engineering at FEIS/UNESP – The University of São Paulo State,
Brazil

José Pissolato Filho
Department of Electrical Engineering, DSCE/UNICAMP – The State University of Campinas,
Brazil

6. References

[1] Microtran Power System Analysis Corporation, Transients Analysis Program Reference Manual, Vancouver, Canada, 1992.

[2] R. M. Nelms, Steven, R. Newton, G. B. Sheble, L. L. Grigsby. "Simulation of Transmission Line Transients", IEEE.

[3] R. M. Nelms, Steven, R. Newton, G. B. Sheble, L. L. Grigsby. "Using a personal Computer to teach power system Transients", IEEE Transaction on Power System, Vol. 4, No. 3, August 1989.

[4] S. R. Newton, B. B. Reid, G. B. Sheble, R. M. Nelms, L. L. GRIGSBY. "Electromagnetic transient simulator for large-scale spacecraft power systems". IEEE.

[5] H. W. Dommel, EMTP Theory Book, Department of Electrical Engineering, University of British Columbia, Vancouver, 1996.

[6] J. R. Marti, "Accurate modeling of frequency-dependent transmission lines in electromagnetic transients simulations", IEEE Trans. on PAS, vol. 101, pp. 147–155, January 1982.

[7] E. Clarke, Circuit Analysis of AC Power Systems, vol. I, Wiley, New York, 1950.

[8] S. Kurokawa, F. N. R. Yamanaka, A. J. Prado, L. F. Bovolato, J. Pissolato, "Representação de Linhas de Transmissão por meio de variáveis de Estado Levando em Consideração o Efeito da Freqüência Sobre os Parâmetros Longitudinais", SBA. Sociedade Brasileira de Automática, Controle & Automação, v. 18, p. 337-346, 2007.

[9] S. Kurokawa, F. N. R. Yamanaka, A. J. Prado, J. Pissolato, L. F. Bovolato, "Utilização de variáveis de estado no desenvolvimento de modelos de linhas de transmissão: Inclusão do efeito da freqüência nas matrizes de estado", XIX Seminário nacional de produção e transmissão de energia elétrica (XIX SNPTEE), p. 1-8, Rio de Janeiro. 2007.

[10] S. Kurokawa, F. N. R. Yamanaka, A. J. Prado, J. Pissolato, "Representação de linhas de transmissão por meio de variáveis de estado considerando o efeito da freqüência sobre os parâmetros longitudinais", XVI Congresso Brasileiro de Automática, v. 1, p. 268-273, Salvador, 2006.

[11] F. N. R. Yamanaka, S. Kurokawa, A. J. Prado, J. Pissolato, L. F. Bovolato, "Analysis of longitudinal and temporal distribution of electromagnetic waves in transmission lines by using state-variable techniques", Sixty Latin-American Congress: Electricity Generation and Transmission – VI CLAGTEE, Mar Del Plata, 2005.

Chapter 10

The MatLab™ Software Application for Electrical Engineering Simulations and Power System

Leonardo da S. Lessa, Afonso J. Prado, Rodrigo Cleber Silva,
Sérgio Kurokawa, Luiz F. Bovolato and José Pissolato Filho

Additional information is available at the end of the chapter

1. Introduction

Transmission lines are the elements of the electric power system that connect the load to the generation joining the production facilities of energy over large geographic areas. You could say that the transmission of electricity is one of the most important contributions that engineering has offered to the modern civilization.

The distribution of current potential differences and the transfer of energy along a transmission line can be analyzed by various methods, and it is expected that all lead to the same result. In engineering problems, in general, it can not indiscriminately apply a single formula for solving a specific problem, without the full knowledge of the limitations and simplifications accepted in its derivation. It is worth mentioning that this circumstance would lead to its misuse. The so-called mathematical solutions of physical phenomena typically require simplifications and idealizations.

Therefore, there are several models that represent the transmission lines and can be classified as to the nature of their parameters in the model parameters constant and variable parameters the models with frequency.

The parameters in the models in terms of frequency are easy to use, but can not adequately represent the line in the entire range of frequencies at which these phenomena are transient in nature. In most cases, these designs increase the amplitude of the high order harmonics, distorting the waveform peaks and producing exaggerated errors.

For adequate representation of the transmission line should be considered that the longitudinal line parameters are strongly frequency dependent, including the variable parameters in the models with frequency, the sum of the effect of soil, developed by Carson and Pollaczek, with skin effect, whose behavior as a function of frequency can be calculated using formulas derived from the Bessel equations.

Models with variable parameters in terms of frequency are considered more accurate when compared to models that consider the constant parameters. The variation depends upon the frequency. This variation may be represented by series and parallel combination of resistive and inductive elements pure.

As transmission lines are inserted in an electrical system that has many nonlinear elements and, thus, it is difficult to represent them in the frequency domain, there is a preference for line models that are developed directly in the time domain.

Another factor, that makes the model lines developed directly in the time domain are most commonly used, is that the majority of programs that perform simulations electromagnetic transients in electrical systems require that the system components are represented in time domain.

Probably, the first model to represent the transmission line directly in the time domain is designed for H. W. Dommel, which was based on the method of the characteristics or Bergeron's method. The model has combined the method of characteristics with the trapezoidal method numerical integration, resulting in an algorithm able to simulate transient electromagnetic networks whose parameters are distributed or discrete. This algorithm has undergone successive developments and is now known as the Electromagnetic Transients Program, or EMTP simply.

In situations where one wants to simulate the propagation of electromagnetic waves resulting from operations carried out maneuvers and switching the transmission lines, it can be represented the same as a cascade of π circuits.

In this model, each segment consists of a combination of series and parallel circuits composed by resistors and inductors. This results in an equivalent resistance and an inductance that depend on the frequency. It is considered in hese equivalent elements the ground and skin effects.

Due to the fact that EMTP-type programs are not easy to use, several authors suggest describing the currents and voltages in the cascade of π circuits by means of state variables. The state equations are then transformed into differential equations and can be solved using any computer language or mathematical software.

The representation of the line by means of state variables can be used in teaching basic concepts of wave propagation in transmission lines, the analysis of the distribution of currents and voltages along the line, and the simulation of electromagnetic transients in transmission lines with non-linear elements.

Although the technique of state variables is widely used in the representation of transmission lines, it can be seen in recent publications, that it was only used to represent the parameters of which longitudinal rows can be considered constant and independent of frequency.

However, it is recognized today that the use of constant parameters to represent the line in the whole frequency range, present in the signals during the occurrence of disturbances in it, may result in responses in which the high frequency harmonic components have larger amplitudes than the real ones.

Thus, in this chapter, it is intended, using the MatLab™, to enter the effect of frequency on a line represented by π circuits connected in cascade and obtain the currents and voltages on the line from the use of the technique of state variables. The method is applied in a single-phase line, which considers the presence of soil and peel effect.

This line is approximated by a cascade of π circuits which will then be represented by state equations. The state equations, which are the voltages and currents along the line, will then be simulated in MatLab™. The cascade will also be implemented in software such as EMTP, used for simulations of electromagnetic transients in power systems. Then the results obtained with Matlab™ and EMTP are compared, considering the single-phase line.

Besides this mentioned modeling, for MatLab™ software users, the main contribution of this chapter is to demonstrate the application of this program for analyzing and simulating transient phenomena in power systems. It is important for undergraduate students for understanding the basic concepts of wave propagation and transmission lines. On the other hand, specific programs, like EMTP type programs, use a specific numeric method for solving the linear systems through numeric integration. With MatLab™ basic tools, the graduate students can apply different numeric methods for solving the same problem, comparing the results and analyzing the accuracy, precision and computational time related to each method.

2. Trapezoidal integration

It is a brief equation that relates the numerical method for lumped parameters used by the ATP. Is an arbitrary differential equation given by:

$$y(t) = k\frac{dx(t)}{dt} \tag{1}$$

The solution between the instants t_0 and t is obtained by the following:

$$dx(t) = \frac{1}{k}y(t)dt \Rightarrow \int_{x_0}^{x} x(t)dx = \frac{1}{k}\int_{t_0}^{t} y(t)dt \Rightarrow x(t) - x_0 = \frac{1}{k}\int_{t_0}^{t} y(t)dt \tag{2}$$

or finally:

$$x(t) = x_0 + \frac{1}{k}\int_{t_0}^{t} y(t)dt \tag{3}$$

The numerical solution of the equation is obtained at discrete instants of time, given:

$$\int_{x(t-\Delta t)}^{x(t)} x dx = \frac{1}{k} dx(t) = \frac{1}{k}\int_{t-\Delta t}^{t} y(t)dt \Rightarrow x(t) = x(t-\Delta t) + \frac{1}{k}\int_{t-\Delta t}^{t} y(t)dt \tag{4}$$

The solution of equation (2.4) consists of numerical integration of a discrete function y(t) which must be performed in discrete steps size Δt, which solution is the area under the curve, limited by the instants t and t-Δt as shown in Figure 1.

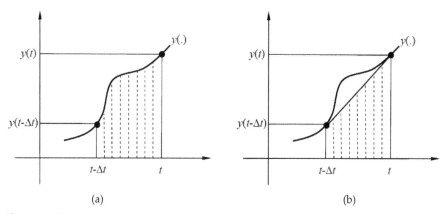

(a)   (b)

Figure 1. (a) function y(t) slight to be integrated; (b) trapezoidal rule integration.

Solving equation (2.5) by the trapezoidal rule integration, which allows a linear variation between y (t-Δt) and y (t) of the integrated, as shown in figure 1 (b), as:

$$x(t) = x(t-\Delta t) + \frac{1}{k}\int_{t+\Delta t}^{t} y(t)dt = x(t-\Delta t) + \frac{1}{k}\frac{y(t) + y(t-\Delta t)}{2}\Delta t \tag{5}$$

or:

$$x(t) = \frac{\Delta t}{2k}y(t) + \left[x(t-\Delta t) + \frac{\Delta t}{2k}y(t-\Delta t)\right] \tag{6}$$

in other words:

$$x(t) = C_{TR}y(t) + h_{TR}\left(t - \Delta t\right) \tag{7}$$

where:

$$\begin{cases} C_{TR} = \dfrac{\Delta t}{2k} \\[2mm] h_{TR}(t - \Delta t) = x(t - \Delta t) + \dfrac{\Delta t}{2k}y(t - \Delta t) \end{cases} \tag{8}$$

It may be noted that the term historical $h_{TR}(t-\Delta t)$ depends on x (t) and y (t) after t seconds, Δt, is already known during the solution.

3. Modeling cascada of π circuits

Discussion will now represent a mathematical model for a transmission line using an electrical circuit. With this model, you can make a study of the behavior of a transmission line for energizing and switching transient simulations. A transmission line, whose parameters can be considered independent of frequency, can be represented in an approximate manner and following a series of restrictions, as a cascade of π circuits.

Each segment of π circuit consists of one resistor and one series inductance in series. Completing the π circuit, there are components in parallel: capacitance and conductance. It is shown in Figure 2.

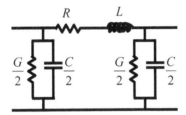

Figure 2. A π circuit.

It's represented a transmission line through this model, connects to n π circuits in cascade. So Figure 3 shows a single-phase transmission line length d represented by n π circuits connected in cascade.

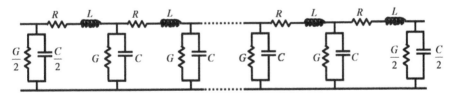

Figure 3. Line represented by a cascade of π circuits.

In Figure 3, the parameters R and L are the resistance and inductance of the longitudinal line, respectively. The parameters G and C are the capacitance and conductance of transverse dispersion, respectively. These parameters are written as:

$$R = R'\frac{d}{n} \tag{9}$$

$$L = L'\frac{d}{n} \tag{10}$$

$$G = G' \frac{d}{n} \tag{11}$$

$$C = C' \frac{d}{n} \tag{12}$$

In the equations (3.1) to (3.4), R 'and L' are the resistance and inductance of the longitudinal row per unit length, respectively while the terms G 'and C' are the capacitance and conductance per unit cross-sectional line in length.

Using this representation of the line, a state model is formulated for the energy system that uses the voltages on the capacitors and the currents through the inductors as state variables. The system that describes the state equations is transformed into a set of differential equations whose solution is given by the use of trapezoidal integration. The state variables are found by solving the set of equations.

Although the technique of state variables is widely used in the representation of transmission lines, it is applied only to depictions of longitudinal lines whose parameters can be considered constant and independent of frequency.

However, it is recognized today that the use of constant parameters to represent the line in the whole frequency range, present in the signals during the occurrence of disturbances in it, may result in responses in which the high frequency harmonic components have larger amplitudes than are actually.

4. Line representation with parameters of frequency dependent

The representation of transmission lines through cascades of π circuits, taking into account the effect of frequency, is usually implemented in EMTP-type programs.

Another drawback of the type EMTP programs is that they limit the amount of π circuit that can be used to represent the line. Thus, depending on the length of the line to be depicted, the quality of results obtained from simulations may be compromised.

To circumvent the difficulties mentioned, it is suggested to describe the cascade of π circuits by means of state equations. However, some authors disregarded the effect of frequency on the parameters of the longitudinal line.

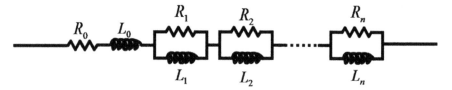

Figure 4. Circuit that represents the longitudinal parameters of the line.

The models proposed by would become more complete if the effect of frequency on the longitudinal parameters of the line was inserted in them.

So, the parameters of a transmission line can be synthesized by means of a circuit of the type shown in Figure 4.

It's used a cascade of π circuits to represent a transmission line taking into account the effect of frequency on the longitudinal parameters. In this case, every π circuit will be shown in Figure 5.

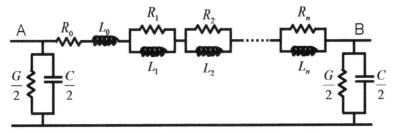

Figure 5. Cascade of π circuits considering the effect of frequency.

In Figure 5, the RL parallel associations are as many as necessary to represent the variation of parameters in each decade of frequency that will be considered. First, arrays are displayed in a state for a line represented by a single π circuit, whereas the effect of frequency is synthesized by n RL associations. Then, the results will be extended to a line represented by a cascade of n π circuit, considering n RL associations to synthesize the effect of frequency.

Before being certain state equations for a line represented by a cascade of n π circuits, it will be shown in detail the development of equations of state considering only one π circuit.

Then, the development done for a single π circuit element can be extended to a generic cascade with any quantity of these circuits.

Considering, as shown in the Figure 5, a transmission line represented by a single π circuit, the effect of frequency on the longitudinal parameters is represented by n RL associations.

In line shown in Figure 5, the voltages at terminals A and B are u(t) and $v_k(t)$, respectively. It is also considering that the currents i_{k0}, i_{k1}, ..., i_{km} are circulating through the inductors L_0, L_1, L_2, ..., L_m, respectively. These currents are dependent time functions and the notations do not include the time dependence for more simplicity. This simplification is also applied to the $v_k(t)$ state variable. From the currents and voltages in the circuit of Figure 5 it can be determined:

$$\frac{di_{k0}}{dt} = \frac{i_{k0}}{L_0}\left(-\sum_{j=1}^{m} R_j\right) + \frac{1}{L_{L0}}\left(\sum_{j=1}^{m} R_j i_{kj}\right) + \frac{1}{L_0}u(t) - \frac{1}{L_0}v_k \tag{13}$$

$$\frac{di_{k1}}{dt} = \frac{R_1}{L_1}i_{k0} - \frac{R_1}{L_1}i_{k1} \tag{14}$$

$$\frac{di_{k2}}{dt} = \frac{R_2}{L_2}i_{k0} - \frac{R_2}{L_2}i_{k2} \tag{15}$$

$$\frac{di_{km}}{dt} = \frac{R_m}{L_m}i_{k0} - \frac{R_m}{L_m}i_{km} \tag{16}$$

$$\frac{dv_k(t)}{dt} = \frac{2}{C}i_{k0} - \frac{G}{C}v_k(t) \tag{17}$$

The equations (4.1) to (4.5), describing the circuit shown in figure 4.2, can be written as:

$$\dot{x} = Ax + Bu \tag{18}$$

For one π circuit, the A matrix is substituted by:

$$A_\pi = \begin{bmatrix}
-\dfrac{\sum_{j=0}^{j=m} R_j}{L_0} & \dfrac{R_1}{L_0} & \dfrac{R_2}{L_0} & \cdots & \dfrac{R_m}{L_0} & -\dfrac{1}{L_0} \\[2ex]
\dfrac{R_1}{L_0} & -\dfrac{R_1}{L_0} & 0 & \cdots & 0 & 0 \\[2ex]
\dfrac{R_2}{L_2} & 0 & -\dfrac{R_2}{L_2} & \cdots & 0 & 0 \\[2ex]
\vdots & \vdots & \vdots & \ddots & 0 & 0 \\[2ex]
\dfrac{R_m}{L_m} & 0 & 0 & \cdots & -\dfrac{R_m}{L_m} & 0 \\[2ex]
\dfrac{2}{C} & 0 & 0 & \cdots & 0 & -\dfrac{G}{C}
\end{bmatrix} \tag{19}$$

$$B^T = \begin{bmatrix} \dfrac{1}{L_0} & 0 & 0 & \cdots & 0 & 0 \end{bmatrix} \tag{20}$$

$$x_k^T = \begin{bmatrix} i_{k0} & i_{k1} & i_{k2} & \cdots & i_{km} & v_k \end{bmatrix} \tag{21}$$

$$\dot{x}_k = \frac{dx_k}{dt} = \begin{bmatrix} \dfrac{di_{k0}}{dt} & \dfrac{di_{k1}}{dt} & \dfrac{di_{k2}}{dt} & \cdots & \dfrac{di_{km}}{dt} & \dfrac{dv_k}{dt} \end{bmatrix}^T \tag{22}$$

In the equations (4.8) and (4.9), B^T e x_k^T correspond to transposed B and x_k, respectively.

The obtained results show that the vesctor x_k have $(m + 2)$ elements and the matrix A is a $(m + 2)$ order square matrix.

Based on the equations and the results for one π circuit, it can be extended the analysis to a cascade of π circuits. Thus, the matrix A will have an order of $n(m +2)$ and the vector x has dimension $n(m +2)$. The A matrix can be written as:

$$A = \begin{bmatrix} A_{11} & A_{12} & 0 & \cdots & 0 & 0 & 0 \\ A_{21} & A_{22} & A_{23} & \ddots & \ddots & \ddots & 0 \\ 0 & A_{32} & A_{33} & \ddots & 0 & \ddots & 0 \\ 0 & 0 & A_{43} & \ddots & A_{(n-3)(n-2)} & 0 & 0 \\ 0 & \ddots & 0 & \ddots & A_{(n-2)(n-2)} & A_{(n-2)(n-1)} & 0 \\ 0 & \ddots & \ddots & \ddots & A_{(n-1)(n-2)} & A_{(n-1)(n-1)} & A_{(n-1)n} \\ 0 & 0 & 0 & \cdots & 0 & A_{n(n-1)} & A_{nn} \end{bmatrix} \tag{23}$$

The elements x_1, x_2, ..., x_n are describe by equation (4.9). In equation (4.11), A is a tridiagonal matrix which elements are square matrices of order $(m +2)$. In this case, a generic element A_{KK} at main diagonal of the matrix A is written as:

$$A_{kk} = A_\pi \tag{24}$$

The A_π matrix is defined in equation (4.7).

An element of any upper subdiagonal in equation (4.11) is a square matrix of order $(m +2)$ which the only one nonzero element is located in the first column of last row and has the value $\left(-\dfrac{1}{C}\right)$.

The structure is:

$$A_{ik} = \begin{bmatrix} 0 & 0 & \cdots & 0 \\ \vdots & \ddots & \cdots & \vdots \\ 0 & \cdots & \ddots & \vdots \\ -\dfrac{1}{C} & 0 & \cdots & 0 \end{bmatrix} \tag{25}$$
$$i = k - 1, \quad 2 \le k \le n$$

The subdiagonal elements in the equation (4.11) are square matrices of order (m +2). These arrays have a single nonzero element which is in the last column of first row. It is a value of $\left(\dfrac{1}{L_0}\right)$. The structure is:

$$
A_{ik} = \begin{bmatrix} 0 & \cdots & 0 & \dfrac{1}{L_0} \\ \vdots & \ddots & \cdots & 0 \\ \vdots & \cdots & \ddots & \vdots \\ 0 & 0 & \cdots & 0 \end{bmatrix} \tag{26}
$$

$$i = k+1, \quad 1 \le k \le n-1$$

Considering a cascade of π circuits, the vector B has the dimension of n(m +2) and if it is connected a u(t) source at the beginning of the line, the vector B has a single nonzero element, which is the first array element and it has the value $\left(\dfrac{1}{L_0}\right)$.

The state equation, that describes a line representation by a cascade of π circuits cant be solved by numerical methods, like Euler and Heun methods. Other numeric methods are described in the next item

5. Other numeric methods

Besides the trapezoidal integration, there are also other numeric methods that can be used for solving state equations related to the modeling of transient phenomena in transmission lines. Among them, it may be mentioned, for example, the Simpson's and the Runge-Kutta's method. The following items will describe these methods. In this case, the MatLab™ is important because it facilitates the comparisons among the mentioned methods. With this software, undergraduate students can analyze the application of different numeric methods for solving an engineering problem, besides the analysis about wave propagation and the transmission line modeling. Graduated students can analyze what it is the best option for specific transmission line characteristics and develop the numeric method related to the simulation of transient phenomena in power systems.

5.1. Simpson's rule

Simpson's rule is based on the assumption that, given short intervals of time the derivative of the function to be integrated, the function (y') can be approximated by a second degree function as shown in Figure 6.

From Figure 1, it is obtained:

$$
y\left(t_{k+1}\right) = \frac{1}{3}\left[y'\left(t_{k+1}\right) + 4y'\left(t_M\right) + y'\left(t_k\right)\right]\Delta t \tag{27}
$$

From (5.1) and (4.6), it is obtained:

$$x\left(t_{k+1}\right) = a_1\left(a_2 + a_3 + a_4\right) \tag{28}$$

Equation (5.2) is applied Simpson's rule for solving the state equation of state of the type shown in (5.1). In this case, the matrices a_1, a_2, a_3 and a_4 are written as:

$$a_1 = \left(I - \frac{\Delta t}{6}A\right) \tag{29}$$

$$a_2 = \left(I + \frac{\Delta t}{6}A\right)x\left(t_k\right) \tag{30}$$

$$a_3 = \frac{2\Delta t}{3}A\,y\left(t_M\right) \tag{31}$$

$$a_4 = \frac{\Delta t}{6}B\left[u\left(t_k\right) + 4u\left(t_M\right) + u\left(t_{k+1}\right)\right] \tag{32}$$

It is defined the following terms:

$$\Delta t = t_{k+1} - t_k \tag{33}$$

$$t_M = \frac{t_{k+1} + t_k}{2} \tag{34}$$

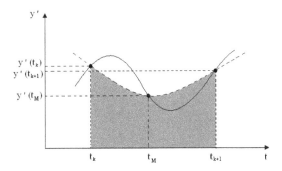

Figure 6. Approximation of the derivative of the function to be integrated (solid curve) by a function of the second degree (dashed curve).

5.2. Runge-Kutta's rule

Runge-Kutta's rule is defined by the following:

$$x\left(t_{k+1}\right) = x\left(t_k\right) + \frac{1}{6}\left(k_1 + 2k_2 + 2k_3 + k_4\right) \tag{35}$$

The terms in the last equation are described by:

$$k_1 = \Delta t \left[A x(t_k) + B u(t_k) \right] \tag{36}$$

$$k_2 = \Delta t \left\{ A \left[x(t_k) + \frac{k_1}{2} \right] + B u(t_k) \right\} \tag{37}$$

$$k_3 = \Delta t \left\{ A \left[x(t_k) + \frac{k_2}{2} \right] + B u(t_k) \right\} \tag{38}$$

$$k_4 = \Delta t \left\{ A \left[x(t_k) + k_3 \right] + B u(t_k) \right\} \tag{39}$$

5.3. Comparisons among the numeric methods

The Matlab™ software is easily applied for the development of numeric routines. Using this characteristic, it is possible to compare different numerical methods. Figure 7 shows the results for the three methods investigated for the simulation of electromagnetic transients in a single-phase transmission line.

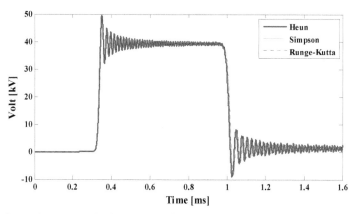

Figure 7. Comparisons among the three numerical methods.

In the last figure, it is shown the result obtained with the application of a step voltage source on the initial transmission line. This is a 20 kV step voltage source. The transmission line is modeled as a mono-phase circuit and the linear system is solved using three numeric methods: trapezoidal rule, Simpson's rule and Range-Kutta's one.

Based on the results shown in Figure 7, the three numeric methods lead to similar results considering the method accuracy. Because of these results, it is necessary to analyze the other characteristics. An important characteristic for the application of the numeric methods for transient analysis in transmission lines is the simulation time. For example, this is important for analysis in very short simulation times. The next table shows the simulation time comparisons obtained with the MatLab™ software.

Step of calculating (μs)	Computational effort (simulation time)		
	Heun	Simpson	Runge-Kutta
0,1	t1	22,52 t1	0,63 t1
0,5	t2	8,94 t2	0,23 t2
1,0	t3	8,40 t3	0,26 t3

Table 1. Simulation time required by numerical methods

Table 1 shows the time relationship between the applied numerical methods. It is possible to carry out these comparisons because the Matlab™ provides a simple way to replace the codes related to the numeric routine without changing the structure of the main code, maintaining the same computational flowchart. Using this characteristic, it is possible to determine the simulation time of each numeric method, because the computational time for introducing the data and other characteristics of the simulated transmission line is equal for all compared numeric methods. Because of this, the MatLab™ is an adequate tool for developing new models and numeric routines used for analysis and simulations of transient phenomena in transmission lines.

6. Model implementation of single phase line

In this section, it is presented the implementation of a single-phase transmission line through a cascade of π circuits, considering the effect of frequency on their longitudinal parameters and using the concept of state variables. Then, the results obtained are compared with results obtained with EMTP.

6.1. Block diagram of the program for single-phase line

The model that represents the single-phase line was implemented in a microcomputer using the software MatLab™.

Data from single-phase transmission line are read in the first part of the program, then the parameters are calculated from the transmission line considering the influence of frequency.

After observing the behavior of single-phase line parameters as a function of frequency, it is necessary to represent this influence on the transmission line model proposed in item 4. This was done using the method called vector fitting and the longitudinal single phase line parameters are fitted by means of rational functions.

With these parameters synthesized and distributed in the proposed model of a single-phase line, it is possible to calculate the voltages and currents at the terminals of this line or at any point of the line.

The model represented by a cascade π circuits can be represented by a linear system that is represented by state variables. For the solution of the system represented by $\dot{x} = [A]x + [B]u$, it's used Heun formula (trapezoidal integration method). This method is widely used in simulations of electromagnetic transients in power systems

Figure 8 is shown a block diagram of the algorithm of the program developed for single-phase line.

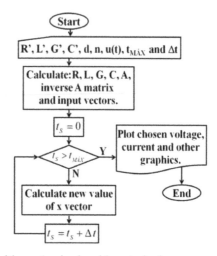

Figure 8. Block diagram of the routine developed for a single-phase.

6.2. Calculation of the parameters of the transmission line single phase

It's possible to bring the longitudinal parameters of single-phase line by means of rational functions. Using the vector fitting method and allowing the fitting the frequency dependence of these parameters, this effect is entered in the discrete parameter model.

The equation that summarizes the parameters of longitudinal single-phase line is given by:

$$Z_{VFIT}(\omega) = R_0 + j\omega L_0 + \frac{j\omega R_1}{j\omega + \dfrac{R_1}{L_1}} + \frac{j\omega R_2}{j\omega + \dfrac{R_2}{L_2}} + \frac{j\omega R_3}{j\omega + \dfrac{R_3}{L_3}} + \frac{j\omega R_4}{j\omega + \dfrac{R_4}{L_4}} \tag{40}$$

The values of R and L in the equation (6.1) found by the method vector fitting are shown in Table 2.

From the values of Table 1, it can view a summary of the parameters of longitudinal line as follows: replacing the values of Table 1 in the expression (6.1) and attribute values are included in the frequency range 10^1 to 10^6 for it is possible to calculate the longitudinal impedance synthesized.

In the equivalent circuit, the values were considered in the frequency range from 10^1 to 10^6, because transients that occur in the transmission line are within this frequency range. So the four blocks RL in parallel, shown in Figure 9, are representing the influence of frequency on longitudinal parameters of single-phase transmission line.

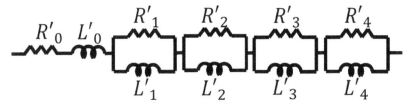

Figure 9. Circuit that represents the longitudinal parameters of the line.

Resistors (Ω/km)		Inductors (mH/km)	
R'_0	0,026	L'_0	2,209
R'_1	1,470	L'_1	0,74
R'_2	2,354	L'_2	0,12
R'_3	20,149	L'_3	0,10
R'_4	111,111	L'_4	0,05

Table 2. Values of elements R e L for a single-phase.

7. Transmission line with corona effect

7.1. General aspects about the corona

The corona discharge mechanism is an electrostatic phenomenon due to ionization in an insulating material, usually a gas, subject to electric field intensities above a critical level.

Electrical discharges in gases are usually triggered by an electric field that accelerates free electrons therein. When these electrons acquire enough energy from the electric field, they can produce new electrons from the collision with other atoms. It is the process of impact ionization. During its acceleration in the electric field, each free electron collides with atoms of oxygen, nitrogen and other present gases, missing, that collision, part of its kinetic energy. Occasionally, it can achieve an electron atom with sufficient force so as to excite it. Under these conditions, the atom is achieved to a higher energy state. The orbital state of one or more electrons and the electron moves colliding with the atom loses some of its energy to create this state. Subsequently, the atom can hit revert to its initial state, releasing the excess energy as heat, light, electromagnetic radiation and acoustic energy. An electron can also collide with a positive ion, converting it into neutral atom. This process, called recombination, also releases excess energy.

7.2. Corona effect representation

After the pioneering work of Peek (1915), several measurements have made on lines and experimental laboratories have examined the nature of the corona and its influence on wave propagation in transmission lines. These works have had fundamental importance, contributing to the understanding of the basic mechanism of the corona.

In 1954, Wagner et al. (1954) and Wagner and Lloyd et al. (1955) published two articles that would be a reference for future work on corona. Voltage experimental measurements were made of in the laboratory of a conductor under corona (project called Tidd 500 kV).

Through these experimental results, it has developed empirical formulas and procedures for considering the effects of attenuation and distortion in the spread of outbreaks. These formulas and procedures are based on the voltage gradient, and voltage curves are obtained from attenuation measurements and the power dissipation due to the corona effect. The usefulness of these methods is limited however, because it requires different approaches and uses abacuses.

The corona model can be divided into three classes: analog models, mathematical models and physical models. The electrical circuit analog models are designed to reproduce the geometric increase in the capacitance of the conductor to the voltage reaches critical ionization.

Like the analog models, mathematical models roughly reproduce the characteristics of drivers under the corona, but by means of mathematical equations. Several authors have empirical formulations for the variation of capacitance of the line based on functions and constants derived from measurements. Most models show a linear relationship between capacitance and dynamic tension.

Due to the complexity in describing mathematically the physical phenomena involved and the insufficient amount of data propagation in corona, it is not available generic models of this nature yet.

7.3. Gary's model

The equations describing the corona effect is not easily implemented in the differential equations of the transmission line in order to obtain a solution formulation easyly. Thus, to obtain responses directly in the time domain, numerical models are used such as the finite difference method and the method of the characteristics. This last category of models has been developed to be implemented in EMTP-type programs. Some of these models use non-linear resistors and capacitors that are dependent on the voltage applied on them. However, most existing models of corona present satisfactory results only for a specific situation.

The mechanism of the corona effect can also be represented by the model of Gary, using a capacitance and a non-linear conductance to represent the accumulation and the pressure drops in the line. The capacitance and conductance mentioned above are variables with the applied voltage on them and are called corona capacitance (Cc) and corona conductance (Gc). Cc and Gc elements are obtained by known analytical function, and, therefore, this representation for the corona effect is called analytical model of the corona effect. This model for the corona effect can be inserted in lines represented by a cascade of π circuits, where currents and voltages along line is described by state variables.

If the capacitance is represented by Gary's corona model, it is defined as:

$$C_C = \begin{cases} C\eta \left(\dfrac{v}{V_C} \right)^{\eta-1} & se \;\; v \geq V_C \\ 0 & se \;\; v < V_C \end{cases} \qquad (41)$$

In equation (7.1), Cc is the corona capacitance, C is the geometric capacitance of the line segment represented by a π circuit, v is the voltage being applied to the line capacitance, Cv is the minimum voltage required to the corona effect accurrance and η is a coefficient defined as:

$$\eta = 0,22r + 1,2 \qquad (42)$$

where: r the radius of the conductor in centimeters.

Thus, given the presence of the corona effect and the effect of frequency, a differential element row can be represented as shown in Figure 10.

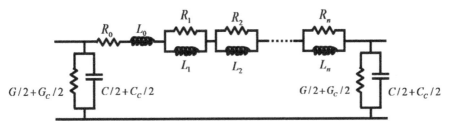

Figure 10. A differential element of line considering the corona effects

The corona conductance to Gary's model is defined as:

$$G_C = k_C \left(\dfrac{1 - V_C}{v} \right)^2 \qquad (43)$$

Gary's model considers that the corona effect is manifested only if the voltage Vc is greater than v and the rate of variation over time v is positive. Thus, if the corona effect is manifested at a given point P of the line, the voltage Vp at this point must satisfy the following conditions:

$$V_p > V_C \quad and \quad \frac{dV_p}{dt} > 0 \tag{44}$$

Thus, for the corona effect is present at a generic point of the line represented by a cascade of π circuits, as shown in figure 10, it is necessary that the voltage at this point satisfying the two conditions shown in equation (7.4). If a condition is not met, this point will not have increased the capacitance and conductance representing corona. Therefore, the A matrix shown in equation (4.6) should be changed for each iteration as a function of cross-line voltage.

8. Testing the model

Checking the effectiveness of the developed model, it is simulated the energizing of a transmission line shown in figure 11, considering frequency independent line parameters and frequency dependent ones.

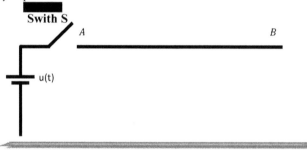

Figure 11. Single phase line representation with opened terminal.

In Figure 11, S is a switch that be closed at time t = 0, energizing the line through a voltage source u(t). In the current procedure, the terminal B is open and the other terminal is powered by a constant voltage source. For frequency dependent line parameters, it is considered that the longitudinal parameters of the line per unit length can be perfectly summed up by a circuit consisting of four RL parallel blocks connected in series. The structure is completed using a RL series block as shown in Figure 9.

The values of R and L used to synthesize the effect of frequency on the longitudinal parameters of the line were obtained using the method proposed by [10] and are shown in Table 1. The parameters of the unit transverse line shown in figure 3 are G'=0,556 μS/km e C' =11,11nF/km.

9. Simulation analysis of transmission lines with single phase representation

In all simulations, it is used the following values: the transmission line has 10 kilometers. It is represented through 200 π circuits. The time step used in the simulations is 50 ns and the simulation period is 600 µs. The voltage in the initial of the line is 1 kV. It can also be considered as 1 pu.

Since the values of R and L elements of the cascade of π circuits that describe the line are known, it can be obtained the state equations that describe the behavior of currents and voltages along the line. The simulations using the model proposed in this chapter were performed in MatLab™ program, using the trapezoidal integration method. Considering the frequency independent line parameters, the circuit of Figure 4 is reduced to the R_0 and L_0 elements. In this case, the values are: $R_0 = 0.05$ Ω/km and $L_0 = 1$ mH/km.

The values of Table 9.1 are written per kilometer for the generic π circuit. For the simulation, it used the values represented in the Table 9.2 that are resistance and inductance [Ω] and [H], respectively. In the Figs 12-21, it is used the values of Table 4.

Figures 12-17 show the relationship between the number of RL parallel blocks and the inclusion of the frequency influence. In Figure 12, the resistance values are obtained using only one RL parallel block related to the high frequencies. Because of this, the resistance values for all frequency values are equal. In this case, the value is equal to the R_4 value per length unit.

Parameter	100 π circuits	200 π circuits
R	5 mΩ	2.5 mΩ
L	100 mH	50 mH
G	556 µS	278 µS
C	1.111 nF	555.5 nF

Table 3. Values of line parameter used in all simulations without frequency.

Resistors(Ω)		Inductors(µH)	
R_0'	0.0013	L_0'	110.45
R_1'	0.0735	L_1'	37
R_2'	0.1177	L_2'	6
R_3'	1.0075	L_3'	5
R_4'	5.5556	L_4'	2.5

Table 4. Values of line parameter used in simulations with 200 π circuits.

From the results of Figures 13 and 14, it is observed that the synthesis of the effect of frequency on the resistance can only be considered when inserted in the cascade of π circuits, at least, two RL parallel blocks, because each block is related to a frequency set point.

So, if more blocks are used, more frequency set points are obtained. It is confirmed through the results shown in Figures 15, 16 and 17 where the inductance values are presented. So, it is concluded that the synthesis of the longitudinal line parameters is improved with the increase of the number of RL parallel blocks.

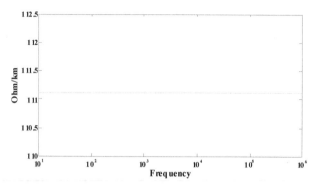

Figure 12. Synthesis of resistance per unit length using $R'_4L'_4$ parallel block.

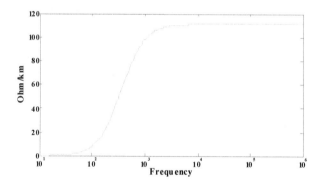

Figure 13. Synthesis of resistance per unit length using $R'_1L'_1$ and $R'_4L'_4$ parallel blocks.

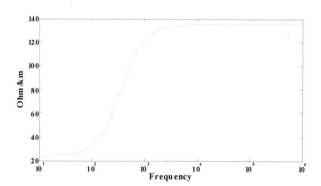

Figure 14. Synthesis of resistance per unit length using four RL parallel blocks.

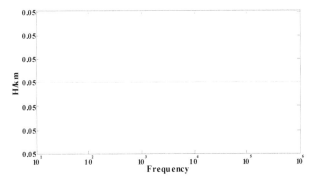

Figure 15. Synthesis of inductance per unit length using only R′₄L′₄ parallel block.

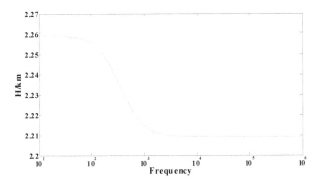

Figure 16. Synthesis of inductance per unit length using R′₁L′₁ and R′₄L′₄ parallel blocks.

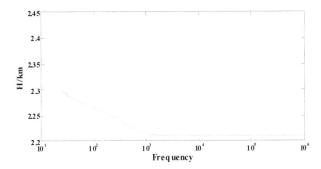

Figure 17. Synthesis of inductance per unit length using four RL parallel blocks.

The result of the simulation made for the voltage input signal u(t) can be seen in Figure 18. It is shown the output voltage at the receiving end terminal of the line without the frequency influence. Using the routine without the influence of frequency from the results of Figure. 18, it is observed that there is a period of time related to the time of signal propagation through the line.

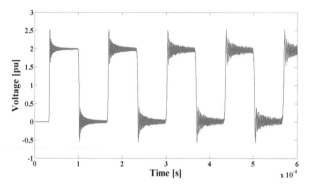

Figure 18. Energization of the transmission line without the effect of frequency considering 200 π circuits.

Thus, it represents a time delay between input signal and output signal. After the delay, there are oscillations associated with wave reflections on the transmission line terminals that make up the output voltage shown.

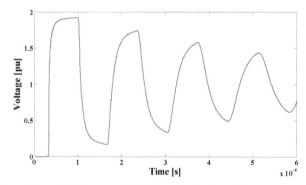

Figure 19. Voltage at the end of the transmission line with the effect of frequency considering 200 π circuits.

Using the routine with frequency influence in longitudinal parameters, it is obtained the results of Figure 20. In this figure, comparing to Figure 19, the voltage signal is attenuated because the inclusion of the frequency influence.

Figures 21 and 22 show the influence of frequency on the current results. Without the frequency influence, the obtained signal current is not attenuated and is highly modified by numeric oscillations (Figure 14). On the other hand, when the routine considers the influence of frequency (Figure 22), it is clear that the current signal could not contain those oscillations shown in Figure 21. So, those oscillations are numeric oscillations and they can be associated to the representation of the longitudinal line parameters which does not consider the frequency influence.

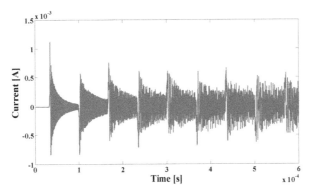

Figure 20. Current at the end of the transmission line without the effect of frequency.

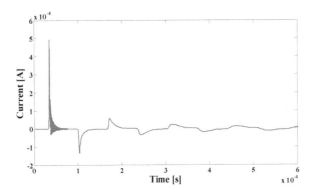

Figure 21. Current at the end of the transmission considering the effect of frequency.

So, for the sequence of this work, it should be investigated what is the saturation point for the number of the π circuits and the number of the RL parallel blocks. It is carried out using the simulation results from several voltage signals that will be used as voltage sources at the initial line terminal.

For Figures 22 and 23, using the routine without the effect of frequency, it is analyzed a particular stretch of the simulation at the end of the line. It is shown the voltage values without frequency influence. In Figures. 22 and 23 it is used the values of Table 2, using 100 and 200 π circuits, respectively.

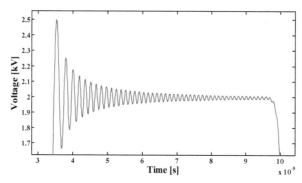

Figure 22. Specific portion of the simulation at the end of the line with 100 π circuits and without the effect of frequency.

Based on the mentioned results, it concludes that increasing the number of π circuits leads to a decrease in the numerical oscillations.

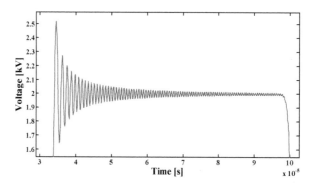

Figure 23. Specific portion of the simulation at the end of the line with 200 π circuits and without the effect of frequency.

In Figure 23, it is clearly a greater condensation of numerical oscillations in both x and y axes in contrast to Figure 23, where the period of the oscillations and the peak value are higher than those obtained in Figure 23. In Figures 24, 25 and 26, it is used the routine with the effect of frequency, analyzing the number of the RL parallel blocks inserted in the cascade of π circuits, searching for reducing of numerical oscillations. In Figures 24, 25 and 26, it was used the values of Tables 3 and 1, as well as, 3 and 4 RL parallel blocks, respectively.

From the results of Figures 24, 25 and 19, it is observed that the used routine including the effect of frequency in the cascade of π circuits obtains considerably fewer numerical oscillations when compared to Figures 22 and 23. From these results, it is evident that if it is increased the number of the RL parallel blocks, it is reduced the numerical oscillations and the voltage in the line end has a smoothly curve in the time domain.

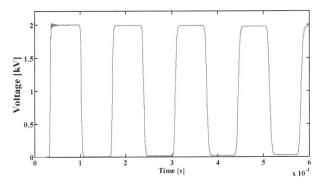

Figure 24. Voltage at the end of the line with the effect of frequency considering 200π circuits and using R_4L_4 parallel block.

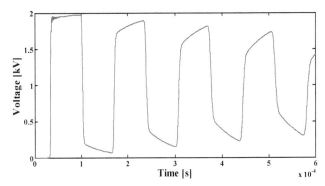

Figure 25. Voltage at the end of the line with the effect of frequency considering 200π circuit and using R_0L_0, R_2L_2 e R_4L_4 parallel blocks.

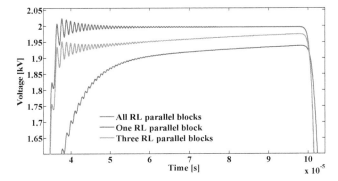

Figure 26. Comparison of figures 24, 25 and 19 of the tension at the end of the line with the effect of frequency.

Concluding the analysis of the results, Figure 26 shows a comparison among the results of Figures 24, 25 and 19, leaving a clear decrease in the numerical oscillations. In this figure, it is shown a time range of the time simulation used at the last three figures. In this case, it is clearly shown that, increasing the number of RL parallel blocks, the numerical oscillations are decreased and the frequency influence is better reproduced through the state equations in mathematical software.

Considering the corona effect, Gary's model is applied with the routine described in the previous items. It is used the line representation without frequency influence, because the representation with frequency influence has not hardly analyzed. The corona effect is introduced by

$$C_C = C \cdot \eta \cdot \left(\frac{V}{V_C} \right)^{\eta-1}$$

$$\eta = 0.22 \cdot R_{COND} + 1.2$$

(45)

In this case, R_{COND} is the conductor phase radius in [cm], C is the transversal line capacitance and the C_C is the new value of the transversal line capacitance because the corona effect. In this chapter, the R_{COND} value is 2.54 cm. The simulations are carried out for some relations between V and V_C. The V value is 1 pu for all following shown simulations.

Considering Figures 27-31, the corona effect is related to the 10 π circuits in the middle line. It corresponds to the 500 m of the represented line. Figures 27-30 show results for different relative values of the corona voltage when compared to the line nominal voltage. In Figure 31, it is shown the comparisons among the results for the voltage values in the receiving end terminal. So, using a simple routine based on π circuits for transmission line representation, undergraduate students can analyze and simulate traveling wave phenomena in transmission lines.

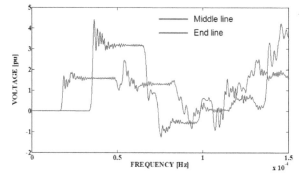

Figure 27. The time domain simulations with the corona effect for V_{CORONA} = 0,35 V.

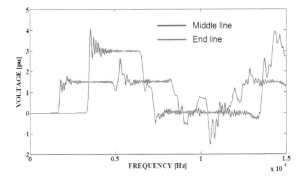

Figure 28. The time domain simulations with the corona effect for $V_{CORONA} = 0,5$ V.

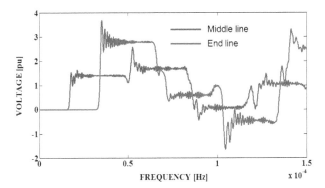

Figure 29. The time domain simulations with the corona effect for $V_{CORONA} = 0,7$ V.

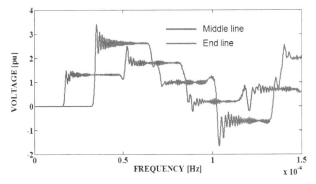

Figure 30. The time domain simulations with the corona effect for $V_{CORONA} = 0,9$ V.

Based on Figure 10, it's simulated the corona effect with effect of frequency for some relations between V and V_C. The V value is 1 pu to the following shown simulation.

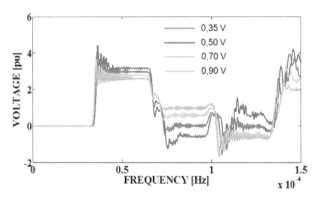

Figure 31. Comparisons of the time domain simulations with the corona effect for some V$_{CORONA}$ values.

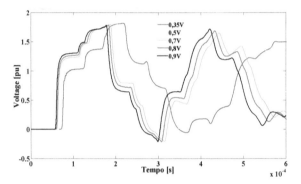

Figure 32. Comparisons of the time domain simulations with the corona effect with effect of frequency for some V$_{CORONA}$ values.

10. Conclusions

It is described the application the MatLab™ software in analysis and simulations of transient phenomena in transmission lines. Using the characteristics of this software, transmission lines are easily modeled as a mono-phase circuit. Transient simulations are also easily carried out. For these applications, it is used basic and simple tools of the MatLab™ software. So, this software improves the analysis of the proposed problem, because it is possible to obtain several types of the graphic results that are not available in the specific programs for transient analysis like the EMTP programs. So, it is possible to analyze the resistance and inductance values that depend on the frequency when it is considered detailed transmission line models. It is possible to analyze the application of different numeric methods for solving the differential state equations by numeric integration routines. On the other hand, with a simple model of the transmission lines and the MatLab™ software, it is possible to develop a routine that is used by undergraduate students, making easy the learning about important concepts as wave propagation, transient phenomena and transmission lines. This routine can be modified, introducing elements that are able to consider the frequency influence in the transmission line parameters. These parameters have their characteristics distributed along the line and this is considered in the mentioned routine.

The shown analysis and results can be used by undergraduate students for learning about the important concepts of power systems, transmission lines and wave propagation, for example. Related to the graduated students, it can be used for analyzing transient phenomena, developing transmission line models, improving numeric routines and comparing different numeric integration methods. So, the MatLab™ software is an excellent tool for basic and profound studies of transient phenomena in transmission lines.

Author details

Leonardo da S. Lessa, Afonso J. Prado, Rodrigo Cleber Silva,
Sérgio Kurokawa and Luiz F. Bovolato
Transient Electromagnetic Studies Laboratory, Department of Electrical Engineering,
UNESP – The University State of São Paulo, Brazil

José Pissolato Filho
Department of Electrical Engineering, UNICAMP – The State University of Campinas,
Campinas, Brazil

11. References

Chipman, R. A. Teoria e problemas de linhas de transmissão. São Paulo: Mc Graw Hill do Brasil, 1976. 276p.

Dommel H.W., Electromagnetic Transients Program. Reference Manual (EMTP Theory Book), Bonneville Power Administration, Portland, 1986.

Dommel, H.W. Digital computer solution of electromagnetic transients in single and multiphase networks. IEEE Trans. On Power App. And Systems, v. PAS-88, n.4, p. 388- 399, 1969.

Faria, A.B.; Washington, L.A.; Antônio, C.S. Modelos de linhas de transmissão no domínio das fases: estado da arte. In: CONGRESSO BRASILEIRO DE AUTOMÁTICA, 14, 2002, Natal. Anais... Natal: [s.n.], 2002. p. 801-806.

Fuchs, R. D. Transmissão de energia elétrica: linha aéreas; teoria das linhas em regime permanente, 2.ed. Rio de Janeiro: Livros Técnicos e Científicos, 1979. 582 p.

Greenwood, A. Electrical transients in power systems. New York: John Wiley&Sons, 1971. 558 p.

Hedman, D. E. Teorias das linhas de transmissão-II. 2.ed. Santa Maria: Edições UFSM, 1983. v. 2 e 3.

J. R. Marti, "Accurate modelem of frequency-dependent transmission lines in 105 electromagnetic transient simulations", IEEE Trans. on Power Apparatus and Systems, vol. PAS-101, nº 1, pp. 147-155, January, 1982.

Kurokawa, S.; Yamanaka, F. N. R.; Prado, A. J.; Pissolato Filho, J.. Using state-space techniques to represent frequency dependent single-phase lines directly in time domain. In: THE 2008 IEEE/PES Transmission and Distribution Conference and Exposition: Latin America, 2008, Bogotá. Proceedings, Bogotá:[s.n.], 2008. p. 312-316,.

Kurokawa, S.; Yamanaka, F. N. R.; Prado, A. J. Representação de linhas de transmissão por meio de variáveis de estado levando em consideração o efeito da freqüência sobre os parâmetros longitudinais. Sba Controle& Automação, Campinas, v.18, n.3, p.337- 346, 2007.

Kurokawa, S.; Yamanaka, F. N. R.; Prado, A. J.; Pissolato, J. Representação de linhas de transmissão por meio de variáveis de estado considerando o efeito da frequência sobre os parâmetros longitudinais. In: CONGRESSO BRASILEIRO DE AUTOMÁTICA- CBA, 16, 2006, Salvador. Anais... Salvador: [s.n.], 2006. v. 1 p. 268-273,

Mácias, J. A. R.; Expósito A. G.; Soler, A. B. A Comparison of techniques for state- space transient analysis of transmission lines. IEEE Transactions on Power Delivery, [S.l.], v.20, n.2, p. 894-903, 2005.

Mamis, M. S. Computation of electromagnetic transients on transmission lines with nonlinear components. IEE. Proc. General Transmission and Distribution, [S.l.], v.150, n.2, p. 200-203, 2003.

Mamis, M. S. State-space transient analysis of single-phase transmission lines with corona. In: INTERNATIONAL CONFERENCE ON POWER SYSTEMS TRANSIENTS- IPST, [s.n.], 2003, New Orleans. Anais New Orleans: [S.l.], 2003. 5p.

Mamis, M. S.; Nacaroglu, A. Transient voltage and current distributions on transmission lines. IEE. Proc. General Transmission and Distribution., [S.l.], v.149, n. 6, p. 705-712, 2003.

Martí, L. Simulation of transients in underground cables with frequency-dependent modal transformation matrices. IEEE Transactions on Power Delivery, [S.l.] , v. 3, n.3, p.1099-1110, 1988.

Nelms, R. M.; Sheble, G. B.; NEWTON, S. R.; GRIGSBY, L. L.; Using a personal computer to teach power system transients. IEEE Transactions on Power Systems, [S.l.] v. 4, n. 3, p. 1293-1297, 1989.

Swokowski, E.W. Cálculo com geometria analítica. São Paulo: Ed. Makron do Brasil, 1994. v. 2, 792p.

Tavares, M. C.; Pissolato, J.; Portela, M. C. Quasi-modes multiphase transmission line model, Electric Power Systems Research, [S.l.],v. 49, n. 3, p. 159-167, 1999.

Yamanaka, F. N. R.; Kurokawa, S.; Prado, A. J.; Pissolato, J.; Bovolato, L. F. Analysis of longitudinal and temporal distribution of electromagnetic waves in transmission lines by using state-variable techniques. In: SIXTH LATIN-AMERICAN CONGRESS ON ELECTRICITY GENERATION AND TRANSMISSION, 16, 2005, Mar del Plata. Proceeding... Mar del Plata: [s.n.], 2005. p. 1-7.

Permissions

The contributors of this book come from diverse backgrounds, making this book a truly international effort. This book will bring forth new frontiers with its revolutionizing research information and detailed analysis of the nascent developments around the world.

We would like to thank Vasilios N. Katsikis, for lending his expertise to make the book truly unique. He has played a crucial role in the development of this book. Without his invaluable contribution this book wouldn't have been possible. He has made vital efforts to compile up to date information on the varied aspects of this subject to make this book a valuable addition to the collection of many professionals and students.

This book was conceptualized with the vision of imparting up-to-date information and advanced data in this field. To ensure the same, a matchless editorial board was set up. Every individual on the board went through rigorous rounds of assessment to prove their worth. After which they invested a large part of their time researching and compiling the most relevant data for our readers. Conferences and sessions were held from time to time between the editorial board and the contributing authors to present the data in the most comprehensible form. The editorial team has worked tirelessly to provide valuable and valid information to help people across the globe.

Every chapter published in this book has been scrutinized by our experts. Their significance has been extensively debated. The topics covered herein carry significant findings which will fuel the growth of the discipline. They may even be implemented as practical applications or may be referred to as a beginning point for another development. Chapters in this book were first published by InTech; hereby published with permission under the Creative Commons Attribution License or equivalent.

The editorial board has been involved in producing this book since its inception. They have spent rigorous hours researching and exploring the diverse topics which have resulted in the successful publishing of this book. They have passed on their knowledge of decades through this book. To expedite this challenging task, the publisher supported the team at every step. A small team of assistant editors was also appointed to further simplify the editing procedure and attain best results for the readers.

Our editorial team has been hand-picked from every corner of the world. Their multi-ethnicity adds dynamic inputs to the discussions which result in innovative outcomes. These outcomes are then further discussed with the researchers and contributors who give their valuable feedback and opinion regarding the same. The feedback is then collaborated with the researches and they are edited in a comprehensive manner to aid the understanding of the subject.

Apart from the editorial board, the designing team has also invested a significant amount of their time in understanding the subject and creating the most relevant covers. They scrutinized every image to scout for the most suitable representation of the subject and create an appropriate cover for the book.

The publishing team has been involved in this book since its early stages. They were actively engaged in every process, be it collecting the data, connecting with the contributors or procuring relevant information. The team has been an ardent support to the editorial, designing and production team. Their endless efforts to recruit the best for this project, has resulted in the accomplishment of this book. They are a veteran in the field of academics and their pool of knowledge is as vast as their experience in printing. Their expertise and guidance has proved useful at every step. Their uncompromising quality standards have made this book an exceptional effort. Their encouragement from time to time has been an inspiration for everyone.

The publisher and the editorial board hope that this book will prove to be a valuable piece of knowledge for researchers, students, practitioners and scholars across the globe.

List of Contributors

Wael A. Al-Tabey
Department of Mechanical Engineering Faculty of Engineering, Alexandria University, Alexandria, Egypt

C.S. Chin
Faculty of Science Agriculture and Engineering, Newcastle University, Newcastle upon Tyne, United Kingdom

Vedran Vajnberger, Semir Silajdžić and Nedim Osmić
Faculty of Electrical Engineering, Department of Automatic Control and Electronics, Sarajevo, Bosnia and Herzegovina

Marian Gaiceanu
Dunarea de Jos University of Galati, Romania

Michal Blaho, Martin Foltin, Peter Fodrek and Ján Murgaš
Slovak University of Technology, Slovak Republic

Nourdine Aliane and Javier Fernández Andrés
Dpto: Sistemas Informáticos Automática y Comunicaciones, Universidad Europea de Madrid (UEM), Villaviciosa de Odón, Madrid, Spain

Rafael Pastor Vargas
Dpto: Sistemas de Comunicación y Control, Escuela Técnica Superior Ingeniería Informática, UNED, Spain

Ian Grout
Department of Electronic and Computer Engineering, University of Limerick, Limerick, Ireland

Abu Khari Bin A'ain
Faculty of Electrical Engineering, Universiti Teknologi Malaysia (UTM), Skudai, Johor, Malaysia

Eric Anterrieu
National de la Recherche Scientifique & Université de Toulouse, France

Rafael Cuerda Monzani, Afonso José do Prado, Sérgio Kurokawa and Luiz Fernando Bovolato
Department of Electrical Engineering at FEIS/UNESP – The University of São Paulo State, Brazil

José Pissolato Filho
Department of Electrical Engineering, DSCE/UNICAMP – The State University of Campinas, Brazil

Leonardo da S. Lessa and Rodrigo Cleber Silva
Transient Electromagnetic Studies Laboratory, Department of Electrical Engineering, UNESP – The University State of São Paulo, Brazil

Printed in the USA
CPSIA information can be obtained
at www.ICGtesting.com
JSHW011450221024
72173JS00005B/1021